Praise for *The Butt*:

'Normal laws of ridiculousness do not apply in Self's invented country . . . like all good satire, *The Butt* avoids easy allegory . . . It's raucously imaginative stuff, full of bite and bile'   *Evening Standard*

'Self writes here with an adroit impersonation of coarse exuberance that makes *The Butt* as readable as a blokeish airport novel . . . Swift, Voltaire and Lewis Carroll are all partly responsible for the ingenious, mephitic invention that is *The Butt*'   *Sunday Telegraph*

'This satire has distinct echoes of the invasion of Iraq and proves as disturbing as it is assured'   *Observer*

'A Kafka-esque descent into nightmarish farce . . . By turns absurd and compelling, *The Butt* is a Swiftian satire for the post-9/11 era'   *Jewish Chronicle*

'Will Self creates worlds that are separate from our own but cunningly similar . . . A tale of the absurd'   *Vogue*

'The writing crackles with stupendous imagery . . . Best intentions, the author seems to be warning us in this savage and stylish novel, can also spawn their very own forms of evil'   *Financial Times*

'[*The Butt*] manages to show modernity and rationalism dissolving into irrational primitivism and still tell some good jokes along the way'   *Word Magazine*

'The atmosphere is powerf~~ul~~ . . . ~~emo~~tions that roil under the story are ~~. . .~~ ~~b~~ig reveal, is wonderfully ingenious ~~. . .~~ ~~Dai~~*ly Telegraph*

'Lurid, discomforting, K~~afka-esque~~ . . . ~~vint~~age Self and handsome proof, should anyone nee~~d it~~ . . . ~~literar~~y fiction can hold its own against rolling news, pixellated exp~~er~~i~~e~~nce and the reality-entertainment industry'   *GQ*

BY THE SAME AUTHOR

FICTION

The Quantity Theory of Insanity
Cock & Bull
My Idea of Fun
Grey Area
Great Apes
The Sweet Smell of Psychosis
Tough, Tough Toys for Tough, Tough Boys
How the Dead Live
Dorian
Dr Mukti and Other Tales of Woe
The Book of Dave
Liver

NON-FICTION

Junk Mail
Sore Sites
Perfidious Man
Feeding Frenzy
Psychogeography (with Ralph Steadman)

the
BUTT

An Exit Strategy

WILL SELF

BLOOMSBURY
LONDON · BERLIN · NEW YORK

First published 2008
This paperback edition published 2009

Copyright © 2008, Will Self

The moral right of the author has been asserted

No part of this book may be used or reproduced in any manner
whatsoever without written permission from the Publisher except in
the case of brief quotations embodied in critical articles or reviews

Bloomsbury Publishing Plc
36 Soho Square
London W1D 3QY

www.bloomsbury.com

A CIP catalogue record for this book
is available from the British Library

ISBN 978 0 7475 9645 5

10 9 8 7 6 5 4 3 2 1

Typeset by Hewer Text UK Ltd, Edinburgh

Printed by Clays Ltd, St Ives plc.

The paper this book is printed on is certified independently
in accordance with the rules of the FSC. It is ancient-forest
friendly. The printer hold chain of custody.

FSC
Mixed Sources
Product group from well-managed
forests and other controlled sources
Cert no. SGS-COC-2061
www.fsc.org
© 1996 Forest Stewardship Council

In memory of John Scott Orr

The author wishes to thank the Scottish Book Trust and its partners, who facilitated the writing of some of what follows.

Who knows, whether, if I had given up smoking, I should really have become the strong perfect man I imagined? Perhaps it was this very doubt that bound me to my vice, because life is so much pleasanter if one is able to believe in one's own latent greatness.

– Italo Svevo, *Confessions of Zeno*

1

Standing on one of the balconies of the Mimosa serviced apartments, Tom Brodzinski sucked on the moist filter-tip of his cigarette, and swore to himself it would be his last.

But then, it occurred to him, that's something I've sworn a whole heap of times before. This time, though, it would be different.

For the three weeks of the Brodzinskis' vacation, Tom had found the prohibitions on smoking, in this vast and sun-baked country, particularly intrusive. There were strident signs in – and on – every restaurant, bar and public building, threatening fines and imprisonment not only for smokers themselves but even for those who – whether wittingly or not – allowed smoking to take place.

Moreover, outside the public buildings, there were yellow lines painted on the sidewalks and roadways, indicating where smokers could legally congregate: sixteen metres from their entrance.

Such measures, of course, existed in Tom's homeland; yet there they hardly seemed so egregious. Besides, the bulk of the population had long since kicked the habit. While here, the whole garish infrastructure of this public-health campaign appeared, even to Tom's indolent ethical eye, to have been imposed on the country's polyglot and heavy-puffing population, in place of any more commanding civic morality.

And so it all had grated on Tom, turning those little interludes of cloudy self-absorption into hurried and unsatisfying liaisons with La Divina Nicotina.

Yes, giving up would free him from such bondages, while, at the same time, he would find liberation in doing the right thing, facing up to his mortality, his responsibilities as a father, a husband and a citizen. No longer would he sustain his individualism with such puerile puffing.

Tom was no fool; he understood that smoking was really only of any interest to smokers – and that, increasingly, that was all that interested them. Once free of the habit, he would be in a new world, where he could see things clearly and understand their significance, rather than being hectored by signs and lines.

Thinking of stubbing his final cigarette out, Tom looked around the balcony for an ashtray, or any other receptacle which could receive the worm's cast of ash. But there was none. Next, he peered over the balustrade, down on to the balcony below, which projected out from the façade of the apartment block that much further.

An elderly Anglo man was spread out on a lounger. The thin legs that stuck out from his Bermudas were lumpy with bunches of varicose veins. The onion-skin sheets of an international edition of the *Wall Street Journal* lay on his deflated chest. From Tom's vantage, the old man's face was foreshortened to a nubbin of a nose and chin, while his bald pate flaked beneath an artificially lustrous comb-over.

Tom tipped the ash into his own cupped hand, tamped it into dust and blew this into the heavy, humid air. From below there came the noise of metal scraping on tile. A young woman had emerged from the sliding doors that, Tom assumed, must separate the balcony from the old man's own serviced apartment. A very young woman – a girl, in fact.

She wore only a sarong, which was wrapped around her slim, sinuous hips, and, from where Tom stood, he could appreciate the orchidaceous perfection of her breasts, the taut purity of her matt-black skin. She must, he thought, be a desert tribeswoman, but what the hell was she doing with this dried-up stick of a guy?

What she was doing was drawing up a small metal table and placing upon it a tall glass, frosted with condensation and choked with fruit. She removed the newspaper, tidied its pages and folded it. What she was doing was unaffectedly ministering to the old man's needs, to the point that she seemed quite unconscious of the way one of her long, pinky-brown nipples pressed against his neck, as she smoothed the sweat-damp hair on his forehead.

'Thanks, honey,' the old man rasped, and the complacent tone of his voice summoned up Tom's righteous indignation, reserves of which were generous to begin with, and always easily replenished by the follies of his countrymen.

Jesus Christ! Tom internally expostulated. That sick creep is one of those disgusting sex tourists. He's come over here to get his gross old body fondled by one of these young girls! It's revolting – he can't be allowed to get away with it!

Tom's grasp on the ethnic complexities of the country wasn't strong, but he did know that the Tugganarong – the copper-skinned natives of the offshore Feltham Islands – came here as guest workers; and that many of the young women ended up prostituting themselves. But this girl was clearly a desert tribeswoman, and he hadn't seen any like her hanging around outside the bars and strip clubs of Vance's small – but savage – red-light district.

In truth, the whole bizarre palimpsest of race and culture in this vast land bamboozled Tom. In theory, the Anglo descendants of the former colonial power still constituted the elite. Yet, only the previous morning, in the highland township where they'd stopped to get gas and cash, Tom had found himself in line at an ATM behind a shambolic, shaking figure that was bent almost double and wearing a dirty-blue patterned native toga. But when his turn came at the brushed-steel keyboard, it transpired that the man hadn't been waiting to make a withdrawal at all. Rather, he stooped to retrieve a half-smoked cigarette butt from the dusty ground.

Tom found himself fixated on the white trough of a scar that bisected the old wino's grizzled head from nape to crown. Was this, Tom wondered, the most extreme of tribal markings? Or had the man stumbled, drunk, into a buzz-saw?

Then, as the figure straightened up, and the turtle head swung up and round, Tom was confronted by the sun-cracked features of an ancient Anglo, whose mouth was crusted with dried yellow goo.

Later on, as Tom struggled to pilot the preposterously large minivan – which he had hired in an excess of foolish grandiosity – through the maddening mêlée of the main street, he spotted the same old Anglo wino, in the shade of a fat-trunked tree set back from the road.

Now, recalling the unpleasant scene that had followed, Tom took a particularly deep draw on his cigarette, and it fizzed and popped in the humid atmosphere. He deposited another quarter-inch of ash into his hand, tamped and blew.

4

Tommy Junior, who, as usual, had been right at the back of the car, had also seen the old wino. More importantly, he'd seen what the indigenes with whom the wino was sitting and drinking palm spirit were selling.

'Dad! Dad!' he had boomed out – why couldn't he control his volume? 'They've got one of those model things we saw back a ways. Can we stop and get this one? Can we? Can we, please?'

Tom was going to give this request no more attention than the previous score, but Tommy's mother had decided to intercede. 'Why don't we stop and see if we can buy it, Tom?' Martha suggested, gently enough. 'Tommy's been real good the last couple of days – and they haven't been easy for him. The other kids have all gotten stuff they wanted; why not get him something too?'

'I don't think they're for kids . . .' Tom began, and then thought better of continuing, because his wife's posture had altered in the way it always did when she was readying herself to bring him into line: her bare shoulders rising up, her elegant neck snaking down, her round golden eyes widening under her thick blonde fringe. Tom had looked for a gap in the throng – with its press of wagons drawn by lama-like auracas, its frenetic pedestrians and clashing rickshaws – aimed the car at it and pulled up by the tree in a cloud of ochreous dust.

Needless to say, the model Tommy had wanted wasn't for sale. Or, rather, it wasn't for sale to them. The native who had made it explained to Tom and Martha, through the slurred intermediary of the old Anglo wino, that it was a cult object, and, as such, could be bought only by a member of a different clan to his own; one that stood in a special – and obscure – relation to it.

'As you can see,' the wino croaked, 'it is an absolute top piece of workmanship, yeah. A Gandaro spirit wagon – but then, you knew that.'

What was knowledge? God knows, Tom always tried to read up on the culture of the places the family visited, and this vacation had been no exception. Before the Brodzinskis left home, he had given himself kaleidoscopic migraines reading stuff on the web. Was it the surreptitious joints he smoked in front of the screen, or the way the luminous info-panels slid across it? Tom couldn't be sure, but, instead of grasping the details, he found them slipping between his numb mental digits.

This much Tom did know: these upland tribes – the Gandaro, the Ibbolit and the Handrey – were less austere and mystical than the desert dwellers. Their magic was tempered, both by the warm rains of their cloud forests and the long history of contact with aliens. They believed in a kind of can-do, can-get approach to their spirits, importuning them through the agency of these talismans: finely wrought models, depicting those goods and attributes that they wished for themselves.

Hence, this particular model, which was a 1:10 scale version of the very four-wheel-drive minivan they were sitting in. Right down to the iridescent blue paint job, the ludicrous flying-vee spoiler, the bulbous wheel arches and tinted windows. It had been fashioned with exquisite cunning from tin cans, hammered flat, seamed and then soldered together. Now it lay in the lap of its Gandaro creator, and he stroked its metallic curves as if it were a much loved child.

The contrast between the primitivism of the model and the sophistication of its subject imbued it with a curious potency, even if you gave no credence whatsoever to its magical properties. Tom, himself, wanted to take it from the thickset hillman with the bone nose plugs. And Tommy Junior – who had extracted his broad rear end from the back of the car with his usual difficulty – stood in the dusty shade, screwing up his gross features, overcome by the loss of that thing that he had never possessed, and began to keen.

The cigarette was finished. All that remained was a fang of ash curling up from its speckled gum. The cigarette was finished – his last – and Tom also felt overwhelmed by the loss of that thing that he had never possessed: some deep and primordial sense of healing satiety, a patch on his ruptured heart. Vainly, he cast about once more for the ashtray that wasn't there; and then, in a moment of utter unthinking, he flipped the butt into the sodden air.

It arced up, end over end, then, for an instant, hung at the zenith. Tom bade it a fond farewell, for, as it described its neat parabola, it was defining his own new moral compass. I'm a better man, he thought, a much better man. Then, as the butt fell towards the balcony below, the dream Tom had had the preceding night, as he fretted in their fetid bed in the Tree Top Lodge, high in the cloud forest of the Handrey, came back to him.

Martha, sitting on a rattan chair, staring down between her parted thighs, as the slick, oily pool of blood on the floor plipped and plopped.

'I'm spotting again, Tom,' she had said in a low, venomous tone. 'I'm spotting again – and it's your fault.'

There was a long, drawn-out howl from the balcony below, as of an animal caught in some fiendish trap. Confused at first, assuming that the kids were fighting in the apartment, and one of them had banged their head, Tom started towards the sliding doors. But Martha, having heard the howl as well, confronted him in the entrance, bulges of fresh-showered flesh cinched by her towel.

Together, they strode to the balustrade and looked over. The old man was balled up on the lounger. His hands and those of his young mistress both clawed at the mess of disarranged hair on his smoky scalp.

Realizing what had happened right away, Tom called down: 'I'm sorry! So sorry – I wasn't thinking.'

The old man was still twitching and howling. Martha looked at Tom with accusatory eyes. The native mistress had found what she was searching for, and brushed clear of the lounger the last smoking shreds of the butt, which scattered on the white tiles.

'Why you fuggin do that?!' she spat up at them. 'Why you? You damn bloody fool, you!'

Later, when they had managed to calm the kids down, Martha took them all out for a walk, and a guilty, junk-food supper at Cap'n Bob's, the open air café on the 'nade.

It took half an hour for Tom to summon up the courage of his contrition; then he tiptoed down the bare stairs, padded along the covered walkway and knocked on the door of the odd couple's apartment. The native girl answered it, and, despite the fluster of his own disgrace, Tom was still disappointed to see that she had repositioned her sarong to cover her breasts.

'Oh, you.' She pointed a damning finger at him. 'What you wan'? Wha'chew doin' down 'ere, yeah? Wha'chew wan' with me?'

'I – I came to see how he's doing.' Tom felt juvenile

8

under the girl's knowing gaze; her brown eyes held the eternal powers of youth and sexual vitality.

And what did the girl see? Another Anglo tourist, the same as all the rest? He wasn't in bad shape for a man of his age – he had all his own hair – but there was no disguising the fact that Tom Brodzinski had only ever had average looks to begin with. His was a face, he knew, that cried out to be ignored: his nose small and lumpy, his cheekbones ill defined, his chin irresolute. His eyes, like the girl's, were brown, but they held nothing more than a certain mildness, together with the bafflement of middle age. Even Tom's height and build were – if such a thing is possible – dull. Average.

Without more ado, the girl led Tom into the smaller of the two bedrooms in the apartment. He knew this was so, because the layout corresponded to that of his own. Here, on a low, narrow, single bed, lay the victim of his butt, apparently naked beneath a thin, floral-patterned sheet. There was a compress, or face cloth of some kind, over the old man's face. He looked corpse-like, and Tom stuttered, 'I – I don't m-mean to . . .'

Rousing himself, the old man removed the cloth. Where the butt had burned his scalp, a blister the size of a grape rose midst the pathetic dyed hairs. A beam of light, hard and metallic, probed between the curtains pulled across the tiny window, clearly illuminating the gleet in this cyst.

The old man's jaw was slack, and turkey wattles shivered beneath it. His hand – which he held out to Tom – was caricatured by arthritis, yet, when he spoke, his voice was surprisingly deep and powerful. 'Reginald,' he said. 'Reginald Lincoln the Third.'

'Tom.' Tom took the hand and subjected it to considerate

pressure. 'Brodzinski – the first of the line. Lissen, I can't tell you how sorry I am about this dumb . . . this dumb thing. Crazy, I don't know what I was thinking; I mean, I guess I wasn't thinking at all.'

'C'mon . . .' Lincoln released Tom's hand, and indicated that he should sit beside him on the skimpy bed. 'We all do dumb things,' the old man continued. 'I know I have. It was an accident; don't be too hard on yourself.'

'But a cigarette, Jesus, in this day and age that's an offensive weapon, even if you don't, like, *hurl* it at someone.'

Lincoln, to Tom's considerable relief, laughed again, then said: 'Like I say, we've all done dumb things, and I used to be a smoker myself. I only gave it up a couple of years ago. With my blood pressure, it was getting in the way of more important things, if you know what I mean.'

Lincoln's black hooded eyes were directed to the doorway, where his teenage mistress was standing. Despite his state of contrition, and his gratitude at being so speedily shriven, Tom still felt a stab of sexual jealousy, mingled with an unreasoning hatred, at the sight of the black-skinned sylph, her discoid hairstyle forming a fetching halo around her pretty head.

Tom took a deep breath, and half smelled, half tasted Vaseline and coconut oil. Could it be, he wondered, that my sense of smell is already more acute?

'You're not going to believe this' – Tom addressed them both – 'but that was my last – my last cigarette. I'm giving up too. I guess that's why I was . . . I was so, uh, preoccupied. Well,' he laughed shortly, in what he hoped was a self-deprecating manner, 'at least if I stick to my resolution, I'll never be in any danger of doing such a dumb thing ever again.'

'At my age,' Lincoln said, levering himself up on one elbow, 'young man, you learn not to make too many resolutions at all. You just take each day as it comes, and try to be grateful if you've hung in there.'

Observing the keen expression on Lincoln's dissipated face, Tom was thankful for the 'young man', which, for once, seemed genuine, not patronizing, and placed him in the same age group as the girl leaning in the doorway.

He got up to depart. 'If there's anything, anything at all I can do for you, please don't hesitate to ask?' Tom said, turning questioningly to the girl.

'Sure,' Lincoln put in. 'Atalaya will be here, she'll let you know if there's anything, but I doubt there will be. It's a blister – that's all. I'll see you at breakfast in the morning. Lemme tellya – they do a good one here.'

When he got back upstairs, Tom found the eight-year-old twins already drooling in front of the riotous, colourful barbarism of the Cartoon Network. His daughter, Dixie, who was thirteen, was sitting at the round table in the dining area of the apartment, threading glass beads on to a leather thong. Tommy Junior was in the small back bedroom, cross-legged on the bed. With his T-shirt as capacious as a robe, his large long-lobed ears and his sagittal crest of greased part-bleached hair, the boy resembled at once the Buddha and an ape. He was fiddling with the toggles of a hand-held-computer games console that was hidden in his big hands.

Tom looked at his eldest son, smitten with the shame and rage that were so habitual as to have formed a callus, jibing his heart.

Tommy Junior looked up, grunted, looked down again.

Was he truly retarded – Tom pondered this automatically,

as any other man might have yawned – or wilfully fucking stupid? The boy seemed stupid to his father, his obsessions and his obduracies determined by some inner-peasant, rather than visited upon him. It was as if Tommy Junior tried quite concertedly to do everything in his power to upset his father. He grunted his way through meals, he ignored the most fundamental social pleasantries. If Tommy Junior spoke voluntarily with anyone at all, it was only in order to regale them with interminable monologues concerning whichever computer game he was currently fixated on.

Besides, it wasn't like he was at some special school. He was in the same grade as other kids his age. He got a little extra help, sure, but he could read, he could write.

Martha came into the vestibule where her husband was standing. She was abstracted, withdrawn into the glossy funnel of a magazine which she held beneath her dripping, freshly showered face. A face hosed of expression as well as make-up. Regarding her sharply, Tom had a bizarre insight: Martha had given up smoking five years before, and ever since then she had seemed increasingly exiguous to him. It was as if the smoke that had once wreathed her beautiful face had given it definition.

'How'd it go?' she asked.

'OK, I guess. He's got a big blister, he's lying down. The native chippy's looking after him fine.'

'Please, Tom–'

'What? The kids? They can't hear – they don't care.'

'No,' she snapped back, 'not the goddamn kids – me, Tom, me.'

'Anyways,' Tom continued, eager to put his wife's sensibilities behind him, 'it looks like he's gonna be OK. I smoothed things over.'

Padding away from him, leaving wet footprints on the white tiles, each one like a blister, Martha said over her bare shoulder: 'Well, that's something, but then you're always good in a crisis.'

Crisis. Crisis averted. A crisis that had happened not to one of his kids – which Tom always feared when they were overseas – but only to the old man, Lincoln.

Well into the cicada-chafed, tropical darkness, when he and Martha had finally managed to get all the kids settled – the twins in the bunks, Dixie on a studio bed grudgingly supplied by the management, Tommy Junior in the back bedroom – Tom allowed himself this positive stroke: the old man was OK, he was safe. Martha and the kids were safe too. They had all survived the drive over the Great Dividing Range, the switchback roads, the slithery mud.

They had survived their adventurous vacation, and the day after tomorrow they would fly home, triumphant, the memory cards of their cameras loaded with digital trophies.

Tom rolled towards his wife. She sighed, and hunkered away from him. He took the rebuff in his self-satisfied stride, and soon enough managed to sleep.

But in the deep of the night there came a hammering on the door of the apartment, and swarming through heavy, humid dreams and misapprehensions – which continent am I on? who am I? – Tom swung the door open to find Atalaya, her breasts swinging free in the warm, damp vee of her lacy nightie, while above this curls were plastered against her furrowed brow.

'He – Reggie, he's fallen,' she said without preamble. 'I can't lift him. Can you? Can you lift him?'

'What time is it?' Tom asked, reaching out for the quotidian.

However, she only reiterated: 'Can you lift him?'

It was worse than he could have imagined. Tom found the little old man crumpled up on the tiles between the narrow single bed and the closet. It was pathetic: the blister had burst, and the flap of skin had peeled away from his pate, on it a clutch of the shoe-polish-coloured hairs.

Tom hesitated for a moment – perhaps moving Lincoln would be a mistake? – then Atalaya urged him on with a none too gentle shove.

The body was as light as a child's, the liver-spotted skin unpleasantly scaly to the touch. Holding the old man in his arms, Tom felt Lincoln's heart fluttering against his hand. He set him down, gingerly, on the bed, as if to wake him would be to disrupt an innocent repose.

Propped up against the pillows, Lincoln breathed in laboured squeaks and nasal squeals. Tom was reminded of a smoker, gasping for breath after an unaccustomed jog.

Atalaya gripped Tom's elbow. 'We must get him to the hospital. Now.'

The old man's eyelids twitched, exposing yellow bloodshot whites. His twisted hands grabbed at the fitted sheet, pulling it back to reveal the mattress, which was garishly patterned with frangipani blossoms.

Out of unusual consideration – or calculated disdain – Martha had let Tom sleep in. He awoke to find the apartment empty, and, staggering from room to room, his damp soles sucking on the tiles, he saw the abandoned chrysalises of sheets and counterpanes on the disordered beds. The fans on the ceiling lazily sculpted the claggy atmosphere. Tom went out on to the balcony, then recoiled from the fanfare of the tropical day: its brassy greens and reds, its hot jazz of sunlight.

The previous few hours came winging in on him: the boxy ambulance, its flashing lights slashing the darkness; the glaring white cube of the hospital; the old man being wheeled in on the gurney; the receptionist – freaky, with coiled braids and projecting, ornamental cones of hair – swiping his credit card. By what means – telepathy? – Tom could not comprehend, but by the time they'd reached the hospital room his Mastercard had secured a gaggle of Atalaya's tribeswomen were already there. Tall, burly women, with pumped-up parodies of her lissom figure, who chattered loudly as the nurses hitched the unconscious old Anglo to tubes and monitors.

The detachment of the desert tribeswomen, and of Martha, had seemed, to Tom, to be two sides of the same strange coin. For, when he finally returned to the apartment, stripped off his short pants, dragged his sore head through the neck of his T-shirt and clambered on to the bed, she only roused sufficiently to hear the sorry tale in sullen silence, before saying: 'Look, Tom, right now I couldn't give a damn how you screwed up this time. The kids'll be up in an hour, and someone – meaning me – will have to look after them.'

Now, observing a long rivulet of dark red leaf-cutter ants that trickled along a branch, bearing upon its crest-wavering, translucent, sail-shapes of vegetation, Tom was ashamed to catch himself – despite all the stress and anxiety of the previous fifteen hours – searching, automatically, through the pockets of his pants.

Perhaps a crumpled paper tube of tobacco would be nestling in there, offering the prospect of temporary repose. Reclusion in a private cubicle, separated from the rest of the world by comforting, hazy, blue, blue-grey, grey and brown drapes.

2

The Consul – whose name was Adams – found Tom sitting in the breakfast room of the Mimosa, warily contemplating a bowl cluttered with sharp-angled chunks of some strange fruit.

Adams, who wore a faded tan seersucker suit and lace-up shoes, and whose button-down collar had trapped a tie embroidered with the insignia of a major institution – university? military formation? corporation? – that Tom half recognized, sat down across from him, offered a hand clasp as cursory as a dog pat, then began withdrawing papers from an old leather briefcase, talking the while.

'This, ah, Mr Brodzinski, is a retention guarantee, this is a visa-rights waiver, and this is a credit-rating form issued by the Interior Ministry. I'll need your signature on all three.'

He offered a fountain pen, which Tom, abandoning his syrup-sticky spoon, took. Adams smiled, exposing bleached teeth in his heavily tanned face. He was, Tom supposed, in his late fifties. Wire-wool hair bunched on top of his long equine head. The Consul sported Polaroid lenses in severe, oblong, wire frames, which, even as Tom contemplated them, were becoming clearer, and revealing watery blue eyes caught in a net of laughter lines. Adams's shirt collar had wing-tips, there was a plastic pen holder in the breast pocket of his jacket, and a heavy gold signet ring on the pinky finger of his left hand.

'But, why?' Tom queried. 'Why have I got to sign them?'

'Purely a formality,' Adams snapped. 'In a case of this, ah, nature, all the relevant departments want to keep their backs covered, just in case you . . . Well, just in case you leave the country.'

'Leave the country?' Tom was incredulous. 'Why in hell would I do such a damn-fool thing?'

Adams sighed. 'People panic – I've seen it plenty of times. They've heard . . . things, rumours about the way the justice system works here. They figure it might be, ah, better to get out while the going's good.'

'Rumours? Justice system? I dunno what you're talking about – what's this got to do with the local authorities? Surely, Mr Lincoln and I, I mean, we're fellow citizens, can't all this be sorted out by you, here, right now? And if Mr Lincoln requires some kind of, well, compensation, that can be organized back home.'

Adams didn't answer this immediately. Instead, he pushed himself back on his chair and, breaking from Tom's fierce stare, trajected a stream of liquid syllables towards a maid who was clearing away the cereal-crusted bowls.

The maid, whose heavily scarred arms and legs gave her the sinister appearance of having been sewn together out of several other people, barked with laughter, then went to the hot plate and poured out a cup of coffee. This she brought straight over to the Consul.

Tom smelled the bitter odour of the five-times-reheated brown gloop. Adams took a slug – unmitigated by milk or sugar – and wiped his mouth with the back of his hand, a gesture at odds with his fastidious manner.

He burbled at the maid once more, and she crossed the room and snapped off the TV. A TV that, until then, Tom hadn't even been aware was on. Although, now he considered it, at least some of his gloominess was attributable to the news footage he had been subliminally absorbing. Footage of a dirty firefight: half-tracks scuttling like scorpions over stony, nameless bled, their machine guns spitting death venom.

'Look, Mr Brodzinski,' Adams resumed, 'ordinarily, what you say would be the case: two guys overseas, one of them assaults the other . . .'

'Assaults?' Tom expostulated, and then heard, issuing from his own lips, the pathetic excuse he had heard so often from those of his children: 'But it was an accident.'

'That's just it.' Adams remained reasonable. 'Or, rather, the two things are interrelated. You see, Mr Lincoln is, in point of fact, a dual-citizen.'

'A dual-citizen?' Tom feared these repetitions made him seem moronic, exactly the kind of dumb hick, confounded by the exotic, who he himself despised.

'Not, you understand' — a little moue flitted across Adams's mouth — 'that he has taken on this status voluntarily; such a thing is incompatible with our own laws. It's simply that by marrying Atalaya Intwennyfortee he automatically assumed her nationality.'

'But . . . Well . . . I mean, I assumed . . . that he — that she was . . .'

Adams put a stop to Tom's floundering: 'No matter what you assumed, they are indeed man and wife. Moreover, as I'm sure you're aware, there's a complex, ah, relationship here between the established and codified system of civil and criminal law, and the customary laws of the indigenous peoples. To get to the, ah, point, Mr Brodzinski, Mrs Lincoln is Tayswengo, and, in common with the other desert tribes, the Tayswengo don't believe in, ah, accidents.'

Adams placed undue emphasis on the word 'accidents'; and to Tom, who was beginning to feel as if he was descending into a delirium, it seemed for a moment as if the Consul, himself, obtained to the same view.

'They don't believe in accidents,' Tom murmured.

'That's right.' Adams gestured to the unsigned papers that lay beside Tom's untouched bowl of fruit. 'Mrs Lincoln, therefore, considers your, ah, flipping of the butt on to her husband's head to have been, ipso facto, evidence of malicious intent. And, I'm afraid to say, the law backs her up on this. If she were a third-, or even a second-generation Anglo, the situation would've been different. If she were an Ibbolit or, even better, a Tugganarong, the legal status of your action would've been different again. However, Mrs Lincoln is none of these things; she is Tayswengo, and therefore you will, almost certainly, face a charge of assault and, potentially, one for attempted murder.'

For some time after the Consul had vouchsafed this terrible information, the two men sat in silence. Tom stared at the milk carton on the table in front of him, which bore a state-funded advertisement for a suicide helpline. Away down the walkway that led to the pool area, Tom could hear more of the liquid burbling, interspersed with bursts of laughter. The breakfast room was empty save for the two of them. A rivulet of ants came snaking across the tiled floor – black ones, this time. Peering down closely at them, Tom saw that every third or fourth worker carried on its shiny back the tiny pustule of a Rice Krispie.

'I don't know what to say,' Tom said at last, superfluously.

'Really' – Adams, having delivered his body-blow, was almost emollient – 'the situation is nothing to worry about. So far as I'm aware Mr Lincoln is making a full recovery, no?'

'When I left him early this morning, in the hospital, he was already sitting up in bed. To be honest, Mr Adams' – Tom winced, he could hear the note of childish self-exculpation re-entering his voice even as he spoke – 'I'm not even sure that his collapse has anything to do with the – the butt. I mean, he is very old.'

Adams exhaled through pursed lips, and Tom was reminded of the first, satiated exhalation of the smoking day.

'Well,' the Consul said, 'that's good. Very good. If he makes a speedy recovery, it will simply be a matter of basic compensation for the Intwennyfortee, and the charges will quietly be dropped.'

'Meaning?' Tom thought of his credit cards, the plastic pacemakers on his avaricious heart.

'I would expect her clan to ask for some new cooking pots, a couple of hunting rifles, maybe ten thousand dollars. These can be very practical people, Mr Brodzinski.'

'What about Mr Lincoln himself?' There it was again, the querulous note. 'Don't his wishes come into this? Couldn't I, like, reason with him?'

Again, the smokeless blow: 'Er, no – not exactly.' Adams leaned forward, steepling long, aristocratic fingers. 'Certainly, Mr Lincoln's goodwill is a desirable thing, but once he's been harmed by another, he becomes inquivoo – which is to say, inert, passive in the matter. For the desert tribes, all important aspects of their existence are governed by this principle: when to act, and when to remain still. Astande and inquivoo. If–'

Adams was warming to his little anthropology seminar. Tom cut him short: 'What if Mr Lincoln gets worse – sicker, I mean?'

'Let's consider that eventuality if it happens, shall we?' Adams hadn't taken kindly to the interruption. He tapped the papers. 'Sign and date, here, here and here. I need to lodge these papers right away at the Interior Ministry.'

Tom picked up the fountain pen and did as he was told. Then he handed the pen and papers back to the Consul, who took a final slug of his coffee, then unfolded himself from beneath the table. Tom accompanied the long drip-dry streak of neatness out into the parking lot, feeling slobbish and juvenile in his short pants and sandals.

Outside the sun was jackhammering down on whitish concrete, viridian grass, bluish blacktop. A mile or so to the south, the pale blocks of Vance's civic centre – the big hotels, municipal and corporate offices, the hypodermic spire of the Provincial State Assembly – flapped in the convection, as if they were the sails of an urban clipper, about to cast off from this protracted and alien shore. Beyond them, the green hills of the Great Dividing Range mounted, in a seemingly endless procession of lush dips and heavily forested spurs, to the horizon.

Tom was surprised to discover that, far from driving one of the ubiquitous SUVs which anyone of consequence in Vance – Anglo, Tugganarong or native – owned, Adams had a distinctly battered old Japanese hatchback. He slung his briefcase on to the back seat of this, then took off his seersucker jacket and folded it with precise movements. Before getting into the car, he turned to Tom. 'Where, may I ask, are your wife and children?'

'I think they went downtown. We're scheduled to fly

home tomorrow, and the kids wanted to see the terrarium, and . . .' he said, tripping into despondency, '. . . a whole lot of other stuff.'

Adams ignored this remark. 'Do you have a local cellphone, Mr Brodzinski?'

'No, and my own can't use the local networks.'

'Then I suggest you, ah, rent one; you may be needing it. Also, you need to consider the possibility of a lawyer.'

Clearly, this was Adams's way of saying that Tom would have to stay behind, while Martha and the kids flew home. As if to emphasize this, the Consul reached into his shirt pocket and came out with a card. 'You can reach me on my cell at any time,' he said, 'or leave a message on the ansaphone. I pick them up regularly.'

Tom took the card with one hand and stretched out the other. Once again, the Consul patted it. Adams got down into the little car. It was going to be an awkward parting. Adams wound down the window, but his gaze was fixed straight ahead, to where sprinkler jets played on the hurting, emerald green of the sports field, with its three anomalous goal posts like keep-fit gibbets. He started the car.

Hating himself for doing it, Tom leaned down and, to prevent Adams from driving away, placed his hands on the car door.

Where has my cool gone? I'm blabbing like a fucking wimp . . . Tom railed at himself, but to the Consul he said: 'I – I didn't realize any of this stuff, you know. About, um, customary law. I though this was, like, a developed country – it certainly sells itself that way so it can rake in the tourist bucks.'

The Consul withered up at Tom. It would have been a relief if he'd given another of his bite-sized lectures, pointing out that ignorance of the law was no defence, or perhaps detailing a few more ethnographic facts. Instead, Adams only withered at him for a while longer, then resolutely put the car into shift.

'Call me later,' he snapped, 'or I'll call you.' Then he pulled away. The tin-pot Toyota halted at the cross street for a moment, then turned right along Dundas Boulevard, towards the ridiculous white marble pyramid of the casino on the seafront.

Tom stood for a while looking after him, then peered down at the card in his hand. It had the usual heavy weave of government service stationery. Underneath the flag, and the mysteriously armed bird of prey – what could it possibly do with those spears and lightning bolts? – was embossed WINTHROP ADAMS, HONORARY CONSUL; then an address, which Tom, despite his ignorance of Vance, recognized as being residential.

'Honorary Consul'? Tom mused. Presumably, this meant that Adams wasn't a full-time government employee, or even that he came under the auspices of the embassy in the capital down south?

Tom was pondering this when a large red SUV swerved into the parking lot and bounced to a halt beside him. He recoiled, then stepped forward, intent on giving the reckless driver a piece of his disordered mind. But before he could, the driver's window was reeled down to disclose a truly striking visage, while the back door of the SUV burst open, and Tom's younger children came galumphing out.

The eight-year-old twins, Jeremy and Lucas, leaped at Tom, pummelling his chest, and both piping at once.

'We saw crocodiles, Dad!'

'And snakes! Big snakes!'

'One had eaten, like, a goat!'

'And you could see hoofs sticking out of its tummy!'

Tom's daughter, Dixie, put one long leg down from the vehicle, and her father noted, with annoyance, that she had had her blonde hair done up in the discoid coif of a desert tribeswoman. Tom had seen other female Anglo tourists affecting this look, and he'd remarked to Dixie and Martha how unbecoming it was: their hair scraped up and oiled, so that their pink scalps were exposed. He would have forcefully expressed his displeasure right away, were it not for the imposing oddity of the SUV's driver.

He must have been ten years or so younger than Tom – a man in the full rude vigour of his mid thirties. Certainly, the copper-skinned torso framed by the SUV's window was highly toned: every pectoral and abdominal muscle clearly defined. That the man was naked from the waist up was not that remarkable, but his Afro of tight, almost white-grey curls was striking, as was the goatee-and-moustache combination he sported, which was beautifully trimmed.

The man also wore wrap-around reflective sunglasses, the cord of which lay on his broad shoulders. Yet, far from annulling his features, this near-clownish mask of plastic and hair only enhanced them.

Tom couldn't tell what ethnic group – or mixture of ethnicities – the man's face betokened. The sharp, flat triangle of a nose and the high cheekbones suggested he was Asiatic, but his skin was too red for this. His sheer bulk might mean he was Tugganarong – or had Tugganarong blood – for the Feltham Islanders often tipped the scales at over 300 pounds. However, the island people, unlike the mainland natives, had only sparse and wispy body hair.

Could the hair be the result of a generous measure of

Anglo genes? Tom considered. Or was the man a member of some grouping previously unknown to him?

The driver forestalled all of this by flicking a finger to his brow in casual salute, and saying a single word: 'Hi.'

This 'Hi' – lazy, apparently unconcerned – brought with it an astonishingly physical sensation of psychic intrusion. Tom felt the hairs rise on his neck – and even his arms. He began to sweat. It was as if the clown-masked man had walked in through one of his eyes, and was now crouching down in the bony cave of Tom's skull. It was altogether uncanny, and Tom couldn't recall ever having had such a vivid first impression of anyone before.

Certainly not of Martha. Martha, who now emerged from the SUV herself. The way she sidled from one haunch to the other, the way she extended a slim foot to the ground, the way her long neck arched – all of it recalled to her husband the first time he had seen her, across a crowded room, at a dull party in their home town. It was this air of languorous self-containment that had attracted him twenty years before, and which now impinged upon him once again. For, just as the clown-masked man had marched into his head, so Martha, quietly and deliberately, seemed to be quitting it.

'Tom,' she said, coming across to him, 'this is Mister–'

'Jethro, Jethro Swai-Phillips,' the man cut in, and reached out his hand. Tom noted that the fingers were of equal length, so that the whole appendage seemed squared off and artificial. Tom took hold of it reluctantly, thinking: how many goddamn times am I gonna have to shake hands today? It's like these people really do have to check that a man's not packing a gun.

'Jethro saw us waiting at the taxi stand in town,' Martha

explained. 'There were no cabs; apparently there's some kind of a race meet on today, so he, very kindly, offered us a ride.'

'It's the least I could do for visitors to my country, yeah,' Swai-Phillips boomed. He had the deep yet ebullient tones of a voiceover for a radio advertisement. 'We have a saying here,' he continued. ' "The wayside inn should have as many beds as there are folk under the setting sun." '

'Is that what you do?' Tom asked, keen to put the conversation on the ground of masculine competitiveness. 'Are you a hotelier?'

'Lord, no!' Swai-Phillips laughed – a big rich laugh with overtones of helpless hilarity. 'No, no, I'm a lawyer. And I hope you'll forgive me, but your good lady here took the liberty of filling me in on your current difficulties, right?'

Christ! How that meaningless interrogative the locals involuntarily added to the end of their sentences annoyed Tom.

'It's nothing,' he snapped at the lawyer. 'Everything's fine.'

Realizing he was overreacting, yet powerless to stop himself, Tom took a twin in each hand, gripping their shoulders as if they were suitcase handles, and started back towards the front door of the Mimosa. Martha sucked her breath in through gritted teeth. However, Swai-Phillips refused to be snubbed. 'No,' he boomed after Tom, 'I don't believe it is nothing. You're not in your own country now, Mr Brodzinski. Personal-injury cases here can be more than just financially costly, yeah?'

Tom let go of the eight-year-olds – who were already protesting at their frogmarch – and whirled about. 'What is this?' he cried. 'Are you some fucking ambulance-chaser? Is that your thing, man?'

Martha made as if to admonish her husband, but Swai-Phillips seemed not in the least put out. 'I mean it,' he said coolly. 'Not just financially costly, although good representation can be expensive.' He extended the strange hand again, a white oblong aligned with its blocky digits. Martha took the card. 'I don't do no win–no fee personal-injury cases,' he remarked perfunctorily. 'In fact, few lawyers here in Vance will, and certainly not if the plaintiff has any connection to traditional people. But then, the Consul probably told you that already, right?'

Swai-Phillips inclined his neat globe of a head towards Martha, as if he were tipping his hat to her. Then he repositioned his sunglasses.

'Good day, madam,' he said. 'It was a pleasure to make your acquaintance, and, of course, that of your children.' Then the mirror-tinted window of the SUV whined upwards, replacing Swai-Phillips's clownish mask with a reflection of the Brodzinskis' own stunned faces, and the big car pulled away.

They stared after its tail lights as it bounced up on to the roadway. Martha was almost exploding with rage, but Tom felt utterly disconnected.

How could he have known? he uselessly interrogated himself. How the hell did he know that I'd seen the Consul?

3

After a full − obscenely costly − hour on the phone in the apartment, Tom managed to secure three days' postponement on their flights home. First he blustered, then he wheedled, and finally he begged the airline clerk. In the end, he was charged only $500 extra, but the changed bookings meant they would have to depart Vance at 4 a.m., then make two stopovers: the first at Faikwong, and the second at Tippurliah, which Tom had never heard of before, but which turned out to be a tiny atoll in the middle of the Pacific.

'How can, like, international flights stop there?' Dixie asked him when he'd come off the call, and was consulting his pocket atlas. 'I mean, it's like the size of a, like, fingernail or something.'

'I dunno,' her father groaned. 'It must be 'cause there's a military installation in that neck of the woods. At the end of World War II, they laid out strips for Superfortresses on some of these flyspecks. Anyway, we're gonna be there for seventeen hours, so we'll have plenty of time to find out.'

'I've gotta, like, jones for Faikwong,' Dixie said, changing tack; 'everyone says the malls there are, like, totally out of this world. I wanna get some cool stuff.'

'Me too.'

Tommy Junior had lumbered into the main room of the apartment and stood gurning up at his games console, which he held in an outstretched hand. 'This thing is way obsolete – they'll have the latest VX90 in Faikwong. It'll be way cheap too.'

'I don't know where you guys think the money for all this is going to come from . . .' Tom began reasonably enough, but as he spoke his voice began to rise and rise, with little aggrieved yelps. 'Neither of you seems to've sicked on to the fact that your father – that's me, guys – is in some serious trouble, here.

'Changing the flights has already cost five hundred bucks; there isn't any money left over for your toys. I may need a lot more money than we've got to deal with this situation at all. I don't even expect Tommy to understand any of this, but you, Dixie, are you as goddamn stupid as him, or are you just INCREDIBLY FUCKING SELFISH!'

The blood drained from the teenage girl's tanned face, leaving bone-white patches underneath her eyes. Her long neck jerked back, and the absurd disc of greased blonde hair, which sat on her head like an ugly halo, knocked against a hotel-chain abstract in an aluminium frame.

The frame rattled on the brick wall. Dixie's hairstyle was now all mashed up, like a bird's nest found lying by the roots of a tree. She bit her lip. Tears lay in her eye sockets – misery bifocals. She bit her knuckles and spluttered, 'You . . . you!' Then she turned abruptly, mashing the halo still further, and bolted into the back bedroom, where, after a few more seconds, Tom heard her begin to wail, with all the mundane anguish of an ambulance siren.

Tommy Junior remained standing exactly where he was, gurning at his games console.

Later on, when the kids had cooled off in the Mimosa's pool, the Brodzinskis walked across the stretch of park to the 'nade.

When they'd first arrived in Vance, three weeks before, the prospect had both charmed and reassured Tom: the neatly mown grass and the oval beds of tropical shrubbery, which spread smoothly down to the 'nade, the long boardwalk that ran clear around Vance Bay, its supporting piles sunk deep in the muddy foreshore.

Now, however, he was conscious only of what an alien imposition this all was: the flowers were too lurid and fleshy, the heavily irrigated grass too green. As for the 'nade, while the weathered wood used to build it was meant to make the serpentine structure harmonize with its surroundings, this effect was ruined by the regularly spaced 'information points' – each with its perspex rain hood, each blazoned with a stentorian NO SMOKING sign, complete with obligatory list of grave penalties.

Alongside the 'nade, there was a beautifully equipped playground. Bright, primary-coloured climbing frames, see-saws and swings stood in safety pits of fine white sand. There was even a water play area, where concealed jets created an artificial stream. Yet, the high-flown municipal pride in inclusiveness, which had even produced a swing for wheelchair-bound children, now seemed strange to Tom, set beside the brackish ooze of the bay, in which wallowed the occasional salt-water crocodile or prehistoric-looking bird.

As they ate their burgers and fries on one of the trestle tables by the café, Martha pointed out what Tom had known only too well – even as he'd wheedled the airline clerk – yet hadn't dared to acknowledge to himself. 'There are only two alternatives, Tom,' she began.

And he, forlornly, tried to stop her, with a 'Perhaps we should discuss this in private. . . ?'

Which she waved away with 'The kids may as well hear it right now. It's a valuable lesson for them' – she turned to include all the children in the homily – 'about how all our actions have consequences. Your daddy has signed a bond, see, and that bond is his word, because he's an honest man; and because he's given his word, he'll have to stay here for a few more days, so he can sort out this business with Mr Lincoln, the man he injured.

'OK. But if we want to get home in time for you guys to start school, and me to start work' – here, Martha darted a particularly sharp look at Tom, who, she maintained, never accorded her career the same importance that he attached to his own – 'then we'll have to go without him. See' – she turned to Tom again – 'wasn't that easy?'

Jeremy squeezed a French fry between his grubby fingers, until it ejaculated white pulp on to his ketchup-smeared paper plate.

'What's a bond?' he said.

On leaving his family, Tom went straight to the CellPoint store that he'd spotted the day before. It was half a mile along Dundas Boulevard, the wide straight avenue that ran from the terracotta block of the Mimosa into the downtown area of Vance.

The CellPoint store, with its plate-glass window plastered with blue and orange decals, and its modular plastic stands that held the gleaming clam shells of the cellphones, was deeply comforting to Tom. There was an outlet exactly like it in the mall near their home town of Milford.

The CellPoint store spoke to him of efficient global

communications and, more importantly, of what was being communicated: namely, certain standards of human decency and best business practice.

As Tom stepped inside, the air con' separated his damp shirt from his back. The workaday formalities of renting a phone were also comforting, yet Tom couldn't stop himself from examining the sales clerks with new and warier eyes.

Whereas, throughout his vacation, he'd been blithely blind to the racial differences of the country's inhabitants – for, was it not, he asked of his flabby liberal conscience, exactly like home? – he now found the woman behind the counter disconcertingly alien. Even though she riffled her computer keyboard, exhibiting all the vapid efficiency of a First World employee, Tom couldn't help fixating on her café-au-lait complexion. Her wrists were encircled with the same raised bands of whitened flesh as the limbs of the maid at the Mimosa. Cicratization, wasn't that what it was called? And how did they do it? By inflicting a regular pattern of burns, then rubbing ash into them? But what kind of ash? Surely not cigarette?

Cicratization. It wasn't the kind of body-modification that Dixie and her friends snuck off to get at that stoners' piercing joint behind the Milford Mall, now was it? Those alien wrists . . . this reeked of wood-smoked firelight, the jumble and thrash of naked limbs, the jabber of alien tongues . . .

His homely fugue dispelled, Tom couldn't wait to sign the papers and get back outside.

As soon as he'd texted Adams with his new cellphone number, the silvery shell in his palm rattled into life. A loud percussive ring tone issued from its little speaker; the noise entirely drowned out the lazy 'pop-pop-pop' of the auto-mated pedestrian crossing. One of the ubiquitous Vance meter maids was passing by: a faded Anglo in a militaristic orange uniform, toting a handheld computer and a digital camera. She looked over at Tom and grimaced.

He answered the incoming call – it was Adams. 'I'm glad you fixed yourself up with a cellphone,' he said, without any preamble. 'There have been, ah, developments. I need you to come right out to my place; the address is on the card I gave you.'

'Developments?' Tom was bemused.

'I don't want to talk about it on the phone,' Adams came back at him. 'Just get a cab and give the driver the address. He'll know how to find it. Come right out. Right out.'

The cabbie was languid to the point of inanition, and Tom could have sworn he drove half the way there steering with his knees. He dropped Tom on a suburban street that curled up into the foothills. Single-storey clapboard houses were set back from the road behind grassy verges. They stood upon stilts, surrounded by stands of palms and bamboo.

At first glance, the lazy S of bluey-blacktop and the neat gardens could have belonged to any suburb in the subtropical developed world. But then Tom noticed the basement areas beneath the houses: there were heaps of old washing machines, discarded TVs and crazy hanks of chicken wire lying on the dirty concrete pans between the stilts. The odour of the place was more decayed than floral, and, sniffing this, Tom made his way between two thorny hedges, then over a rickety wooden walkway that linked the front yard of Adams's house to its single upper storey.

He opened the screen door and, finding the front door ajar with no sign of buzzer or knocker, called out: 'Anyone about?' In what he hoped was a strong assertive voice.

There was no reply. Tom pushed the door open. The

33

room that confronted him was unremarkable: there were woven rush mats on the highly polished floorboards; rattan easy-chairs with padded cushions; a couple of small bookcases, stacked vertically with books and piled horizontally with periodicals. There were native paintings on the plain white walls: jaggy swirls of bright pigments and finger daubs, applied to curved bark shields. With its slight air of bachelor's asperity, and its fussy co-option of native artefacts, the interior was exactly what Tom had expected of the Consul.

Then, above the steady pulse of the cicadas, which had swelled to occupy the sonic vacuum left by the departing cab, Tom became aware of the cooing and tongue slapping of native speech coming from below.

Retracing his steps across the walkway, Tom made his way awkwardly down the steep bank to the underside of the house. Here, in the stripy cacophony of sunbeams, an arresting spectacle met his eyes: five heavy-set hillwomen were seated inside a long black town car. Tom immediately recognized them as being Handrey. This much he did know, for the tourist lodge the Brodzinskis had stayed at in the cloud forest was run by the Handrey Tribal Council.

The women were chattering away to one another, the two in the front seats twisted round, so that they could address the three others sandwiched in the back. Initially, Tom found it incredible that they could have driven down here in the big black car, a vehicle he associated with the downtown of cities back home. But then, on looking more closely, he realized that the car was only a shell: the tinted windows punched out, the bodywork peppered with rusty holes. Two of the doors were missing altogether, and instead of sitting on Firestones, the automobile carcass was jacked up on bricks.

34

The fat, jolly women were wrapped up in their chatter, just as their fingers were twined in each other's wiry hair. They picked and pulled as they yattered, teasing out the cooties, which they then deftly crushed between their finger-nails, before flicking them away.

The women ignored him; Tom stared at them.

He thought of the ads he'd seen at home: big billboards that had encouraged him to fly his family halfway around the world to this island-continent. On these, smiling Anglo servitors, clad in spotless white, were laying out tableware on immaculate linen, while behind them a towering rock formation burned orange in the low-angled sun. 'We've set the table and checked under it for flippers,' the slogan read. 'So where the hell are you?'

What was missing from these huge photographs, with their groups of grinning models, was the myriad of bit players: the insects. Tom thought of the leaf-cutter ants he'd seen from the balcony that morning, the black ants porting the Rice Krispies in the breakfast room, the crickets filling Adam's backyard with their monotonous fricative noise. Up in the hills, he'd seen the gothic mounds of termites, which were five and even six yards high.

And, of course, the billboards – which also featured laugh-ing surfers on the beaches down south, and bubbling snorkellers on the Angry Reef up north – were devoid of black or brown faces. The natives, like the insects, were not a tourist attraction. It occurred to Tom that if the government had had its way, all visitors to the country would have seen of its indigenous people were their bright, naive patterns: black and white stripes, red dots and blue spirals, on T-shirts, sarongs and the tailfins of aircraft.

The kids had all got cooties – Martha too. The foul-smelling chemicals Tom got at the drugstore had no effect, so, in the end, Martha had spent a good part of her vacation combing her children's hair and her own. Martha's patience frayed, as she pulled at the infested locks.

These Handrey women were different. As he watched them, Tom began to appreciate that their delousing was part of an unforced intimacy, one in which their happy conversation was complemented by the reassurance of touch. They reminded him of the hefty Polynesian maidens painted by Gauguin, but what were they doing here?

At last he ventured to speak: 'Is this . . . Mr Adams's place . . . the Consul?'

The women went on ignoring him, and Tom felt himself succumbing to irritation, when Adams himself emerged from the dense shrubbery of the backyard.

The Consul was sporting a broad smile, and a small, leather apron. He held a pair of garden shears in one hand, while the other parted the lush, ridged fronds.

'Ah, Mr Brodzinski!' he cried, 'Glad you're here. Let me put my gardening things away and we'll go upstairs to, ah, talk.'

Tom thought he might come to loathe Adams's 'ah', a tic that suggested everything the Consul said was judicious, considered and yet never the less utterly provisional. Adams's arrival didn't stop the women's chattering, and he'd had to raise his voice to be heard above it.

Tom thought it odd that the Consul's tone was so light-hearted – joyful, even. Taking him in more fully, he noted further transformations: Adams's eyes were bright, and there was a happy slackness to his stride.

Tom waited while the older man took off his apron and placed it, together with the shears, in a battered cupboard behind the town car. He then followed Adams's narrow rump up an open flight of stairs, which emerged into the room he'd already seen from the front door.

'Drink?' Adams asked, with what Tom felt was unseemly levity, given the urgency with which the Consul had impelled him to come.

'Round this time I normally have a long cool one, a Daquiri mixed with the local palm spirit. Some Anglos say this climate doesn't, ah, allow for early drinking, but I say, they can't handle it.'

'Um . . . I dunno, yeah, OK, then,' Tom mumbled; and then, finding his tongue, continued: 'Those women downstairs in the town car – are they, kind of, clients of yours, or what?'

Adams, who had opened the front of a drinks cabinet, and was mixing the cocktails with near-professional bravura, snorted at this. He paused and looked over at Tom. For a moment, it seemed as if he was going to launch into an explanation of their presence, but he only snapped: 'No, friends.'

Tom, although understanding full well that Adams wished to avoid discussing his private life, couldn't forbear: 'What about the town car?' he pressed. 'Strange place to see one.'

The Consul took a long slug on his Daquiri before answering, and Tom, who had grasped the chilly pole of the highball glass, followed suit, unthinkingly. The drink was a physical wrench, jerking him right into the present, slamming his face against hard reality.

Was the palm spirit like mescal, or something? Tom wondered, because at once the pulsing of the cicadas was that much louder, the heat more insistent; the swirls of Adam's native daubs threatened to rotate like pinwheels.

37

Adams tugged at his long U of a chin, in lieu of a goatee. 'I was working in the south, at our embassy in the capital. When I had to take early retirement . . .' Adams paused and, deliberately and unselfconsciously, lifted one hand high above his head, then brought it down to gently pat the back of his head. He resumed: 'The town car was offered to me as part of my, ah, termination package. Only just made it here. Not the best set of wheels for, ah, off-roading.'

He took another pull on his drink and sat down in the rattan easy-chair opposite the one Tom had collapsed into. He set his glass down on a matching side table and leaned forward, caging the fluttery moment with his wiry hands. 'Two points, Mr Brodzinski.' Adams drew one long finger far back with another. It looked painful. 'One: Mr Lincoln has, very unfortunately, developed an infection.'

'Infection?'

'Two: the Assistant DA has already visited the Mimosa, together with police ballistics experts–'

'Ballistics?'

'Mr Brodzinski, I'd be grateful if you didn't interrupt. The ballistics people have established – to the satisfaction of the Public Prosecutor at least – that the trajectory of your, ah, cigarette end would've taken it inside the exclusion zone that forbids smoking within sixteen metres of all public buildings.'

'I don't understand.' Tom was more than incredulous: he was oscillating in and out of hysteria. 'Smoking is permitted in our apartment; I made sure of that when we checked in.'

'It's simple, Brodzinski.' All laughter was now gone from the Consul's eyes; they bored into Tom. 'While the immediate confines of the apartment are a private space – so long as you're paying for it – the complex, as a whole, is a public space. As the, ah, butt, left your apartment – and before it entered that of Mr and Mrs Lincoln – its parabola took it, albeit briefly, into the exclusion zone that surrounds the Mimosa.

'As I'm sure you can appreciate, this fact, in conjunction with the, ah, victim's deteriorating condition, has distinctly severe consequences for your own, ah, situation.'

Tom, knowing it was a mistake, took another pull on his own Daquiri. Surely, at any second, the great wave of need-for-nicotine would engulf him? And, perhaps, despite all his resolutions, Tom should let it drag him away? Only the absurd irony that discarding a cigarette was to blame for his awful predicament prevented Tom from running from the house and down the road in search of a pack.

Luckily, this time the liquor worked, and Tom felt himself detaching and floating a little way off. He was able to ask, fairly calmly: 'What consequences?'

'Well' – Adams, Tom now suspected, was actually enjoying himself – 'It's complex, and the case may even set a new precedent; but, suffice to say, it's no longer possible to resolve the matter through direct negotiations with Mr Lincoln, or even his wife's, ah, family. The DA has made it clear that he intends to take on the case, and he will almost certainly institute a prosecution for . . .'

Without warning, Adams, who had seemed in full flood, trailed right off. The horsy face tipped forward, and the Consul fretted with the lace of one of his suede shoes.

'What! What? Prosecution for what?' Tom was gabbling.

Adams sighed. 'For attempted murder, Mr Brodzinski, and, should the worst happen, naturally for murder itself.'

Tom stood up abruptly and walked to the back window of the room. The fly screening transformed the view without into a sepia image: an old photograph of a verdant, tropical hillside. Beyond it were the inapposite buildings of the colonial power, which were doubtless teeming with thin, feverish men wearing outsized solar topees.

The hillwomen beneath the house had begun to quietly chant 'Bahn-bahn-bahn-boosh. Bahn-bahn-bahn-boosh . . .' over and over again.

Tom turned back to Adams. 'I guess this means I won't be going back home this Thursday.'

'This Thursday, or any time soon, Mr Brodzinski. Lissen.' Having dropped his latest bunker-buster, Adams was, once more, conciliatory. 'I don't for a second believe these charges will stand for long. There'll be a plea bargain. There's also the delicate matter of making restitution – the form of justice, ah, favoured by the Tayswengo – within any, ah, retributive parameters. The DA is part-Tugganarong, the Mayor two fifths Inssessitti. Both are facing re-election campaigns within the next six months; all of these factors must be taken into consideration.'

Suddenly, Tom crossed to Adams's chair and, heedless of any dignity, fell to his knees. He even grasped the Consul's bare forearm in both of his hands. 'For Christ's sake, Adams,' he blurted out. 'I know you're a kind of a diplomat and you can't screw with the locals, but you could at least advise me. Wouldn't it be better for everyone if I just slipped away? No one's taken my passport; surely they can't be posting a watch at Immigration. I mean, I'm no murderer, ferchrissakes, I flipped a goddamn lousy butt!'

Tom stopped. Adams disengaged his arm in a feminine way, as if he were rejecting the importuning of a lusty suitor. He stood. 'Mr Brodzinski, they most certainly will have your details on the computer system at the airport. Even if you could effect, ah, departure from this country in some other way – and may I remind you, while the coastline is vast, the ocean distances to any other landfall are correspondingly so – you're forgetting the papers you signed this morning.

'We have no extradition treaty, but there is something called an Asset Transfer Convention, which both nations are signatories to.'

'W–What does that mean?'

Tom was squatting on his scrawny legs, back at summer camp, querying the Mohawk tribe's field game task.

'It's . . . well, it's unusual – perplexing even.' Once again, the Consul was enthralled by the fathomless complexities of his adoptive country. 'I can only imagine that it was an oversight on the part of the State Department, or that they didn't understand exactly what the Convention would mean when applied to customary law, but, candidly, should you, ah, abscond, your chattels to the value of your presumptive bond would be liable to destruction – not confiscation, mind, destruction – by the plaintiffs' agents.'

'I – I don't understand.'

'The Lincolns could, should they so wish, destroy any of your assets up to the value of the bond, which is \$2 million. And', Adams snorted, 'unbelievably, this has been known to happen.

'A renegade Aval clan insisted that the Westphalian authorities blow up the house of a German tourist who had run into a herd of their auraca in the interior, then absconded. And they – fearing a diplomatic incident – obliged. I'm told the German ended up in the bauxite mines at Kellippi. He's not very well.'

Adams stood and began to walk up and down. He stopped and looked over at Tom. 'But this is all academic, Mr Brodzinski. Pull yourself together. You aren't going to do anything to imperil either yourself or your wife and kids. You wife is, by all accounts a very lovely woman . . .'

Was it Tom's fevered imagination, or did Adams actually lick his thin lips at this point?

'This morning, I suggested that you get yourself a good lawyer. Have you taken any steps in that direction? If necessary the consulate can recommend some practitioners here in Vance . . .' Adams's voice sank, then disappeared.

Tom turned from the window. The Consul had picked up a wooden flipper lizard from the floor and was running a finger round the whorls incised on the back of the carving. Tom had a moment of compassion for this man, who, he suspected, might be trying to do the decent thing by him.

'And once I've engaged a lawyer, what do I do then? Please advise me.'

'You'll need to present yourself at police headquarters. There, you'll be arrested, formally charged and – if there's a judge available – almost certainly immediately bailed. Have you any means of getting funds transferred to the state's account? There are no bail bondsmen here, Mr Brodzinski.'

'I think – I presume my bank manager will, um, oblige.'

The 'presume' and the 'oblige' sounded good, the kind of measured terminology that the Consul himself might use. Tom felt he was regaining his composure.

'And the lawyer?'

At the exact moment Adams said the word 'lawyer', Tom, who hadn't even been aware of his hand being in his pocket, felt the edge of the card Jethro Swai-Phillips had given him. A card that, out of contempt, he hadn't bothered to put in his billfold, but merely shoved down into this sweaty, lint-filled darkness.

He pulled it out and, without any thought, handed it to the Consul, saying: 'What about this guy, is he any good?'

Adams took the card, and glanced at it. 'Swai-Phillips?' he laughed shortly. 'He's one of the best, and, in point of, ah, fact, for your particular case he's the very best. He has Gandaro and Aval blood; hill and desert. There's a dash of Tugganarong in there as well, and, of course, his mother's mother was Belgian. So, he covers the, ah, waterfront. If anyone can get you bail, he can.'

'Bail . . .' Tom muttered, wonderingly. For the first time he took in the fact that he might actually be seeing the inside of a police cell, before the setting sun splurged, molten red, on to the mudflats of Vance Bay.

'Call him on my phone,' Adams continued, 'and if he's able to meet you down there, I'll give you a ride. Then we must call the DA's office, get the relevant account details and arrange for the transfer of these funds.'

'H-How much d'you think they'll want?'

Tom could already hear his bank manager's incredulous voice echoing from the other side of the world: 'You want what?'

'I should think it'll be a minimum of, ah, $100,000 – maybe even twice that.'

Having sounded this financial death knell, Adams set down the lizard on the polished floorboards. He beckoned to Tom: 'Come back in here to my office, we'll make the calls.'

An hour or so later, Tom levered himself up out of the passenger seat of the Consul's Toyota, to find the lawyer already waiting for them on the brilliant white concrete steps of police HQ.

Tom was relieved that Swai-Phillips had put on a shirt,

but surprised that it was such a loud one: the Manhattan skyline encircled his powerful chest. The skyscrapers were black and studded with hundreds of tiny yellow oblong windows, like a negative image of gnashing teeth.

Swai-Phillips waved away Tom's proffered hand, at the same time politely dismissing a reiteration of the apology his new client had already made to him on the phone. He put one huge and corded arm about Tom's shoulders, while vigorously shaking Adams's hand with the other. The two men exchanged bursts of pidgin, the consonants flying like buckshot, then laughed together.

'OK from here in, Jethro?' Adams said, switching to English.

'Yeah – yeah, no worries, mate,' the lawyer replied, and, still embracing Tom, he wheeled him round and marched him up the steps and under the massive marble portico – a feature that Tom, even in his shocked and sozzled state, could recognize as being absurdly grandiose for a provincial station.

In the lobby, which was equally imposing – shiny marble floor, inset with gold brilliants forming the outline of the southern constellations – Swai-Phillips embraced Tom still more closely. 'You,' he breathed, his sandalwood-scented Afro tickling Tom's cheek, 'say nothing. Keep it zipped.'

Then the lawyer advanced on the reception desk, which had been roughly, but artistically, hewn from a block of rusty-red native rock. Behind it sat an Anglo cop in camouflage uniform. She also wore a bulletproof vest that was cut low, like a décolletage. An assault rifle was propped beside her computer terminal, while leaning against the wall behind her was a bundle of hunting spears, some at least twelve feet long.

Once Swai-Phillips had explained their business, another

officer ushered them into an interview room. Here, there were a couple of plastic chairs and a steel table that had built into it some kind of apparatus; this, judging by the buttons and LED displays, Tom assumed to be recording equipment. Surveillance cameras were mounted in all four corners of the room; they were the same compact models that he'd seen all over town, loitering in alleyways, squatting on top of poles like remote-control stylites.

Feeling the effects of Adams's Daquiri, Tom sat down heavily on one of the chairs. Swai-Phillips went to the window and, parting the slats of the Venetian blinds, pointed out to him a powerboat moored in the marina. The high white superstructure was trimmed with silvery aluminium, and a thicket of whiplash radio antennae sprouted from the wheelhouse roof, while a stand of thick sea-fishing rods was planted by the stern.

'Mine,' Swai-Phillips said casually. 'I'll take you out one day.'

The door whooshed open behind them, and Tom turned to see a very stocky brown-skinned man enter. He was clearly a high-ranking officer, for, while he wore the same military-style uniform as the state police, and his massive head was surmounted with the same shiny origami cap – all sharp angles, with a peak like a stork's bill – his was festooned with ornate enamelled medallions.

The officer – who Tom assumed, rightly, to be a Tugga-narong – marched up to him, smelled his breath through pump-action nostrils and spat out: 'Drinking, eh? Anglo's ruin over here.' Then he laughed and turned to the lawyer. 'Gettinoff on your pot an' stuff, are you, Jethro?' He jerked a thumb towards the marina. 'I ken tellya 'ow that tub ainfor the thing. You gotta veep-creep up on 'em fishy-fellers.

Veep-creep awlways. I bin out lass Satenday for tuckerbully, an' gotta 500-pounder juss offa me skiff.'

Swai-Phillips guffawed. 'Me? I took two 700-pound tunny off Piccaboy's 'fore lunch the same day. Gaffed 'em, filleted 'em, an' served 'em up to the old folk at me veranda. I tellya, Squolly, that pot 'o mine don' juss find de fish – it *lures* dem in!'

The two men – one, two heads taller than the other – continued their hobbyists' boasting for another five minutes or so, their claims becoming more and more fantastical.

At some point Swai-Phillips must have passed the officer, whom he called Squolly, the Milford Chemical Bank's faxed notification of Tom's asset transfer, because he no longer had it in his hand when he broke off and said to Tom, 'We're off now'; then to Squolly, 'Gotta get this diddy one back 'fore 'e karks wiv de stress of itall.'

The two friends – for, clearly, that's what they were – then touched palms, and, grasping his client's shoulder as if it were the tiller of a sluggish sailboat, Swai-Phillips guided Tom out of the building.

Once they were in the lawyer's SUV, and a fair way off from police headquarters, cruising along the wide boulevards through the commercial district, Tom recovered his thick tongue and asked Swai-Phillips: 'What happened there? I mean, Adams said I'd be arrested.'

'You were.'

'Then what about Miranda? He, S-Squolly, he never read me my rights.'

'Rights!' Swai-Phillips laughed. 'The only rights here-abouts are the ones we make!'

And to illustrate this witticism, he signalled and took the next right into a cross street.

Tom absorbed this for a while, then said: 'When will the judge decide if I get bail?'

This time the lawyer laughed long and hard; a series of independent bellows of such force that even the oversized car rocked.

'Oh.' He recovered himself and patted Tom's bare knee. 'You got bail alrighty, no worries there, my friend, yeah. With a hundred K down flat, Squolly would've given bail to a kiddie-fiddler!'

And Swai-Phillips erupted all over again, his preposterous silvery Afro shaking like the foliage of a birch tree.

Put out, Tom almost inquired whether, since there had been no sign of a judge, a bribe had been involved. But then he thought better of it: he was beginning to understand how far out of his depth he was. To ask his own lawyer such a thing would only be to flounder still more in this treacherous quicksand.

The shock, the heat and the leaden charge of Adams's palm spirit Daquiri were all puddling together into a bad headache, when the SUV pulled into the Mimosa's parking lot. Swai-Phillips hit a button on the dash, and the native music that had been unobtrusively playing – and which, Tom now realized, had the same, insistent bing-bong beat as the ring tone on his hired cellphone – cut out.

The lawyer stopped the car and turned in his seat. Tom looked into the wrap-around shades and saw in their bulbous lenses his own pale face, leeched of any colour or composure.

'OK, Brodzinski.' The lawyer was all business now. 'Come by my office tomorrow morning, as soon as you've moved your stuff over to a longer-let apartment. Budget will be a consideration for you now, yeah? I can recommend the Entreati Experience on Trangaden Boulevard.'

'I'll be needing a deposit from you. Another wire transfer would be fine, although I'd prefer cash. Either way, say $5,000. My secretary will make sure you get an itemization at the end of every week.

'Luckily for you, I'm called to the local bar as a solicitor-advocate, so there'll be no need to take on a trial lawyer. I'm going to see the DA this afternoon, and I'm hoping to persuade him to set an early date for the combined hearing, right?'

'Combined hearing?' Tom queried weakly.

'That's right. Bail has to be confirmed by a senior judge; at the same time traditional makkatas will rule on the combo. The judge is no prob', but the makkatas have to come in from over there.' Swai-Phillips jerked a thumb over his shoulder; then, seeing his client's incomprehension, qualified this: 'Y'know, from the desert. Anyways, so long as you've been deemed astande, you can immediately begin restitution to the Intwennyfortee mob—'

Tom waved the lawyer down; none of this arcane legal stuff was getting through to him. What had registered, however, was Swai-Phillips's earlier assumption. 'What makes you so certain' – Tom chose his words carefully – 'that I'll be moving out of the Mimosa in the morning? My wife and kids aren't set to fly until—'

'Please, Mr Brodzinski, look behind you.'

Tom whipped round: the twins, Jeremy and Lucas, were playing in the flower bed at the front of the apartment block. As he watched, Jerry picked up a handful of bark chips and slung them at his brother. Tommy Junior was preoccupied, lost in a solipsistic frolic, leadenly cavorting at the kerbside, his partner a wheeled flight bag that he jerked back and forth by its handle.

At that moment, the double glass doors swung open, and

Martha and Dixie emerged, between them manhandling the enormous suitcase that conveyed the bulk of the family's effects.

Tom swivelled back to face Swai-Phillips's bug eyes. It was a disconcerting reprise of the scene that had been played in the same location, by the same cast, that morning. Only this time, Tom voiced his unease: 'How did'ya know they were leaving? How! Are, are you . . .' he said, floundering, '. . . psychic or something?'

Swai-Phillips began to utter his maddening, stagy laugh. However, he was forestalled by Martha, who let go of the suitcase and came barrelling across to the SUV. She wrenched the passenger door open and, leaning across her husband, began shouting at the lawyer: 'What the fuck's your game, mister? Have you got your hooks into my husband? Whaddya want from us, money? Slimy, fucking money!'

Even the imperturbable Swai-Phillips seemed taken aback by this turn of events. Involuntarily, he reached up and swept off his glasses. It was as if – it occurred to Tom later – he was refusing a blindfold, the better to impress his insouciance on this one-woman firing squad by staring her down.

Except that the lawyer couldn't really stare anyone down once his mask was removed. For, while one of his eyes was keenly green and steady, the other was rolled back in its socket, and half obscured by a pink gelatinous membrane that cut obliquely across the white. The three of them froze, shocked in different ways by the revelation of this deformity. Certainly, neither Tom nor Martha Brodzinski had ever seen anything like it before.

4

Later on, as the Brodzinskis waited at the check-in for an elderly Anglo couple to redistribute their hoard of native knick-knacks, Tom asked his wife why she'd reacted with such vehemence.

It was a mistake. Up until that moment they'd been getting on. Tom had accepted there was little to be gained by Martha and the kids staying, while, if they left immediately, they'd be able to fly home direct, with only one brief stop for refuelling in Agania.

For her part, Martha had refrained from berating her husband in front of the children. She had even, as they sat jammed beside each other in the back of the cab, taken Tom's sweaty hand in her own cool one and given it a series of rhythmic squeezes, as if seeking to pump into him a little of her steely resolve.

However, when Tom raised the issue of Swai–Phillips, Martha's expression hardened. She turned away from him, completed the check-in procedure, then sent the kids over to the gift shop with a couple of bills. Motioning to Tom, she led him in the opposite direction, towards a towering shrubbery: entire trees, strung with creepers, were planted in an enormous container, together with a basalt boulder.

Once they were concealed behind this, Martha let him

have it. 'I understand you made a mistake, Tom,' she began reasonably enough, 'but the way you insist on compounding it is beyond me. It's like you've got some kinda urge to drag yourself down – and the rest of us with you. Jesus Christ!' she spat, then gnawed with perfect teeth at the heel of her hand, a pathetic signal of distress that Tom couldn't remember her making since the dark days, shortly after they'd adopted Tommy Junior, and he was – albeit tentatively – being diagnosed.

'I – I . . . I'm not sure I know . . .' He groped for the right formula to appease her. 'I mean, I thought you – you were angry when I was rude to him, to Swai-Phillips.'

'Jesus-fucking-Christ!' she spat again. 'I wanted you to be *polite* to the man, not sign away our entire fucking livelihood to him. Don't you get anything? Don't you realize where you are? These people are laughing at you – laughing all the way to the fucking bank.'

Tom ran a hand over his brush-cut hair; its thickness reassured him, and his headache had succumbed to two hefty painkillers. He felt gutsy enough to come back at her: 'Look, Martha, maybe you're right, in part, but I do know where I am – right here, and Swai-Phillips is a local attorney, he knows all about this local stuff, the way native and codified laws work together. Shit, even Adams, the Consul, he says Swai-Phillips is the man in Vance – or one of them.'

'The man, the man,' Martha mocked him. 'And what does that make you, a man's man? No, lissen to me, Tom. I told you before we came here to read those books, really read them, not just drift off over them 'cause you'd had your evening toke and your Seven and fucking Seven. This is a big, dangerous, confused country, and these people are not your friends – none of them.

'While you were getting in with them, I was making my own inquiries. Seems Adams hasn't been with the State Department for over ten years – he's just the Honorary Consul, he hasn't got any more leverage than you.'

Tom was unmanned. He stood face down to the polished floor of the terminal. The scissoring brushes wielded by a downtrodden-looking Tugganarong pushed a sausage of lint past where they stood.

Eventually, he said what he thought she wanted to hear: 'What should I do, then?'

Martha pursed her lips; her long neck kinked in irritation. It had been the wrong thing to say.

'Do? I dunno, Tom, but if I was you, I'd at least check with the embassy down south. If they can't advise you by phone, I'd get on a goddamn flight and go see them. You've got bail, haven't you?'

'Yes, but I'm not sure if–' He was going to explain about state and federal jurisdictions in this part of the world, thereby demonstrating that he wasn't completely ignorant.

After twenty years of marriage Martha could anticipate this from tone alone. 'One thing I need you to realize, Tom, is this: this is all your own doing, one hundred per cent. You've screwed this one up, just like you screwed up that real estate business in Munnings, and my goddamn brother's health insurance.'

'That–'

'I don't want to hear it. You've screwed this up like you've screwed up your relationship with Dixie, with Tommy Junior, and the way you're on target to do the same with the twins . . .'

Now she was under way, Martha could have kept going indefinitely, had not Tommy Junior discovered them in their toxic bower. He stared at his quarelling parents, his brown eyes shiny and indifferent, then he forcibly turned his mother by her shoulders to face the departures board.

Martha said, 'Oh, my God!' Snatched up her carry-on bag and started towards the line that snaked into the roped-off pens which directed passengers towards security.

Tom stood sulking for a few moments, then tagged along behind, his arm across his son's shoulder, which was higher and more solid than his own.

At the barrier there was a confusion of goodbyes and kisses that missed their mark – bouncing off cheekbones, lost in hair. Martha was contrite. She leaned into Tom and whispered: 'I'm scared, honey, that's all.'

'Me too,' Tom replied, and he would have sealed the rapprochement with a longer embrace had the twins not grabbed his hands and attempted to swing on them. By the time he disengaged, his wife had disappeared, and Dixie was standing on the far side of the metal detector, calling to her father to propel her little brothers through:

Two days later, waking in the deathly monochrome of a tropical dawn, Tom lay listening to the clickety agitation of the roaches in their motel. He thought back to those last few minutes at the airport. Even though Dixie had called him during the family's lay-over at Agania, Tom couldn't rid himself of the unsettling notion that Martha hadn't left the country at all. He hadn't seen his wife go, and now he felt her presence acutely in the seedy, overheated bedroom of the minute apartment.

The Entreati Experience had turned out to be a back-packers' hostel, with a few short-let apartments on the top storey. The backpackers' cubicles were ranged round a grimy courtyard, across which were strung clotheslines festooned with their garish T-shirts and brightly patterned sarongs and Bermudas, which flapped in the bilge-laden breeze from the nearby container port.

Down here, at the rougher end of Vance, there were few Anglo faces to be seen on the streets. Across the road from the Experience, there was a bar frequented by natives, where surly drunks squatted all day and evening, before, in the small hours, beginning noisily incompetent fights.

Swai-Phillips had been right, though: the monthly rate for Tom's apartment was nugatory; a fact explained by the manager, who reminded him that the tourist season was ending. Soon, all the tanned kids would shoulder their packs and flip-flop halfway across the world back to college.

Tom felt ambivalent about this. The college kids were infuriating, revving the engines of their Campervans at all hours of the night, touristic vehicles that were incongruously pitted with bullet holes.

Beardless blond giants cornered Tom in the dank corridors of the hostel and spun him yarns of their adventures in the interior. Their girlfriends loitered near by, snickering, chewing gum, rearranging the straps of their bikinis to expose more of themselves.

Still, once the kids had finally gone, Tom would be all alone. He felt an aching nostalgia for the very idea of air travel, as if the computer-targeted silvery fuselages belonged to a bygone era. Here he was grounded: that most pitiful of things, a left-behind tourist. In his pitiful suitcase were his pitiful effects: half-squeezed tubes of sun cream, trunks with a big word written across them, airport novels that would never go through an airport again, a digital camera loaded with pin-prick-sharp images of ghostly happiness.

The sheet of paper listing his lawyer's impositions was stuck to the scabrous door of the fridge by a magnet in the squashed L-shape of the great desertified island–continent itself.

Each day now the humidity was building and building towards the monsoon. Most days, it took Tom until noon to rouse himself, pull on some clothes and venture out into the hot sponge of Vance. Standing on the sidewalk, he looked up at enormous cumulo-nimbus formations coasting in from the ocean; their bulbous white peaks and horizontal grey bases mirrored the superstructures and hulls of the cruise ships out in the bay – vessels that were readying themselves to depart, scooting out from beneath the gathering storm and heading for safer waters, busier cities, better shopping.

At the quayside Tom took the roach motel out of the plastic bag. He opened the little perspex door, and the roaches, their feelers probing liberty, fell end over end into the scummy water. The waves washing against the concrete gathered their bodies into an agitated raft. Tom turned and scuttled off in the direction of the nearest mall.

Here he had doughnuts for breakfast in a coffee shop, while scanning the paper. The local news he ignored, preferring to peer the wrong way down a 15,000-mile-long telescope, at events diminished out of all significance.

After a few days of this, Tom felt himself sinking into swampy inertia. It was now so humid in Vance that the atmosphere seemed as thick and moist as a hot towel; it was a relief when his lawyer called and summoned Tom to his office.

Swai-Phillips's office was in the Metro-Center, the 22-storey block that towered over Vance's relatively low-rise business district. Ushered in by a furtive, brown-skinned man, who introduced himself as Abdul, the lawyer's clerk, Tom discovered Swai-Phillips with his bare feet up on his desk, his sunglasses clamped on and his impenetrable gaze levelled at the big windows along the far wall. Tom assumed that, like the rest of Vance's dwindling population, he was mesmerized by the anticipation of the rains.

Swai-Phillips was also smoking a large loosely rolled cigar, the outer leaf of which was partially detached. As Tom watched, appalled, he dabbed spittle on to a finger, then applied it to the vegetative glans.

There must have been eight notices detailing Vance's anti-smoking ordinances between the elevator doors and the frosted ones of the lawyer's suite. Yet, when Tom pointed this out, Swai-Phillips only belched smoke and laughter. 'Ho! Ho! Ho! They don't apply in here; this is a *home* office, yeah, special zoning.'

'But what about Abdul?' Tom asked.

'Him? That feller . . .' Swai-Phillips grinned wolfishly. 'He's my son, kind of, right.'

Tom asked about the building: why was it so much higher than all the rest? This was an earthquake zone, wasn't it?

The lawyer did his Father Christmas shtick again. 'Ho! Ho! Ho! You may well ask – not only is this an earthquake zone, this building is slap on the crack, man. I've been sitting here one time, yeah, and seen the streets rucking up like a rug that's been kicked! I tellya why it's so high – the Metro-Center, it's 'cause the pols in this town are so damn low, that's why!'

Tom felt shaky and sat down abruptly on a low chair.

'I would ask if my cigar bothered you,' Swai-Phillips continued, 'but why bother, I know the answer.'

Was it mere rudeness or sheer arrogance on the lawyer's

part? Tom shook his head, uncomprehending. The thick coils of smoke lay so heavily on the carpeted deck of the office that when Swai-Phillips's secretary came in with a cup of coffee for Tom, she appeared tangled up in its bluey-grey hanks.

While the lawyer continued to puff on the monstrous stogie, it dawned on Tom that his own alternations between belligerence and passivity in the face of this whole grotesque situation could be entirely accounted for by the effects of nicotine withdrawal. That's why he'd been so emotionally labile: whining, inveigling, then inveighing. That's why his encounters – with Adams, Swai-Phillips, even the clerk in the cellphone store – had the vibrant, darkly hilarious character of hallucinations. That's why his judgement had been so clouded: for, instead of the smoke venting from Tom at regular intervals, it was backing up inside his head, getting inside his eyes.

'It wouldn't matter a damn, right,' Swai-Phillips hectored him, 'if you were to take up smoking again, so far as the traditional people are concerned. Engwegge – that's the native tobacco – is used so widely here. Shee-it, they don't only smoke the stuff, they chew it, sniff it, rub it on their gums. They even mix it up into enemas and squirt it up their black arses, right. No, it isn't the Intwennyfortee mob you need to worry about on that score.'

He took his feet off the desk and, dropping the cigar in an ashtray, adopted a more lawyerly air. 'However, should we go to a full trial – which I hope won't happen – we'll more than likely be facing a majority Anglo jury; the defence has no rights to veto jurors here; and, as you've probably realized, the whole anti-smoking drive is, at root, racially motivated. The Anglos have a lot of things stuffed up their arses, but engwegge ain't one of them, yeah.

'So, if you don't want to risk smoking, yeah, you can

always chew a few engwegge leaf-tips. I've gotta batch of the finest here.' The lawyer opened a desk drawer and slung a packet made from a banana leaf on to the blotter. It lay there: grossly organic on the workaday surface.

Tom grimaced. 'If it's all the same to you, Jethro,' he said, 'I think I'll take a rain check.'

'Please yourself.' The lawyer sounded miffed. 'This ain't just a fiery little treat – it's ritual stuff. My old feller sends them from over there. The tips are dew-picked, then fire-baked. The makkatas of my dad's mob chew quids as big as tennis balls; then . . . past, present, future' – he dug his spade-like hands into the ineluctable modality of his own engwegge trance – 'they can see 'em all at once. Still' – the lawyer hunched forward and quit desert mysticism for the prosaic office – 'none of that need concern you – not yet, yeah. I want you to come up to my place tomorrow; there's a bloke you need to see, right.'

Tom grunted non-committally. He looked at the bland wall: a print of a nineteenth-century hunting scene hung beside a magnetic year planner. The red-jacketed huntsmen were on horseback, racing after a flock of moai, the giant indigenous flightless birds.

'What're you gonna do when you leave here?' Swai-Phillips barked.

'I – I hadn't thought . . .'

'You should go over to the hospital and see Lincoln,' the lawyer commanded. 'You may not be able to after tomorrow, yeah.'

When Tom entered the room, he found Lincoln reading a golfing magazine. There was no sign of Atalaya or her desert sorority. An Anglo nurse squeaked hither and thither on the shiny floor, changing the old man's saline drip with studious efficiency.

'Lissen,' Lincoln said, putting his reading material aside and taking Tom's hand in his own. 'You must've maxed out your credit card getting me in here – and there was no need – my insurance'll cover it.'

'I thought, I mean – given that you're a Tayswengo, it'd be part of the payback.'

The old man laughed. He certainly looked frail, and there was a thick dressing taped to his now shorn head, but his hand continued to gently pressure Tom's, and his eyes twinkled with amused affection. 'I'm not Tayswengo,' Lincoln said. 'Don't get me wrong – I love Atalaya, she and me . . . well.' He shook his head on the snowy pillow. 'We're soul mates . . . I wish, I wish I'd met her twenty years ago . . .'

Except for the fact that she'd then have been minus-two, Tom thought – then checked himself, for the old man was being so sweet, he felt craven for not having come to see him before.

He cleared his throat and indicated the supermarket bag he'd put on the bedside cabinet. 'I brought some fruit, magazines and candy. I got a selection, 'cause I don't know what you like.'

'Thanks.' Lincoln smiled but made no move to look in the bag. 'Don't get me off the point, young man, this is important. You probably think – or you've been told by that tight-ass Adams – if you lay out for my medical bills, it'll play well with the Intwennyfortee mob, but it ain't that way at all . . .' He tailed off, and Tom realized that even this short speech had exhausted Lincoln.

He made to disengage his hand from the old man's, while muttering, 'I don't want to tire you out–'

But Lincoln gripped Tom's hand tighter. 'I'm inquivoo, see, nothing I say or do counts for any damn thing any more. Thing is' – he looked at the door through which the nurse had exited, as if he suspected she might be eavesdropping – 'you're nothing until you've had the cut.' His hand tightened still more, his voice grated up the scale. 'The cut, Tommy boy, the cut – you gotta have it! Now, Tommy boy, now!'

Lincoln's insistence on 'the cut' – whatever that might be – jarred Tom, as did his bad-mouthing Adams. On leaving the hospital, he finally followed Martha's advice and called the embassy, which was in Capital City, 5,000 miles to the south, across the desert heart of the crumpled island-continent.

After holding and holding again, being transferred from this clerical assistant to that secretary, he finally spoke to a junior attaché. To begin with the woman's chirpy tone was as redolent of home as a ball-game commentary. 'Uh-huh, sure, I see,' she interjected as Tom explained his predicament. He tried not to sound as if he had misgivings concerning the Honorary Consul, but the attaché still picked them up. 'Look, Mr Brodzinski,' she sighed. 'I appreciate that you're in a pretty lousy situation, but there's not a lot we can do from way down here. Adams is the man on the spot, and he has the full support of the Ambassador. He's sent us a report, and he's confident it can be settled without any jail time.

'If I were you, Mr Brodzinski, I'd go with him on this one. Should anything left-field emerge from the prelim' hearing, either someone from my department will come up or, if the judge permits it, you can fly down here for a meeting.

'One thing's for sure, sir, and that's our mission: we never, ever, leave our citizens out in the cold. Citizenship is a sacred bond for us – you should appreciate that. No matter what one of our own is accused of, he remains exactly that: one of our own.'

Out in the cold. What a ridiculous expression, Tom thought, as the cellphone slipped between his sweaty fingers.

But then, as Tom tried to convey the absurdity of a mere accident being treated as a crime, the attaché's manner changed abruptly, her tone becoming clipped. 'See here,' she said. 'I'm not in a position either to judge your intentions or even to know exactly what it is you did. One thing I do know is that Mr Lincoln is an elderly man, and a very sick one. Another thing I know for a fact is that cigarette smoking is both personally and publically injurious–'

'I was giving up!' Tom spat into the cell. 'It was my last goddamn cigarette!'

'I'm going to have to stop you right there, Mr Brodzin-ski.' The attaché's prissiness was shot through with menacing self-righteousness. 'Embassy staff have the right to undertake our work free from the threat of physical violence or verbal intimidation. I'm going to have to terminate this call immediately, as a direct result of your speech acts. I suggest you cool off and pay a little more attention to your own responsibilities, rather than seeking more victims for your dangerous hostility.'

Later, sitting on his corpse of a bed at the Entreati, it occurred to to Tom that this conversation had been a sickening replay of the butt-flick itself: an unthinking ejaculation into the attaché's ear, followed by a massive overreaction.

Musing in this way brought Tom Brodzinski closer to the essence of what had happened to him. Standing on the balcony of the Mimosa, convincing himself that this would be the last acrid dug he'd ever suck, Tom hadn't been considering his,

his family's or indeed anyone else's health; he hadn't plotted the steeply rising curve of medical expenditure against the slowly declining one of chronic disease. No.

Tom now realized, with mounting horror, that his carelessly discarded cigarette butt had flown on its – perhaps fatal – trajectory powered by one fuel alone: a tank of combustible pride. He was Doing the Right Thing – and for that alone should be accorded the uttermost respect.

So the butt had described its parabola and hit its target, creating a minor entry wound, a tiny blister. But oh, the exit wound! The massive, gaping and bloody exit wound, through which the butt had sped on, fragmenting into scores of smaller butts, which were now hitting his children, his wife, and causing terrible collateral damage.

Tom ate at the café on the 'nade. It was empty, and they served him an underdone burger, still frozen at its core. Too cowed to complain, he nibbled its edges. The waiter stood at the sixteen-metre line smoking and looking out to sea: the last of the cruise ships was sinking into the horizon, and above its fo'c'sle reared a mile-high genie of gibbous thunder cloud, struggling to escape from the tropical night.

In that night, Tom dreamed he was staying in the roach motel. It was fully booked, and the other guests, who wore zooty batik T-shirts and tinted shades, tickled him mercilessly with their antennae. It was a relief when the warder of this plastic prison bent down to pick it up and empty them all into the sea. Tumbling end over end, Tom looked up to the quayside and saw the giant Swai-Phillips, his grey Afro coruscating like the corona of the eclipsed sun around his dark impassive face.

★   ★   ★

The lawyer's house was further out of Vance than the Honorary Consul's, at the top of the Great Dividing Range's first foothills. As the cab laboured up the hairpin bends of the single-track road, Tom was confronted first by walls of impenetrable shrubbery, then by vistas of the city below growing smaller and smaller, reduced from its dirty, confused status as a place of human habitation to a mere scattering of pristine white cubes beside the aquamarine bay.

When the cab eventually stopped, so did the road. The blacktop looped through the scrub and petered out in deep ruts of reddish dust. Struggling to turn his vehicle, the cabbie, an obese Tugganarong, grunted, 'This is it.'

And when Tom queried the location, saying, 'Are you sure?', the man laughed increduously. ''Caws I'm fuggin sure. Phillips 'ouse bin 'ere longest time. Longer than bloody Vance, yeah.'

Tom watched as the cab bounced back on to the road and disappeared down the hill. There was a mailbox nailed high up on a tree trunk, and beyond this a path led into the indecipherable bush – so many plants and trees Tom didn't comprehend, their myriad leafy foreign tongues still further complicated by parasitic mosses and squiggling creepers.

Reluctantly, Tom summoned himself and began to pick his way into the jungle. It was oppressively still – not a breath of wind. The sun's rays struck down through the foliage, spearing the back of his neck. His sandals slithered through leaf fall and caught on tree roots. He tried not to think about the seven species of venomous snake, or the three kinds of venomous spider.

Tom came upon a kennel. Two of the sharp-muzzled, brindled, native dogs lay asleep in it. He crept past. Next, the lawyer's Landcruiser emerged from the greenery, parked on an apron at the end of a metalled drive.

The dogs must have been roused despite Tom's wary tread, because there was an anguish of yelps and the crash of heavy paws through the undergrowth. Tom took flight along the path, staggering and tripping, until he was propelled into the full glare of noon.

He found himself by a fence of corrugated-iron sheets, beyond which spread a large compound that occupied the summit of the hill. He was on the point of throwing himself over this — for he could see no other means of access — when the yelps were throttled off. Turning, Tom saw the big dog, its muzzle dashed with saliva, dancing frantically on its hind legs: it had reached the end of its long chain.

Tom laughed callously, then took his time discovering the stile and mounting it, looking back with each step in order to taunt the watchdog still more.

On the far side he expected to meet the lawyer, or one of his retainers, but there was no one, only cracked earth, and scattered across it bits of scaffolding, a cement mixer, piles of cinder-blocks and mounds of hardened mortar. Towards the far side of the compound, projecting out where the hill fell away, there was a concrete platform upon which a few negligent courses of bricks had been laid. An indication, Tom thought, of where a house might be sited if anyone — in this stifling heat — could be bothered to build one.

Tom walked across and stood on the platform. He checked his cell. There was a signal — if Swai-Phillips didn't appear, he'd call him. Then he heard a skittering noise, as of a lizard's flit, and, peering over the edge of the platform, saw that he was not alone.

Ten feet below, in the thin wedge of shadow at the base

of the platform, sat a very tall, matt-black man. Even at a glance, Tom could see that he was extremely thin, his long thighs no thicker than his calves. All the man's limbs were tucked in, so that he resembled a collapsed umbrella.

Tom slithered down the friable earth of the hillside. Up close the man was still more outlandish. He sported only a dirty leather breechclout, which called to mind Adams's gardening apron. Apart from three long tufts of hair above either pendulous ear, his head was shaven; it was like a fifth, etiolated limb, the face as dimpled as an elbow, the almond eyes glazed. A swelling in the man's cheek was the only part of him which moved, revolving slowly. Tom could almost taste the bitter sloosh of the engwegge, and he understood that this must be the makkata.

Not wanting to disrupt the sorceror's trance – it might be prejudicial – Tom turned away. Yet, reluctant to leave, he sat down a few feet away on a tree stump. Into the shimmering oppression of the tropical noon came the rhythmic slurping sound of the makkata's mastication. Tom wondered if he was deep in a vision of the future and, if so, whether he could see Swai-Phillips's new house, its terrace strewn with loungers tenanted by the lawyer's influential friends? Was the makkata watching while topless party girls dove into the pool, their breasts swaying as they went off the springboard? But no – a springboard was out of the question. Tom hadn't seen one in years, and here in Vance – of all places – such a dangerous pleasure would surely be illegal.

Swai-Phillips, as was his gift, popped up from nowhere. One instant he wasn't there – the next he was, looking frowsty and unshaven, in dirty-white jeans hacked off at the knee and nothing else. There were small balls of greying hair on his chest, Tom noted, each one a mini–Afro. Had he forgotten to shave this as well?

Swai-Phillips was standing some yards down the hill, beckoning and calling to someone up on the platform. 'C'mon, Prentice!' he cried. 'Get your sorry white arse down here, yeah!'

Earth and pebbles rattled. Swai-Phillips pushed up his sunglasses and winked at Tom with his bad eye. Tom got up from his stump and turned to see an Anglo of about his own age making his way, very unsteadily, down the slope.

The man had a preposterous coif: the top of his head was completely bald, while there was brown hair not only at the sides but also on his forehead. This fringe wasn't a few straggly threads that he'd combed over; rather, it appeared to have been left behind when the rest of his hair retreated.

The Anglo came right up to Tom with a waddling gait – he walked like a fat man, even though he was not. He offered Tom a hand at once thin and yet fleshy. 'Brian Prentice.'

'Tom,' Tom said, reluctantly taking the hand. 'Tom Brodzinski.'

Prentice wore very new, very stiff blue jeans, cut narrow in the style favoured by the country's cattlemen. On his feet were steel-toed, elastic-sided boots, on his back a khaki bush shirt. The whole authentic outfit was rounded off by a wide-brimmed hat with a neatly rolled fly net attached to its brim, which Prentice carried in his free hand. The gear pegged Prentice as a wannabe adventurer, determined to strike out for the lawless wastes of the interior – or at least to give that impression. Tom instantly despised him, for Prentice's face belied any such resolve.

It was, like his damp hand, thin yet fleshy. The eyes were

equally unresolved: pinkish lids, reddish lashes and wet pupils like those of an embryo. When he spoke – with his irritating, braying accent – his plump yet bloodless lips rolled back from his gums. Either the man had a bad shaving rash, or he'd picked up a fungal infection in one of Vance's rank shower stalls, for his weak jaw and turkey neck were lumpy and corrupted. All in all, Tom couldn't recall ever meeting a more distasteful individual.

Prentice's handshake was predictably furtive: one finger bent back and caught in Tom's palm, as if he were an accidental Mason. When Tom let go, the hand fell limply back to Prentice's side.

Swai-Phillips observed this meeting with ill-concealed mirth. 'Dr Livingstone,' he quipped, 'this is Mr Stanley. Stanley, this is the celebrated Dr Livingstone. I hope you'll be very happy together!' Then he turned his attention to the tranced-out makkata and spat a long stream of clipped consonants and palate clicks in his direction.

Tom wasn't surprised that the lawyer spoke one of the native languages; never the less the vehement sound of the tongue struck him anew. The desert peoples didn't use the same parts of their mouths to speak as Anglos; or, rather, they hardly used their mouths at all. Teeth, palate and larynx conspired together to produce this percussive noise.

The makkata came out of his reverie at once, ejected the chaw of engwegge into his palm, tucked it into his breech-clout and, gathering his stick limbs under him, rose. His wide black eyes were limpid but showed no sign of intoxication. He pointed at Tom and Prentice while rapping away still more emphatically than Swai-Phillips.

The lawyer grinned. 'He says that he'll do the ceremonial test right away – you first, Brodzinski.'

Tom quailed; he was a skinny boy once more, being pushed towards the vaulting horse by a sadistic phys. ed. instructor. He wished he could deflect the makkata's steady gaze.

'What about Prentice, here? I mean – no offence, Prentice – but what the hell *is* he doing here? Is he a client of yours, Jethro? I think I have a right to know.'

'Rights!' Swai-Phillips guffawed. 'Rights, rights, rights – it's always your bloody rights with you people. Property rights, personal rights, human rights, animal-bloody-rights. Brodzinski, I'm your lawyer, for pity's sake, and let me tellya, this has absolutely nothing to do with anyone's bloody rights at all, yeah. This is a very simple, very quick ritual procedure. This man has come thousands of clicks to perform it. He's an extremely important man, and, strange as it may seem to you, yeah, he's actually in a bloody hurry. So, if it's all the same to you' – Swai-Phillips paused, the better to impress on Tom that this was not negotiable – 'I think my advice, as your lawyer, is that you do exactly what he wants, which is for you to drop your strides – *now*. Please.'

Swai-Phillips took Prentice by the arm, and they went down the hill towards the jungle wall. Even as he was unbuckling his belt and letting his pants slide down, Tom was wondering if such feeble compliance was still because of nicotine withdrawal. He had no idea what the makkata was going to do to him. The awful thought occurred to Tom, as he stood half naked in the glaring sun, that it was a show, put on for the lawyer's perverse enjoyment. That he was bent on humiliating Tom, simply because he could. Maybe Prentice was really a crony of Swai-Phillips, brought along to witness this shaming.

The makkata closed in on Tom and knelt. He was clickety-clacking with his slack dry purse lips. Tom – although he couldn't conceive of anything less likely – admonished himself not to become aroused. Yet this thought itself was arousing: he felt the familiar prickle on the backs of his thighs, his scrotum tightened. The makkata's breath was now on the front of his shorts, and Tom could smell it despite the vegetal rot of the jungle. It was a spicy smell, mixed with the ferrous dust of the desert.

Tom let his head fall back on his sweaty neck. Heavy storm clouds were piled up above, their spongy masses saturated with rain-in-waiting. His fellow tourists – and the native Anglos when they'd had a drink – hymned the beauties of this mighty land. Yet, now that he was left behind here, Tom thought he might be looking at it with the more realistic eyes of the natives, seeing the scarred hillsides of the coastal ranges, smelling the faecal decay of the mangrove swamps. Certainly, there was nothing picturesque in the parts of the interior he had driven through with his family: the salt pans that flaked like eczema, the warty termite mounds, the endless charcoal strokes of the eucalyptus trees on the wrinkled vellum of the grasslands. Even here, on the coast, Tom sensed this alien landscape to his rear, an apprehension of a door ajar in reality itself, through which might be glanced seething horrors.

The makkata, grasping the flesh of Tom's inner thigh firmly between his thumb and forefinger, said 'I'll protect you' in accentless English. Tom felt a searing stab, jerked his head forward and, appalled, watched as the sorceror slowly withdrew the blade of a steel knife.

Blood coursed from Tom's thigh. He felt dizzy, staggered and, hobbled by his pants, almost fell. Then Swai-Phillips was supporting him.

'Be a man,' the lawyer said. 'It's nothing, a flesh wound.'

He gave Tom a wad of Kleenex, which he clamped to his thigh. While Tom rearranged his clothing, the lawyer squatted down by the makkata, who was examining the patch of bloodstained earth, already lucent with feeding flies. The makkata stirred this into red mud with his knife blade while clicking an incantation.

'B-but, he speaks perfect English,' Tom said irrelevantly. He moved a few shaky paces off. Prentice was still fifty yards away, his kinked back resolutely turned.

Swai-Phillips came over. 'C'mon,' he said. 'I'll take you up to the house. My cousin'll bandage that scratch, and I can tellya, mate, you'll enjoy that, yeah.'

As Tom was led away, he asked, 'What about Prentice?'

'Prentice?' For a moment the lawyer was confused – then he barked, 'Oh, him! Right! It's his turn now, isn't it? Silly bastard's got the same problem as you, needs a makkata to judge whether he's astande.'

The lawyer half dragged Tom up the hill, then began marching him across the open ground. Tom shook himself free. 'And am I?' he spat. 'Am I astande? Because if I'm not, I'm gonna sue you and that fucking witch doctor, you better believe it, man.'

'Yeah, yeah.' The lawyer swept off his sunglasses, and his good eye twinkled. He was enjoying himself. 'No worries, mate, you're good.'

Through the living jalousie of the jungle, Swai-Phillips's house came into view. Given its size, Tom was astonished that he hadn't spotted it from the top of the hill. It was three storeys high, with a wide veranda at least a hundred feet long. The entire structure – including the covered walkways that connected the main house to a number of outbuildings

– was riveted together out of corrugated iron. Great slabs of this material, streaked with rust, had been bent and bashed into copings, windowsills, pillars, roofs, chimneys and balustrades. There was even a corrugated-iron pool.

The effect was at once silly and magnificent: it was the dwelling of an idiot-savant *bricoleur*, who, having glimpsed a picture of an antebellum mansion, had then fashioned his own copy, using whatever came to hand.

Despite the electric throb in his wounded thigh, and the growing anxiety that the makkata's knife might have had tetanus on it – or worse – Tom still felt like laughing at the lawyer's absurd pile. Until, that is, it impinged on him what the house was still more reminiscent of: the model minivan Tommy Junior had wanted him to buy, the one the old Anglo had told Tom was a Gandaro spirit wagon. The deftly fashioned artefact that was taboo for an Anglo to even touch, let alone possess.

A few minutes later, sitting in one of the galvanized gazebos, on a galvanized bench, Tom's breathing began to shudder into some regularity. Swai-Phillips, who was sitting opposite, clapped his hands loudly and cried out: 'Gloria! Betsy! Drinks, goddamnit! Now!'

From deep within the metallic bowels of the hulk, there came the sound of women's voices and the clanking noises of their bare footfalls.

Tom studied the house more: creepers thrust between the corrugated-iron sheets of the walkways, while saplings poked through their balustrades. Still larger trees punched through warped walls and rusty roofs, their limbs chafing and squeaking against the metal, as the onshore breeze rose in the gathering darkness.

'Will he be – I mean, who will . . .' Tom couldn't frame

his question; he began again: 'Prentice, will he be able to get up here after . . .'

'He's been speared? Oh, yeah, the makkata'll give him a hand – so long as he's astande too, that is. 'Course, if he's inquivoo, he'll have to leave him where he lies, yeah. That's the size of it.'

Tom was going to ask the lawyer what Prentice had been accused of, when footfalls sounded loud on the veranda and Martha Brodzinski came towards the two men, a tray held on her upturned hand, as if she were an insouciant waitress in a citified brasserie.

At the sight of Martha's willowy figure, and her thick dirty-blonde hair swishing against her long neck, Tom gripped the arm of the iron bench. Despite the heat, cold drops of sweat fell from his eyebrows to his cheeks. As Martha advanced along the walkway Tom's heart burgeoned. Was this why he hadn't seen her go through the metal detector at the airport? Why she hadn't come to the phone when he called during their lay-over?

Why had she stayed behind? For moments Tom allowed himself to believe it was because she had decided to be with him, to support him; and that she had hidden out at the lawyer's house with a view to suprising him, as if they were playful young lovers once more.

The paper dart of this fancy flew true for milliseconds, then hit an iron stanchion, buckled and fell. That wasn't it at all, Tom realized. On the contrary, Martha was here because she was in cahoots with Swai-Phillips – having an affair with him as well. She'd sent their children back, alone, halfway round the world, so that she could dally here with the moustachioed creep, the laughing cavalier!

He stood up to confront her . . . and fell back, because

when the woman came into the gazebo, Tom was presented not with Martha's pale plate of Puritan features but a face parodic of them: the lips thicker, the nose more bulbous, the eyes smaller. The woman who handed him the tall glass jammed with fruit wasn't exactly ugly, but she was coarser – grosser, even – than Martha.

Though Swai-Phillips was laughing, he still managed to make an introduction: 'Brodzinski, this is my second cousin Gloria; she grew up in Liège, Belgium, but she's been here with us for a while now.'

'G'day,' said Gloria.

'Y – you could've warned me!' Tom rounded on him.

'Warned you? Warned you of what, exactly?' The lawyer dipped a finger into the drink his cousin had given him and traced a circle of moisture on his bare chest. 'Oh, by the way Brodzinski, I have a cousin who's the spit of your wife . . . You'd've thought I was crazy. Better you come up and see her for yourself, right. Still,' – he paused, took a slug of his drink and placed it on the table – 'it does explain one thing to you.'

'What's that?' Tom hated himself for playing along with the cruel joke.

'Why it was I was so taken with Mrs Brodzinski, yeah. Believe me, if she's anything like as, um, accommodating as my cousin, then you must be – in ordinary circs – a very happy man indeed.'

Tom sat marooned in his own passivity. What was happening to him? Why were events barracking him with his own impotence? The makkata had mixed his blood with the earth and pronounced him astande, yet he sat inert, while Gloria knelt before him, encouraged him to raise his buttocks so she could pull down his pants, then swabbed and dressed the wound.

Sometime later darkness had fallen utterly. Flying foxes chattered in a mango tree at the front of the veranda. Tom could just make out their oilskin wings opening and closing, the shine of their feline eyes. He thought of the makkata – and so it was that he appeared in the circle of light thrown by a hissing gas lamp Gloria had lit before retiring. He was leading Prentice by the hand – the other man seemed devoid of volition as he staggered along the veranda. There was a brutal streak of red mud on Prentice's cheek, and he'd mislaid his stupid affectation of a hat.

5

om holed up at the Experience and waited for the wound in his thigh to heal. Bored, he ventured out to a book store he'd noticed in the nearby mall. When he let slip to the clerk that he might be going 'over there', she pressed upon him a fat volume called *Songs of the Tayswengo* by O. M. and E. F. von Sasser.

'It's the bizzo,' the girl said. 'The Von Sassers have been over there for decades – first the father, then the son. They know all there is to know. They've collected all the stories – they write beautifully as well.'

Her eyes were a little crazy; her words came in enthusiastic spurts.

Tom didn't find *Songs of the Tayswengo* to be beautifully written at all. It was turgid, loaded with anthropological jargon, and the songs themselves seemed at once silly and incomprehensible: 'Jabber up to me, flipper lizard / Let me rub sand on your sad gizzard' was a representative couplet.

Every time he started reading the heavy hardback, Tom fell asleep – only to wake with a start, having dreamed that a malevolent child was sitting on his chest.

Fed up with the Von Sassers, Tom bought more books and scanned them on his sweat-damp bed at the Experience, a mosquito coil smouldering by his elbow. But these writers were just as bewildering. One would propose an outlandish psychological model of the hill tribes, while the next would say this was nonsense: the Handrey were as similar to the Anglos as any one individual is to the next.

There was dispute even about the fundamentals: some experts categorically stated that the desert people had been there for as long as 100,000 years; while others insisted that when the first Anglo explorers crossed the interior, they encountered Inssessitti makkatas, who told them that their people had only been in the region for the past decade, having themselves arrived by sea from the Felthams.

The very shifting sands of the deserts and the sliding rivers of mud in the tropical uplands served to obscure whatever material evidence there might be to support or deny these competing contentions. And so it was that the land itself was amnesiac, forgetful of its own history; and ignorant, even, of its own terrifying extent.

After a couple of days Swai-Phillips called.

'I've no date yet for the prelim' hearing, right,' he said without any preamble.

'Well, when will you?'

'Hard to say.'

Tom pictured the lawyer in his offices at the top of the Metro-Center, puffing on a stinky engwegge cheroot and bullshitting from behind his mask of a face.

'But so long as the court accepts the makkata's evidence you can make the first reparation trip over there, right away, right.'

'First?'

'There may have to be several, but the good thing is you can head off while the criminal prosecution continues – which may take many weeks.'

Seeking to deploy his new knowledge, Tom asked, 'Am I, like, initiated now?'

Swai-Phillips was dismissive. 'Don't be under any illusions, Brodzinski,' he said. 'If you'd been foolish enough – and some Anglos are – to have gone through initiation to one of the desert mobs, you wouldn't be idling your days away reading, while waiting for a fair trial. That makkata would've broken every bone in your body with a punishment stick – then Atalaya's women would've pissed on you – by way of humiliation.

'Anyway, when're you gonna come up to the house again? Gloria's been asking after you. Squolly's coming up Sunday with his mob, gonna do a big barbie. There'll be heaps of fish, heaps of beer, shitloads of kids in and out of the pool. Do you good, mate, have a slice of the old family life.'

Tom didn't want to see Gloria again; he wasn't certain he'd be able to cope with her travesty of his wife's features in broad daylight. Nor was the idea of sinking a few beers with the policeman appealing.

Tom had to report to police HQ every other day. Squolly – or Commander Squoddoloppololollou, as he was properly called – was always laid-back and friendly. Even when the grandiose marble hallways filled with the clatter of steel-shod boots, and open-topped trucks full of paramilitaries screeched in and out of the parking lot, the barrel-shaped officer still found time to get Tom a soda, then sit with him while he sipped it in the pleasantly cool confines of the interview room.

Squolly disdained the Intwennyfortee mob's ritual business. 'See, Tom,' he told him, 'our belief is that it's a man's intentions that count, yeah. We don't judge an offender for what he's done, yeah, only for what he thought he was going to do.'

'But I thought that's what the native people believed too?'

Squolly laughed and exhaled a patch of condensation into being on the shiny peak of his cap, which he was holding. 'No, no, the desert mobs – the Tayswengo, who you're mixed up with; the Aval, Jethro's dad's people; the Inssessetti and the renegades, the Entreati – well, they're harsh, man. Very fierce, yeah. Their line is that every single act a fellow makes is willed, right enough: a hiccup, or a murder.'

'I knew that much. I've been reading the Von Sassers' *Songs of the Tayswengo.*'

'OK, sure, very . . . *authentic.*' The policeman grinned, revealing teeth as strong and squared off as his own torso. 'The hill tribes, yeah, they're different again. They believe in spirits big time. A spirit gets between a man and his wife, a man and his kiddies, a man's hand and a can of bloody peaches! They're praying all the time, making offerings – trying to get these bloody spirits to stop 'em spilling their grog.

'If a Handrey or an Ibbolit does a big bad one – a rape, a murder – we have to get 'im down here, yeah, get his bloody makkata and get *him* to summon the right spirit, so he can tell the makkata why he made the fellow do it!'

Squolly shook his head at the very idea of such foolishness. He drew a handkerchief covered with brownish engwegge stains from his pocket and began polishing the peak of his cap. 'Now, with us coastal peoples – Anglos, Tugganarong – we're more rational, right. Man's accused of doing something bad – like you, yeah – we don't pull him in and 'terrogate 'im. We don't duff him up, right. No, we ob-serve him. We send our blokes out after him – quiet, yeah, no fuss – and check out how he conducts himself in the world. How he orders his morning coffee, buys his paper, deals with all the little irritations of his day. Then we compile a report on what kind of intentions the fellow has. There's nothing high tech', we don't use no fancy psychologists or profilers, it's just good old-fashioned police leg work.'

Oddly, the surveillance didn't bother Tom – even though Squolly's men were trying to read his mind in a way not usually attempted by anyone save for a mother or a lover.

On the contrary, as he splashed through the first storms of the monsoon to buy his newspaper, or sat beneath bulging awnings drinking his coffee, the sight of a cop, loitering by the doors to the mall, dumpy in his rain cape, was almost reassuring. Often his tails would come over to chat with him, mulling over the strength of the previous night's wind, musing as to whether this year's monsoon was heavier than the last.

In the afternoons, in the brief interval between one swishing curtain of rain and the next, Tom would put on his old sweat-pants and go for a run. Leaving the dock area, he jogged through the shopping district. At this time of the year the chilled malls were empty but for a few Anglos. The tourists were all gone, and the miners wouldn't come in from the interior until shortly before Christmas. Nor was the business district buzzing; the occasional clerk or manager, dressed in their tropical version of a suit – jacket and pants both cut short to reveal pale arms and paler legs – would scamper along the sidewalk, leaping over puddles, their faces set, as if to say, 'This business of leaping over puddles is bloody serious, right.'

Tom slopped by them. He glanced up at the Metro-Center to see if his lawyer was in his office; then, head down, took the wide Trangaden Boulevard, which ran through the outskirts of town, where glass barns sold agricultural equipment, then on between billboards that grew tattier, until it declined into a single strip of concrete, before eventually terminating in the long sable strand of the town beach.

Usually, there would be a couple of other afternoon exercisers out there with Tom, while sea fishermen whipped the slack waves with their lines. The gnarled shapes of the offshore atolls, which in fine weather were lovely ornaments cast down on the azure baize, now resembled crumpled refuse adrift on this oceanic puddle. The clouds shrouded the foothills, obscuring the more elevated suburbs of Vance. So Tom took his constitutional along a sable corridor, between vaporous walls.

To swim in the sea was, of course, out of the question. In the dry season there were sharks and box jellyfish, while the monsoon brought with it the Sangat, or bladder, clams. When the wind rose and the waves pounded, they drummed up these avid crustaceans from the sea bed. Anyone unlucky enough to have one fasten on his skin would soon become the host for a thriving population of necrotic bivalves. Tom had seen bladder–clam victims in Vance, clunking along the sidewalks with their bared arms or legs warty with nacre. They looked like medieval knights, unhorsed and stripped of their armour save for brassards or greaves.

Each afternoon Tom jogged the length of the beach, then back to the Experience. Overall he was covering six or seven miles. But while the first few runs left him heaving for breath, after a week he was managing it easily.

With every breath the humid air was discovering new tissue to invigorate. Tom had read somewhere that, if fully unfurled, the human lung would cover two football fields, and now he felt as if he were reoccupying this living turf, which for so many years had been ploughed over with tar.

Before the rains swished back in there was a small window of opportunity, and gratefully Tom thrust his head into it, breathing deeply with each pace. At these times he was almost glad of his protracted sojourn. He felt a stupefying pride at his own achievement: would I, he wondered, ever have cracked the smoking habit if all this shit hadn't gone down?

When he'd got back to the apartment, showered off and drunk a couple of bottles of mineral water, Tom ventured out once more. This was the most onerous part of his daily routine: the call home.

There were several call stores in downtown Vance. In these strip-lit caves, the Tugganarong who did the city's menial jobs paid over their wages for a few minutes' chit-chat with their families in the Feltham Islands.

The call stores doubled in function, also offering money-transfer services. Tom often saw some downtrodden Tugga-narong pay over half his wages to Western Union, then half of the remainder to Bell Telephone. Squolly had told him that the Tugganarong were paid minimal wages, the justification being that their employers – whether domestic, municipal or business – provided accommodation and food. So, once they'd visited the call store, they had only a handful of change left; enough for a brown-bagged bottle to be drunk in the street, then they'd lurch back to their dormi-tories, festering sheds on the far side of town.

The Tugganarong smelled of the lanolin they used to mould their thick hair into Anglo hairstyles. They were also loud, conducting their calls home with a mixture of frus-tration and anger. As they shouted in the flimsy booths, their language was impenetrable to Tom, and seemed to consist of sharp consonants, interspersed with syllables that all sounded like 'olly'. Making his collect calls, which involved negotiating with up to three operators, all on the line simultaneously, Tom had to contend with this background roar: 'Gollyrollyfollytollybolly!'

When he heard the familiar tone of the wall-mounted phone in his own bright, open-plan kitchen, Tom's frustration fell away, and he simply felt miserable. On answering, his children dutifully passed the handset, one to the next. He pictured them in a row of descending height on the red-tiled floor: Von Trapped.

The twins prattled on about school and friends – the shiftless, shifting alliances of eight-year-olds – then passed Tom on to Tommy Junior, so the lumpen fourteen-year-old could drone on about his computer games and his trading card collection. 'Gollyvollytolly . . .' Tommy Junior seemed to be saying, while all around Tom the Tugganarong kept up the same incomprehensible jabber. Tom pictured Tommy Junior as a Tugganarong, his white skin darkened, his mousy crest greased. And wasn't it true – Tom mused while the boy babbled – that Tommy Junior was his own guest worker? Foisted on Tom to perform the menial job of stabbing his conscience.

The hardest exchanges were with Dixie. When she came on the line, Tom pressed the handset so hard against his ear that he could hear the cartilage crack. Dixie, who was charged with explaining to her father, half a world away, why it was that at this early hour – 8 a.m. by his reckoning – her mother was not in the kitchen cooking breakfast, cutting sandwiches or combing hair. Not, in short, doing any of the things that a now sole parent might be expected to.

The first few times Tom called and got his daughter in lieu of his wife he was understanding. How could he be anything but? Yes, Martha was already at work, yes, he understood. Of course she had to leave early – he saw that. She was still asleep . . . ? Dixie would wake her if he insisted . . . But no, he didn't insist, because he entirely understood, you see. Her mother must be tired after getting in so late.

So it went on, for day after day; until Tom at last cracked and shouted at his wife's proxy: 'Dixie! Dixie! Where is your goddamn mother? I haven't spoken to her since you guys got home, and that was more than two weeks ago! Get her for me now. Now! D'you hear me?'

Dixie chose not to hear this outburst.

'Dad? Dad? What is it, Dad?' Came echoing under the sea, or through the stratosphere. 'Dad? Dad?'

Then the line went dead, and the 'Gollybollyfolly' swelled up, engulfing Tom Brodzinski with the Tugganarong's own exile on this fatal shore.

That night, lying in the sweat box of his apartment, the monsoon pouring through the night outside, Tom began thinking about the butt again. He was back on the balcony, looking down on Atalaya Intwennyfortee. Had he examined her breasts too intently? To glance – surely that was only natural; but had he perhaps ogled her lasciviously? He couldn't recall her seeing him, yet that wasn't the point – it was his intentions that mattered.

Then there was the butt itself. Lying in bed, the heavy volume of the Von Sassers tented over his belly, Tom pressed the nail of his index finger against the pad of his thumb. How much tension had there been? How much pressure had he exerted? This much – or this? Gloria's cool fingers had moved expertly, swabbing at the crescent-shaped incision the makkata's blade had made in Tom's thigh. Tom had felt no arousal – only relief.

Now he was aroused. The natives who drank in the bar opposite were being herded away by the low squawk of a squad car's siren. The rains drummed. The first roaches to check into the motel were fretting in their chambers, already regretting their choice of accommodation. Tom sought to yank the handle that delivered repose. Under the sheet it was not his hand but Gloria's. It went lower, seeking out the raised scar tissue on his thigh . . . Gloria's fingers probed it – or were they . . . Martha's?

He shot upright and squeezed on the light that tore into sharp being the nasty walls, the nylon curtains and the late check-ins to the roach motel, skittering and whirring for cover.

'I was in shock.' Tom said aloud. 'I was in shock and she was wearing make-up – perhaps even a prosthesis.'

His wife of nearly twenty years was conniving with that lawyer. Her performance at the Mimosa Apartments had been just that, put on to throw Tom off the scent. He'd never seen her go through security, because she never had; and there Martha was, up at Swai-Phillips's creepy tin mansion, pretending to be someone else altogether.

'And for why?' he implored the night and the roaches.

Too shaky for sleep now, Tom got up and pulled on his clothes. Outside in the street, he gathered the folds of his rain poncho around him and splashed towards the 'nade. He welcomed the company of his tail, although he was surprised to see the cop putting in such late hours. When they reached the boardwalk, they sheltered in the adjacent perspex hoods of two information points. The audio recording in Tom's was a history of the first colonists, but he didn't want to hear it again. Instead he waited for the grey dawn, and for the green tide to ebb across the mudflats, exposing the ugly crocodiles.

Once or twice he considered taxing the policeman with the hypocrisy – and possibly even illegality – of his smoking while on assignment; but then he thought better of it, and went back to cursing his own folly and stupidity, his wife's perfidy and treachery.

The following evening Tom had dinner with Adams, at the Honorary Consul's house. He took with him a decent bottle of Côte du Rhone that he'd managed to search out from the dusty shelves of a liquor store. Tom presented it to Adams, when his host came bounding along the walkway from his front door and opened the passenger door of Tom's cab.

'Excellent, excellent,' the Consul muttered to himself, while Tom paid off the driver. Then, when Adams turned to face him, he said: 'This will go very well with the main course. My, ah, friends have scared up some binturang for us.'

He leaned into Tom, as if seeing him for the first time. 'You're not a, ah, vegetarian, are you, Brodzinski?'

By night Adams's house achieved a certain elegance. The dark floors reflected the fan blades, and the splashes of colour which were the Consul's native daubs glowed in the lamplight. Seated in a rattan chair, Tom accepted a Daquiri and resolved to make it last. As if by unspoken agreement, the two men didn't discuss the business of the butt at all. Instead, Tom told Adams how struck he'd been by the bladder-clam victims who clonked through downtown.

'Yes, distressing, isn't it?' Adams took a sip of his drink, his tone suggesting that he found it anything but.

'The research centre here is doing some first-rate work on the problem. They already have an effective palliative; however, it's expensive, well beyond the means of any but the, ah, elites – and they don't tend to be the ones foolish, or desperate, enough to swim in the sea.' He smiled insidiously. 'They have pools.'

Tom was content to sit like this, getting gently soused on the Consul's Daquiris and talking of this and that. As long as he didn't require anything from Adams, the man was a decent companion. Besides, he had something he wanted to give his host: a revelation he kept to himself, as a child does a guilty yet treasured secret.

The rains started up outside, as sudden as a twisted faucet, and the Consul raised his voice to combat the pounding on the wooden roof. He was telling Tom, at considerable length – and with certain embellishments suggesting either that he was extrapolating from something that he had written down or that this wasn't the first time he had recounted the tale – about his trip up to Vance in the town car.

From time to time one of the Handrey women came into the room, her bare feet sucking on the floorboards, and bent over Adams to whisper in his ear. On each occasion this happened, he'd report to Tom: 'Nearly there, binturang's damn tricky to cook – it's the timing that's crucial.'

Once, Tom thought he saw Adams cup the heavy breast of one of the women and give it a squeeze, but he couldn't be sure. He took it as read that Adams's involvement with these native women was exploitative – probably on both sides.

Adams was describing how the car broke down and he became trapped in the Tontine Townships of the bauxite belt. 'Parts were impossible to get hold of locally, and it took several weeks for them to be freighted in. The situation at that time was . . . well, to be frank I was frightened. But there was no question of my abandoning the car. It had become' – he smiled in a self-deprecating way – 'well, become part of my, ah, quest to discover this country. To truly be part of it.'

Tom couldn't have cared less about Adams's quest, nor was he eagerly awaiting the binturang. He'd seen the animals in the wild, when the Brodzinskis toured a nature reserve in the Highlands. Binturang was the native name for these large arboreal mammals, which were anthropoid in their form and bulk, yet feline in their movements and manner of reclining, usually full-length on the horizontal limbs of the high jungle canopy.

While Tom had been keen to sample the local cuisine when his family had been with him – the thick creamy stews of the hill tribes, the fruity curries of the Tugganarong – now that he was alone he yearned for down-home junk food. He went into fast-food joints and sat there uptaking hydrolysed fat and corn syrup, his hands wrenching at the bolted-down tables. Sipping on his waxed-paper bucket of soda, Tom hearkened to the familiar gravelly sounds of the ice chips inside and, narrowing his eyes, attempted to screen out anything in his visual field – a spike of alien greenery against the plate-glass window, the oiled pompadour of a dining Tugganarong – that jibed with this homeyness.

A spindly gateleg table had been set for the two men in the Honorary Consul's bedroom. In the corner of the austere room, with its white walls and polished wooden floor, stood a narrow army cot, made up with a brown blanket and a neatly folded sheet. On top of a chest of drawers, in front of an oval mirror, were arranged silver hairbrushes and crystal scent atomizers.

Tom would have commented on the oddness of all this, were it not for the presence of the cooked binturang. The long pink glistening skinned corpse lay on an enormous chopping board that had been placed on the table, which hardly seemed strong enough to support it.

The Handrey women had removed the binturang's head before they spit-roasted it. It rested to one side in a heap of arugula, its eye sockets black and crispy, its needle-sharp teeth bared. Tom thought the animal looked like a faked photograph of an alien's corpse lying in a secret military installation. He steeled himself with a slug of Daquiri before sitting, then set his glass down with a clonk, hoping one of the women would get him a refill.

Adams registered this and said irritatedly, 'I think I'll ask for that excellent vino you brought to be poured, Brodzinski. Liquor doesn't sit well with binturang.'

He began to sharpen a long carving knife with slow, deliberate strokes on a cylindrical whetstone. Then Tom watched, repulsed, as Adams began sawing through one of the fully extended back legs. The table moved back and forth under the impetus, the claws of the leg Adams was severing flicking droplets of grease across the front of his tan cotton pants. He stopped for a moment to wipe the sweat from his forehead, then bent back to his task.

'Wayne?' said a Handrey woman, passing Tom a brimming goblet. He took it gratefully.

The Binturang turned out to be very tasty. The flesh was so tender it could be forked apart into long filaments as twirlable as spaghetti. The flavour was between that of partridge and of pork. With the assistance of half a bottle of Côte du Rhone, and the Handrey women who ladled taro paste and vegetable curry on to his plate, Tom ate most of a leg, together with a little of the belly meat, which Adams told him was the most prized part of the beast.

The woman who served them stayed in the bedroom,

squatting against the baseboard. She slowly exposed the knuckle bones of the paw Adams had carved for her. Occasionally, Tom glanced across and observed the way she gently held the paw, as if it were the hand of a small child.

They were silent while they ate. Adams bent low over his plate, his jaw knotting with steady effort. The fan thrummed, the rain drummed. After a few false starts the Handrey women's chanting got going underneath the house. The volume rose until the beat of their 'bahn-bahn-bahn-bahn-boosh' competed with the overhead percussion.

Tom was half-cut when the chopping board, bearing most of the binturang still intact, was borne off below to feed the chanters. Because of this, he considered his conversational gambit fairly astute. Wiping his mouth with a starched napkin, he asked his host: 'D'you know this guy, Brian Prentice, that Swai-Phillips is representing?'

Adams seemed not to have heard. 'I think we may as well have our coffee next door,' he said, fastidiously wiping his own downturned mouth. 'I didn't ask them to trouble with dessert; I hope you don't mind?'

Tom grunted that he didn't and stumbled back into the other room, where he collapsed into one of the creaking rattan chairs. After fiddling with a music deck on one of the shelving units, the Consul slumped down opposite him. A trickle of New Age music – wind chimes, flutes and a theramin – percolated through the heavy rhythmic soundscape of the house. Tom thought the choice a modest revelation, not what he expected from the tightly buttoned Adams. His host absent-mindedly fluttered his fingers as if conducting the puny tune, then said: 'Prentice? Well, he's not one of ours, so he's no direct concern of mine. Obviously, I take a closer interest than I would with other foreign nationals, and, as it happens, I have spoken to their attaché here in Vance, Sir Colm, ah, Mulgrene. Without in any way being loose-mouthed, we were able to ascertain that your situations had certain, ah, similarities.'

'They have an attaché right here in Vance?' Tom was surprised; this hardly tallied with the respective global reaches of the two nations.

'It's a hangover, of course,' Adams said. 'Not that they were the colonial power here, but they had extensive interests over many years. Incidentally' – his horse lips puckered – 'I'm aware you harbour doubts concerning my own, ah, capabilities–'

Tom tried to issue a denial, but Adams wouldn't permit it. 'I may no longer be a salaried official of the State Department, but, believe me, this is a fully functioning consulate, and I am empowered to do anything that's necessary to assist you. Anything.'

He regarded Tom icily, before adding, 'The same does not apply to, ah, Prentice.'

'What's he accused of?' Tom asked bluntly.

'I can't tell you,' Adams snapped back.

'Can't or won't?' Tom needled him.

'Can't. Won't. Mustn't. There are strict laws here, criminal cases can't be, ah, bruited about – especially when the charges involve the traditional peoples. You'll be grateful for such a, ah, close-mouthed approach when it comes to your own preliminary hearing. It means that the judges can't be influenced by knowledge of what the defendant has been accused of, right up until he steps into the dock.'

Tom swam up through the watery music towards the light. 'Swai-Phillips said Squolly would give a child abuser bail if he could come up with the right cash. Is that true?

Is that what Prentice has done, screwed a native kid? He certainly looks the type.'

Tom would have gone on if a Handrey woman hadn't come in carrying a tray with coffee things and a small dish of truffles on it. When the coffee had been poured and she had withdrawn, Adams slowly inclined his teaspoon so that some large granules of the Turkish sugar tumbled into his tiny cup. Then he sighed. 'Look, let's not fence, Brodzinski; we both know it's not Prentice who's bothering you, it's Swai-Phillips.'

Tom regretted having taken a truffle. His thumb and fore-finger now had pads of melted chocolate on them as shiny as paint. He sucked these in what he hoped was a sage and meditative fashion, before replying: 'Martha – my wife. I saw her up at Swai-Phillips's place. She's still here. I think – I think . . .' A pause, then the words came in a rush: 'I think she's mixed up with him in something. I've tried calling her again and again – she's sure as hell not back in Milford.'

Tom stopped. Adams had stood up abruptly and now loomed over him, a queer half-smile on his diffident lips. 'First off,' he said firmly, calming a fractious child, 'I know who you mean – at Swai-Phillips's place, that is – his cousin Gloria Swai-Phillips. Remarkable lady, runs several orphanages in the Tontine Townships. And yes, there is a striking resemblance between her and your wife.' He paused, sighed. 'If you want the truth, the reason why you and your family were, ah, noticed in the first place, was because of that resemblance.'

'Noticed?' Tom said wonderingly.

'Well,' Adams laughed shortly, 'we get a lot of Anglo tourists through here in the season, and one bunch looks pretty much the same as the next. Your wife made your family stand out – Gloria Swai-Phillips is a very popular, very influential person.'

Adams crossed to his drinks cabinet. 'I believe a Seven and Seven is your poison,' he said, holding up the whisky bottle. 'I'm afraid I don't have any 7 Up; will you take a little branch water with your Seagram's?'

Adams saved his clincher until the drinks were poured and he'd sat down once more. 'The thing is, Brodzinski, your wife can't possibly still be here in Vance.'

'Oh, really?' Tom sipped the drink; it didn't taste right without the sugary gloss of the soda. 'Why's that?'

'Because I've spoken to her myself. She called me – and I called her back in, ah, Milford.'

'She called you? Why? Was she worried about me?' The rains stilled, a fissure opened up in the lowering sky, and through it shone the reinvigorated sun of Martha's regard.

Adams put a stop to it: 'Look, I appreciate that this must be painful for you, Brodzinski; that I, a comparative stranger, should be, ah, privy to your wife's estrangement; but facts are, ah . . .' He pulled on a long bony finger. ' . . . facts. She wishes to reassure you of her, ah, concern – but not to speak to you. She called on another matter, in some, ah, distress because of something – or, rather, somebody – she had seen in your local mall.'

'In the mall? Who?' Tom had definitely had too much to drink. His words lurched from his mouth and found themselves suddenly on the glossy floor.

'It would', Adams said, shifting to academic mode, 'have been almost exactly at the time the makkata was doing the astande ceremony at Swai-Phillips's place – perhaps twenty minutes later. Your wife saw – or thought she saw – a Tayswengo man in L. L. Bean.'

'In L. L. Bean?'

'In L. L. Bean, trying on a pair of, ah, pants. Which was

just as well!' Perversely, Adams seemed to be enjoying himself. 'Because, apart from his breechclout, he was completely naked.'

'Let me get this straight,' Tom staggered on, following the Consul's crazy logic. 'You're saying my wife called you because she saw . . . . the makkata in Milford Mall, in L. L. Bean?'

Despite the ludicrousness of this, Tom realized that he too had no difficulty in picturing the wizard right there: beside an aluminium rail, hung with jeans and slacks, while on the other side of the plate glass zitty teenagers in their lumpy puffa jackets watched the guy riding the resurfacing machine describe bold figures on the ice rink.

'Magic', Adams said, 'is a much misunderstood, ah, concept. Besides, Brodzinski, I'm not even necessarily saying that's what this was. But no one can live here for long without becoming aware of the traditional people's ability to, ah, shall we say, influence certain coincidences.'

Tom didn't know how to reply to this – so he said nothing. This, in terms of Adam's recondite etiquette, must have been the right thing to do. Because, after looking at Tom from under his wire-wool eyebrows for a while, the Consul said: 'Good, I'm glad you understand. Now, to more mundane business. Jethro dropped off some of the prosecution's depositions earlier on.'

Adams rose, went back to the shelving, picked up a plastic wallet and lobbed it into Tom's lap. 'They're ballistics reports, witness statements – that kind of thing. Jethro's over there' – a thumb jerk over one shoulder – 'right now. He'll be back in time for the prelim' hearing, which is now set for this Friday. In the meantime, he asked me if I'd go through these with you.'

Adams hooked a bamboo stool between them with his

foot, then began dealing forms and diagrams out of the wallet.

'See here,' he began. 'This is a computer-generated diagram of the, ah, butt's parabola; these figures are the force estimated to have been exerted on it by your fingers, and these the velocity the butt reached before impacting with Mr Lincoln's head. Should the DA decide to push an evidential-intentional line, it will be necessary for the defence to take issue with them.'

Tom took a judicious sip of his whisky, then said: 'Why?'

'Why?' Adams echoed him witheringly. 'Why? Because, Brodzinski, if these, ah, calculations are allowed to stand unopposed, they would suggest that you employed more force in, ah, flipping the butt than a negligent act would imply. The prosecution then has you lining up the butt like a – like a grenade launcher, or any other offensive weapon.'

Tom allowed this absurdity to wash over him for a while, together with the New Age tinkling, the Handrey women's chanting and the drumming of the rain. It was up to him, he grasped, to think outside of the box. Adams wasn't capable of it – he'd gone native. Swai-Phillips wasn't either – he *was* a goddamn native. There was a crucial piece missing from this crazy jigsaw.

Tom hunched forward and, taking the diagram from the stool, flapped it in Adam's horsy face. 'What', Tom demanded, 'could possibly be my motive for attacking Mr Lincoln?'

'Motive? Motive?' Strange wheezing sounds issued from Adams, his eyelids flickered, his pale-blue eyes watered. He was laughing. 'There's motivation in abundance, Brodzinski,' he managed to choke out at last. 'Jealousy, for one. Atalaya has already told Commander Squoddolop-polollou that you were looking at her, ah, breasts, before you flipped the butt–'

'Oh, ferchrissakes!' Tom cried.

But Adams continued: 'Or, should the police choose to paint you up, ah, blacker still, they could say this was a race-hate crime.'

'Lincoln's not black!' Tom expostulated.

'Mr Lincoln is an initiate of the Tayswengo, Brodzinski.' His lips twisted with the irony. 'And, so far as they're concerned, they only come in one, ah, colour.'

An hour or so later Adams escorted Tom along the slippery walkway to where a cab was idling at the kerb. The Consul had only a small umbrella, and it was awkward manoeuvring it so as to protect them both. Adams kept on bumping against Tom's behind. Drunkenly, he wondered if Adams might be a little drunk.

Tom opened the car door and turned to face his host. 'Look,' he said, 'I'm sorry I kinda lost my cool back then. You've – you've been decent to me, Adams – I know you're trying your best to help, and thanks for the dinner – the binturang was great.'

The rain was now falling so heavily that it was as if the two of them were standing under a waterfall. Adam's hand, clenched round the umbrella's handle, was within an inch of Tom's cheek.

'Well, ah, thank you, Brod – I mean, hell, let me call you Tom, d'you mind?'

'N-No.' Tom was taken aback.

'And you'll call me Winnie, yes?' There was a pathetic eagerness in Adam's eyes.

'S-Sure, Winnie,' Tom said.

Then, as if to seal this contract, the Consul inclined his head and kissed Tom on the forehead, his lips remaining there for several seconds. Tom was struck by how wet and plump Adam's lips felt, considering how dry and diffident his mouth appeared. When he removed them, it was with an audible 'plop' of un-suction.

Tom stood, staring at the Consul's face, grey and washed out in the sodden night. He felt a bead of consular saliva trickle down the bridge of his nose.

'W-Winnie,' Tom said to break the spell. 'Is there anything else I can do, anything at all?'

Adams inclined his head once more, coercing Tom's eyes to his own. 'You know, don't you, who Astande is?' he said.

'No.'

'He is "the Swift One" in Tayswengo cosmology, the "Righter of Wrongs"; so there's always more you can do. You've been to visit Mr Lincoln; well, go again. However off-putting he may be, keep talking to him. If anything can mitigate the charges levelled against you, it's the, ah, willingness to be astande despite his inquivoo. So, go. Go now.'

With this, Adams placed a hand on Tom's shoulder and pressed him down into the ear.

Tom rolled down the window so he could say goodbye, but Adams was already slipping back along the walkway to his front door. By the time the cab drove off, the lights on the small veranda had been extinguished. Adams and his five fat Handrey women were bedding down for the night.

Tom pictured the Consul stretched out full length on his army cot, the rough blanket pulled up under his long chin.

'But how?' he asked out loud. 'How did he know that I drink Seven and Sevens?'

'Whozzat?' the cabbie interjected; however, his passenger didn't explain, only asked him to drive to the hospital.

6

The cabbie let Tom off in the hospital parking lot. Ambulances backed and filled, their revolving lights throwing spangles into the curtains of rain. Tom picked his way between gurneys, upon which lay all manner of drunk and wounded native people. All were soaked to the skin – none were stoical: their moans and groans were plangently theatrical. Each gurney also had its attendant posse of keening womenfolk who tried to push it forward. The paramedics and police in their glistening rain ponchos did battle with these recumbent jousters, forcing them back from the double doors to the Emergency Department.

Seeing the cop who'd tailed him to the 'nade the previous morning, Tom approached and was waved through. After the mêlée outside, the silence of the white-tiled corridors was eerie. There was no sign of any staff as he walked towards the central elevator lobby. Through head–height windows in the ward doors, Tom could see rows of beds, most of which were empty, although here and there was the outsized foetus of a sleeping patient.

As he waited for the elevator, Tom wondered why it was that so many casualties were being left out in the rain, while inside the hospital snoozed, dreaming its dreams of antiseptic purity.

There was more activity on the fifth floor. An orderly carrying a kidney dish full of foul-smelling fluid got into the elevator as Tom stepped out. An Anglo nurse stood by the nurses' station chatting with an Anglo patient in a bathrobe. She left off and asked Tom what he wanted.

Without understanding why he did so, Tom pulled up the leg of his short pants and pointed to the three-inch scar left by the makkata's blade.

'A-Astande,' he said. Both Anglos nodded vigorously, as if to say: that explains everything.

'Go through, yeah,' the nurse said to Tom. 'I think the Intwennyfortee mob have finished their ritual now.' He thanked her and moved on.

By night the corridor that led to Lincoln's room seemed longer. It kinked and turned, passing bays in which stood mysterious machines, their coiled electrical flexes and rubber wheels suggesting they were deadly as well as silent. Then Tom heard the pitter-patter of water falling on to the tiled floor and the crackle of flames.

He rounded the next corner: someone had built a small fire in the corridor by piling twigs up against the wall, then setting them alight. The smoke curled up into the sucking mouth of a ventilation duct; a fire sprinkler had been activated and the spray from this was splattering the floor. Where the water splashed the fire, it hissed into steam, which diffused the harsh strip-lighting into its component colours, so that a small rainbow arced from wall to floor.

Tom was transfixed by this indoor weather system. Then, seeing an alarm button, he reached for it, only to have his hand detained.

'I shouldn't do that if I were you, right.'

It was a doctor, wearing a white coat of military cut. A stethoscope was tucked beneath one epaulette.

'Why not?' Tom asked.

The man, who had the strained yet authoritative air of hospital doctors the world over, seemed flummoxed for a moment, then explained: 'It's the Intwennyfortee mob: they're doing their business along here, yeah. The engwegge – it has to be seared.'

The doctor knelt and, picking up some greenish stalks that were lying by the fire, raised one to his lips and nibbled it. 'Good stuff,' he said, smiling up at Tom. He was very young, with a helmet of auburn hair and thick black-rimmed glasses. The doctor's magnified eyes – at once jaded and quizzical – were trapped in these little tanks.

'I'm, um, surprised,' Tom said, choosing his words with tipsy circumspection. 'That you allow the traditional people to hold such, um, ceremonies in the hospital.'

'We've got no choice, right.' The doctor rose and faced Tom. 'Once they're in – they're bloody in. Besides, fires in hospital corridors, criminal charges for blokes disposing of cigarette ends – it's all part of the same topsy-turvy sitch, right.'

'You – you know who I am, then?' Tom wasn't that surprised.

'Yeah, obviously. With the state the old man's in and you astande, you'd be a fool not to pitch up. I'll ask Atalaya's spiritual manager if it's OK now for you to see him, yeah.'

'Manager?' Tom was bemused.

The young doctor laughed. 'Her spirit intercessor. No Tayswengo can talk directly to her makkata; ritual business is organized by a manager, right. 'Course, that's not their own term; a literal translation is something like "informed explicator of the mind–world–body conundrum" .'

'It's incredible to me how much you guys–'

'Know about the bing-bongs' shit?' The doctor grinned, while Tom searched his open face for irony. 'It goes with the territory, yeah. You can't doctor them if you don't.

'I'm Vishtar Loman by the way.' He held out his hand and Tom took it.

They slopped along the corridor to the door of Lincoln's room. Dr Loman opened it and slid inside. Tom waited. A smell of meat cooking tickled his nostrils. The little fire succumbed to the sprinklers and they cut out. The shreds of smoke and steam were inhaled by ventilation ducts. It fell silent, replete, and once more Tom could hear the natives in the parking lot baying for admission.

The doctor was back.

'You can come in now.' He leaned forward and whispered: 'Lissen, mate, I'm not gonna bullshit you, yeah. Your man's in a bloody bad way. No matter what antibiotics we pump into him, we can't seem to get on top of the septicaemia. If it carries on like this, we're gonna have to try to drain the core of the infection.

'That's why the Intwennyfortee mob're here; Atalaya's makkata's gotta, like, purify me and Mr Bridges – that's the house surgeon – before we do the op'.'

Peering into the darkened interior of the room, Tom could see that a battery of equipment had been installed since his last visit: metallic boxes with winking LCD readouts, a pump that kerchunked with machine vigour, a monitor upon which undulated eight real-time graphs. Yet, jibing with this high-tech were tiny oil lamps, each fashioned from half a tincan. They had been set upon every available flat surface, and the room was thick with their sooty smoke.

Still whispering, the doctor drew Tom inside. 'I've given

Reggie a shot of diamorphine so he can cope with the ritual, yeah. He's a bit high.'

Growing accustomed to the gloom, Tom saw Reginald Lincoln's etched features well up on the white pile of pillows. The old man's eyes glittered feverishly as he lifted a claw from the snowy covers and beckoned. 'Tommy.' His voice was oddly strong and confident. 'C'mere, kiddo, we need to have a pow-wow.'

As he made his way across, a body surged up and wiry arms bound him. Tom was drawn in to breasts so resolute their nipples felt like probing digits. Atalaya Intwennyfortee's hair was arranged in the Tayswengo style, and the edge of the discoid coif brushing against Tom's neck sent an erotic jolt from his nape to his base.

'I knew you was coming down,' she husked into his clavicle. 'Now youse astande, any damn thing can go up rightways.'

Tom was rigid in her circling arms, but when she introduced her leg between his thighs, he enfolded her, his hands swarming over the dry matt of her beautiful black skin.

Reluctantly lifting his eyes from Atalaya's hair, Tom saw that he could see – and be seen. The functional furnishings of the hospital room – its high bed, the Venetian blinds on the wide window, a brutal commode, an articulated electric light – were exposed in all their obscene prosaism.

In addition to Lincoln, Dr Loman, Atalaya and himself, there were five others in the room. A naked makkata sat beside the bed leafing through a golfing magazine. Side by side on the couch below the window were three Tayswengo women, all with discs of hair set at jaunty angles on their long, thin skulls. Standing by the glass door that opened on to the balcony was a fifth Tayswengo woman. Or was she a Tayswengo – or even a woman – at all?

She stood, cocksure, one skeletal leg advanced. She was naked and entirely hairless, with her eyebrows and pubis shaven as well as her head. A long time since, she'd had a radical double mastectomy, the scars of which marked her chest like two badly sewn darts in the back of a dress. In one hand she held a long-handled spoon, while between her scissor shins Tom could see a camping stove with a bubbling aluminium pot on top of it.

'Intwakka-lakka-twakka-ka-ka-la!'

Tom half understood what the woman said. He somehow comprehended that she was an Entreati sorceress, from the wildest and least assimilated of the desert tribes; and, further, that she was Atalaya's so-called manager.

Tom felt his scrotum tighten and one of his knees began waggling uncontrollably. There was no one in the hospital room save him and the sorceress: the night, the rain, the others had all receded. The sorceress was standing in the lumber room of Tom's life, her feet like blades cutting into the poorly cherished memories of forgotten friends. She stooped to pick up a rusty ice skate, a mildewed college year book. Clearly, she was searching for anything she might use.

One of the Tayswengo women got up and opened the door to the balcony. It broke the spell. Rain and wind gushed in, the oil lamps guttered and went out. Dr Loman snapped on the overhead lights. Everyone started; their hands went to their eyes. Muttering, the sorceress retreated to the balcony.

The infection on the old man's head had swelled massively. It rose to an angry red summit, and lava flows of sepsis wended into his sparse hair. The infection had a distinct and malignant psychic presence. Lincoln's eyebrows and one of his cheeks were swollen and taut – yet still the eyes glittered, the arthritic finger beckoned. 'C'mere, Tommy-lad,' he said. 'C'mere.'

'Iss OK, you go fer 'im.' Atalaya squeezed Tom's arm. 'You get smeared now – you astande.'

Another of the Tayswengo women rose from the couch and passed her a small pot. Atalaya poked a finger into this and withdrew it coated in a viscous substance. She reached up and anointed Tom on either cheek and on the bridge of his nose.

'You go fer 'im,' she reiterated. 'Go.'

Tom approached the high bed warily, but Lincoln croaked, 'C'mon, sit beside me.'

Careful not to disturb his tubes and wires, Tom propped himself on the mattress. Lincoln smelled meatier than the meat stewing on the sorceress's stove. His decrepit body had been tenderized by thousands of carnal pummellings, cured by the smoke of sixty times that many cigarettes. Now it was putrid. He grabbed the neck of Tom's shirt and pulled his face to his own. There was shit and mischief on the old man's breath.

'Get in there, boy,' he grated.

'I'm sorry?' Tom queried.

'Get in there, boy,' Lincoln said again; and, following the pinpricks of the old man's pupils, Tom noted first the preposterous engorgement tenting the bed covers, and then, beyond it, exposed by the wifely act of placing a urine bottle on a shelf, the gaping vulva of Atalaya Intwennyfortee.

'Get in *there*, boy,' Lincoln said, rasping the emphasis. 'And when you've got out of there – get out of here! Don't pack, don't call anyone – just skedaddle . . .' Lincoln's voice became croakier still, and ratcheted up until it sounded like a sheet of galvanized iron banging in a gale: 'I've spoken to the Ambassador down south in Capital City – that pantywaist Winthrop Adams organized it.' Dr Loman came over, but

Lincoln waved him away. 'You've got your pardon now, so get while the getting's good, Tommy.'

Tom tried to pull away, but the old man's grip on his shirt tightened. Gravy-coloured spittle spattered Tom's chest. 'Fix her up real good,' he was almost shouting. 'I need you to, boy – then get out. Get out!'

Lincoln spasmed, then collapsed back on the pillows. Atalaya came with a cardboard dish, and her husband coughed brown matter into it.

'Engwegge,' Dr Loman sighed. Then, turning to Tom, he said, 'I think you'd better leave now.'

Atalaya smiled broadly at Tom as he followed the white coat out of the room.

The hospital had returned to some semblance of normality. There were medical and support staff in the main lobby. Drunken and damaged patients were slumped on moulded plastic seating.

'What was going on earlier?' Tom asked Loman. 'They weren't admitting anyone.'

'It's the engwegge,' the doctor explained. 'Look here.'

He led Tom out through Emergency, then pointed to the black gloss of the parking lot. 'You see those little brown dollops?'

Tom could just make out the discarded engwegge chaws sixteen metres off, disintegrating in the rain.

'Thing is,' Loman continued, 'engwegge isn't allowed in the hospital, yeah. We have to get 'em to spit their plugs out before they can be seen to.'

'No matter how hurt they are?'

'They can be bloody dying, mate, but we won't treat 'em while they're damaging their health. Look,' Loman said, shrugging, 'I've gotta go back in. You can prob'ly get a cab down by the main gate – there's usually a few loitering, even this late.' He moved off.

'What – I mean, the engwegge,' Tom called after him. The doctor turned and eyed him quizzically. 'They had it up in the room – they were giving it to Mr Lincoln.'

'Oh, that,' Loman laughed. 'There are exceptions to the rules so far as the desert mobs are concerned – very important exceptions.'

The clerk in the convenience store where Tom got his groceries had a name badge on her lapel. It read HITLER. Tom asked Swai-Phillips about it, and the lawyer said. 'Sure, that'll be her name, right enough. What was she, Ibbolit? Gandaro p'raps?'

'I – I guess so,' said Tom, who, although he could now distinguish the hill from the desert tribes, still had difficulty with further subdivisions.

'Bastard hill mobs.' The lawyer took a swig of beer and beckoned over the barman, who brought a fresh thimble-sized glass and took twenty-five cents from the pile on the bar. Then he retreated to his own perch, a high stool next to a peanut dispenser shaped like a peanut. The chiller cabinets ranged along the back of the bar cast a forensic light on the barman's shaven and cicatrized scalp. The raised white scars must, Tom thought, observing his ugly scowl, indicate the seats of his ill-will and bad character.

'They don't think anything much is what it damn well is, yeah,' the lawyer continued enigmatically. 'There's that cargo-cult nonsense, and these damn-fool names they take. Think it'll give 'em power, see, keep the bad spirits offa their backs, right.' He snorted. 'Nonsense! Total bloody superstition. Anyways, Brodzinski, what're you doing shopping?'

Tom took a sip of his own beer before replying. They were both on beer – the weather demanded it. But Tom had also had a few shots before Swai-Phillips showed up. He was a little drunk and tried to conceal it by speaking deliberately. 'I've taken to cooking for myself at the Experience. There's a kitchenette, and it's cheaper.'

'Bullshit!' the lawyer expostulated. 'You can eat good for a few cents at the food court. What's the real reason?' He rounded on Tom, lifted his shades, gave him the bad eye.

'Well, if you must know, it's Prentice.'

'He bothering you – or, what, interfering?' As so often with Swai-Phillips, Tom had the uneasy feeling he was being laughed at.

'No, not exactly bothering, it's more that he kind of fastens on to me whenever I step outta the goddamn hostel. Where's he staying, anyway?'

'Prentice?' Swai-Phillips seemed confused by the question. 'I dunno – with Mulgrene, their attaché, I think. You'd have to ask him yourself – or Squolly. Prentice is on more restrictive bail conditions than you.'

Everything Swai-Phillips said concerning Prentice appeared to tease Tom with his ignorance of the other man's crime. Not that he felt ignorant any longer, as he'd had enough hints: Prentice was a sex-offender of some kind, probably what the lawyer termed a 'kiddie-fiddler'. He certainly looked the part, with his crazy fringe, his doughy face and his dude's outfit.

Prentice must, Tom thought, be staking out the Experience, just like the cops. For the past week, whenever Tom left the hostel, Prentice was there, strolling towards him along the sidewalk, his dumb hat – or a dumb replacement – tucked under his poultry wing of an arm.

'Mind if I take a turn with you?' he'd say, and, even if Tom demurred, he'd insist: 'Look, old chap, I haven't a pal in Vance to speak of, so I'd be awfully grateful for a little company.'

Little company, eh. Tom nearly slapped him in the face, a face that was becoming increasingly corrupted by the rash spreading up from his jaw. Perhaps it was pity, but Tom always gave in, and together they would thread their way between the other, less culpable pedestrians.

In instalments that lasted the time it took to get to the mall or the call store, Tom heard Prentice's story.

'My lady wife', he said, 'is staying down south. Cousin of hers has a little spread a couple of hundred clicks from Capital City. He migrated here for the good life – you know how it is. My countrymen, well, we have strong links with this place, as you know. It's not exactly a sense of ownership, more, well . . . stewardship. We need to keep an eye on it, make sure the local Anglos aren't too rash.'

'You really believe that bullshit?' Tom was incredulous; Prentice was coming on like some lordling, sent out to the colonies to tote the white man's burden.

'Oh, absolutely.' Prentice was unfazed. 'You take my wife's cousin's station. He's got almost a whole section – but he can't make it pay any more. You see' – he leaned in conspiratorially – 'those bing-bongs, they burnt off the scrub for bloody years. It's completely messed up the water table, leached all the nutrients out of the soil and replaced them with salt. Gerard – that's my wife's cousin – he needs a square mile or more to raise a single head of cattle.'

And Prentice, bandy-legged, clumped on along the sidewalk, lost in his fantasy of stewardship.

Tom wondered what he made of his bing-bong-blooded

lawyer. Prentice was beyond caricature; the lines that described him were too distorted. In every exchange Tom had with him, he was on the verge of blurting out: 'What exactly is it that you've done? Tell me now – right now!'

Yet he never did. Moreover, as their desultory promenades continued, Tom found a curious respite in this mutual circumspection. It was as if their inability to talk of what held them here, in Vance, was a kind of stoicism – manliness, even.

Swai-Phillips had an alternative explanation, one he tossed out as he tossed back another beer: 'The makkata, yeah. Well, he divines degrees of astande: astande por mio, astande vel dyav, astande hikkal. Some are for men, some for women, some only for the Tayswengo – others the Inssessitti. There are cross-over, or hybrid, mobs as well, and every degree of astande relates in a different way – both to all the degrees of inquivoo and to each other, yeah.'

'It sounds bewildering,' Tom observed idly. He'd read as much in *Songs of the Tayswengo*, but then – as now – he'd found it impossibly fiddly to link the hooks of this byzantine magical system to the eyes of his own numb understanding.

There was a flapping noise from outside the bar. One of Squolly's men was shaking the water off his rain cape. He came in, sat down at the bar and nodded familiarly to Tom and Swai-Phillips. Then he unslung his automatic rifle and checked the safety, before placing it carefully on a towelling bar mat. The magazine curved up like a penis machined on a lathe. The cop began chatting to the barman, who, without needing to be asked, had brought him a beer.

Swai-Phillips continued in an undertone: 'It is bewildering – even to me, and I grew up with it. But the strangest thing is that you find out which degree of astande you are in action, by the things you can do for other people – and they can do for you. You and Prentice, 'cause you're both mixed up with the Tayswengo, you'll discover, if you haven't already, that there are things only you can do for him – as well as vice versa.'

'Like buying his goddamn "fags",' Tom muttered derisively. For it had occurred to him that maybe this was why Prentice was dogging him. Every time they were on one of their forced promenandes, Prentice would slap the pocket of his khaki bush shirt and exclaim: 'Bugger! I've forgotten them again. Look here, Brodzinski, you wouldn't mind popping into the shop for me, would you? Thing is – I don't know exactly why – but I can't bring myself to buy a pack of fags. You wouldn't mind, would you? Terribly grateful and all that. Thirty Reds'll do the trick.'

Standing at the counter, Prentice's $10 bill cocked in his hand, Tom wondered why it was that he agreed so readily to fetch the 'fags', an epithet he found at once risible and sinister – exactly like Prentice himself. Moreover, his asking Tom to buy them implied that the other Anglo, despite what their lawyer had claimed, knew full well what the charges against him were.

Watching Prentice scrabble with his quick-bitten fingers at the cellophane on the fat red pack of cigarettes, his fish-belly-white face haunted by cellular need, Tom felt, once again, a surge of righteous pride at his own sterling efforts to break the addiction. Efforts that had already been rewarded with this pay-off: not having to look at the medico-horror photos with which the health authorities disfigured the pack-ets – lurid pictures of mouths eaten out from within and noses picked to a cancerous mush.

Swai-Phillips was staring intently at Tom, a smudge of beer foam on the fleece above his full top lip. 'Yeah, well,' said the lawyer. 'After tomorrow's prelim' you may never see the bloke again. I dunno that I'll be able to swing it for him, yeah.'

'What d'you mean? Are you saying Prentice is in court tomorrow as well?'

'That's right,' the lawyer drawled. 'I managed to square it with the DA and the Tayswengo mob – guess you'd call it a block booking. Suits the court – the Tayswengo too. There are the makkatas, the managers, the witnesses . . .'

'Witnesses? What witnesses? D'you mean Atalaya?'

'The witnesses,' Swai-Phillips continued, ignoring the interruption. 'They've all gotta come in from over there.' He jerked a thumb over his shoulder. 'Besides,' he continued, raising his fresh glass of beer to the cop, 'Squolly's blokes can't go off patrol too long to testify, or who knows what hell might break out round here!'

The cop guffawed at this and downed his beer. The barman laughed too, and Swai-Phillips, naturally, was mightily amused by his own feeble joke. Unwilling to be left out, Tom laughed as well and, sinking his beer, slid further into the nauseating jacuzzi of drunkenness.

Later, Swai-Phillips drove Tom back to the Experience. Sitting outside in the Landcruiser he asked: 'You've got your dress kit sorted out now, have you?'

'Yeah.' Who is this man? Tom wondered. My mother?

He'd been to the tailor Swai-Phillips recommended: a jaundiced Asian who ran his business out of his house, which was in among the dive shops by the jetties where, in the season, the boats set off for the Angry Reef. Prentice accompanied Tom, for he too needed to be outfitted.

Tom opted for a cotton fabric, but Prentice had picked up a swatch of woollen cloths and, flipping through them, selected a pinstripe that a bank president or a CEO would have worn back home.

Tom laughed at him. 'You can't wear a suit cut from that! It'll be wringing wet with sweat before they've even sworn in the jury.'

Prentice's face darkened, and with unaccustomed sharpness he snapped back: 'There's aircon' in all the courts, Brodzinski, you'll see. And no jury for a prelim',' he added as an after-barb.

Up in the crappy little apartment, Tom lit a mosquito coil and sat down on a chair covered with diarrhoea-coloured vinyl. Within minutes it was slippery with his own sweat. The aircon' in the apartment sounded like a stick running along a picket fence – and it leaked brownish fluid. Most days Tom didn't even bother to switch it on, preferring to suffer the soupy humidity.

He sat staring at the ludicrous truncated suit, which was hanging from the closet door. Perhaps, he mused, I should've gone for a darker fabric? The judge may be a bing . . . the judge may have some blue taboo I know nothing about.

He sighed, then picked up a brown-paper bag, the mouth of which had been folded into a ruff. He set the fifth of whisky down again: it wouldn't be a good idea to have a hangover.

Tom picked up his digital camera. He couldn't recall having unpacked it when he moved over from the Mimosa. He certainly hadn't used it these past three weeks – what would he have photographed? Prentice? The makkata making the cut?

He switched it on, selected the archive and began clicking his way through the photographs of the Brodzinskis' family holiday. There they all were, Martha, Dixie and the twins, sporting in a swimming hole in the cloud forest, striking poses next to the car, eating at a road stop. The pictures were crisp and vivid – far more so than the sodden world he now trod water in. Despite his hefty bulk, Tommy Junior was hardly present in this album. There were one or two shots that showed the broad expanse of his back but none of his face.

Tom scrutinized that back – or, more exactly, the back of Tommy Junior's neck. In one photo the vertical scar that ran from the base of the boy's skull up to his crown was clearly visible, exposed by the way he'd gelled his hair. Tommy Junior had come to them with it – an ugly mark on a pretty baby. Martha, who handled all the particulars of the adoption, had implied to Tom that what lay behind the scar explained, in part, why an otherwise perfect – and more or less white – baby was available through this particular agency, which usually sourced children from poorer, browner regions of the world.

The scar . . . Tom had seen one like it very recently – but where? Then it came to him: the old Anglo, bending to pick up the butt by the ATM in the hill town.

Tom sighed and switched off the camera. He unscrewed the whisky and took a slug. He gathered up his cash and the key to the apartment, then he set off for the call store to make his evening visit to his family.

In his tipsy state it seemed to Tom that the 'Gollybollyfolly' of the Tugganarong was even louder than usual. He had to stick a finger in one ear and press the handset hard against his other, so as to hear Dixie tell him: 'I kind of stood . . .

like, next to . . . not Stacey, but, uh, Brian, and he picked up one, like, medium and two supersize, yuh? So that was, like, it sucked.'

She halted and Tom, heedless of her feelings, asked her to put one of her brothers on.

'They're, like, out, Dad,' she explained. 'But Mom's right here – d'you wanna speak with her?'

Since Adams had seen fit to notify Tom of his wife's estrangement, Tom had stopped bothering even to ask if Martha was in the house. He was taken aback and could only mutter: 'Uh, yeah, OK, I guess.'

There was a 'clonk' down the line, followed by a hiss of static so loud that Tom jerked the handset from his ear. When he replaced it, Martha was saying, 'Are you there, Tom?' And sounding concerned.

'Yeah, yeah, I'm here, honey,' he blurted. 'I'm here, how're you? I was getting worried.'

Again, there was a clonk, then a hiss.

'I'm fine.' Martha's voice emerged from the sonic fog, poised, imperturbable. 'But it must be nearly time for your court hearing. The kids have told me all about it.'

Tom waited, assuming she would add to this. She didn't – the thousands of miles separating them twanged.

'It's tomorrow,' Tom said eventually. 'It's only a prelim' hearing. Swai-Phillips says I can then make, uh, reparations to the Intwennyfortee mob – to Mrs Lincoln's people – then we can proceed on a, uh, better basis.'

Clonk–hiss.

'I've heard he's a good lawyer.' Now Tom thought he could detect a peculiar flatness in Martha's intonation. 'I'm sure if you put your full trust in him, then he'll reward it.'

This wasn't Martha's way of speaking at all. Confused,

Tom let the handset drop. It clonked on to the ledge the phone sat on, then there was another static hiss and, reedily, he heard Martha's voice reiterate: 'I've heard he's a good lawyer. I'm sure if you put your full trust in him, then he'll reward it.'

Slowly and carefully, Tom replaced the venomous snake of the handset on its cradle. He stood smearing the sweat from his brow into his hair. The 'Gollymollydolly' of the Tugganarong swelled up like the chafing of crickets. Tom went to pay the call store's manager, who sat in a booth watching a TV show set among surfers and lifeguards, which was beamed from down south.

Late that night, when Tom was dreaming of a desert corroboree – hundreds of naked Entreati women, their breasts missing, howling at a bloody moon – his cellphone was taken with ague. It shook, then fell from the compartmentalized headboard on to his head. Dazed, he snatched it up and held it to his sleepy ear.

At first there were disordered noises, then they resolved into a rhythmic jingling trudge. Assuming that someone had left their cell unlocked and it had dialled him automatically, Tom was about to break the connection, when over the trudge came a tinkling laugh.

'Ah! Tee-hee-hee!' Followed by Martha's voice: 'Well, y'know how it is, you've gotta say these things to keep 'em happy, yeah? I mean, their pathetic little egos require it, yeah?'

Except, it couldn't be Martha – unless, that is, she was deliberately impersonating the local Anglos' accent, its raucous vowels and the useless affirmatives with which every other statement was concluded.

7

Feeling conspicuous in his sky-blue tailored suit, with its short-sleeved jacket and short pants, Tom arrived at the court at what he hoped was an early hour. It was only 7 a.m., yet Vance's office workers were already hurrying through the rain-soaked streets.

The Central Criminal Court stood on Dundas Boulevard. It was an ugly lump of a building five storeys high. The concrete façade was textured so as to resemble the intricate pattern of logs seen in a Gandaro longhouse. Slitted windows like the embrasures of a medieval castle laid waste to the architect's pathetic delusion: this was an Anglo building, at once threatening and ridiculous – a dictator wearing a party hat.

An escutcheon was fixed over the chunky pediment. It was an enlarged version of the badges on the cops' shiny caps. With mouth and beak, an auraca and a moa held aloft the Crown of the Republic against a field of southern stars. Beneath hooves and claws undulated a stylized strip of parchment, upon which was inscribed the motto of the Criminal Justice Department: ABYSSUS ABYSSUM IN VOCAT.

Like a gawky schoolgirl, Tom bent to pull up the white knee-socks that completed his outfit; socks that he had hand-washed in the kitchenette sink at his miserable apartment. A slow hand clap of thunder rolled in across Vance Bay.

Straightening up, Tom saw that, far from being early, he was barely on time; for ranged in a semicircle sixteen metres from the main entrance were a number of suited men smoking with studious concentration. At the middle of this arc was Jethro Swai-Phillips, and, despite the engwegge cheroot stuck in his full lips, the lawyer looked dapper in his dress kit.

Was it coincidence or had Prentice – who stood puffing alongside, basking in the lawyer's reflected elegance – been primed? For Swai-Phillips's suit was cut from the same cloth as his own. On the lawyer the dark pinstripe was magisterial: brilliant white cuffs were turned over the short sleeves of the jacket and fastened with oval gold cuff links. Swai-Phillips's knee-socks were held up with gold-tasselled garters, while from his broad shoulders hung a short pleated gown, decorated with purple and pink ribbons. On top of his Afro perched an antiquated horsehair wig – yet even this only confirmed the dignity of his bearing.

He was accompanied by an Anglo with a jolly Celtic face; bat ears, gap teeth, freckled cheeks. The man had a drinker's red nose. Tom assumed this must be Mulgrene, the attaché, and wondered where Adams, his own government's representative, was hiding himself.

As Tom approached, he realized that Swai-Phillips's trademark shades were gone, and the glaucoma had miraculously vanished from his right eye. In its place there was a glazed copy of an eye: the white too white, the pupil too black, the brown iris fixed and unwavering. Seeing Tom's consternation, the lawyer snapped, 'It's a contact lens, Brodzinski, no need to be afraid.' And Prentice snickered.

'You're mighty cool,' Swai-Phillips continued. 'The lists will be posted any minute now, and we'll find out who's up first.'

He turned to the man smoking beside him in the line, and Tom recognized the clerk he'd met at the Metro-Center. 'Have you got the depositions, Abdul?' Swai-Phillips barked, and the clerk displayed a leather valise bulging with scrolls that were tied up with the same kind of ribbons that dangled from his boss's gown.

'OK.' Swai-Phillips drew Tom and Prentice into a huddle. 'That fellow over there' – he used the nub of his cheroot as a pointer – 'is the DA, Tancroppollopp.'

The man was enormous – six and a half feet of taut solidity. Adams had said the DA had Tugganarong blood – Tom suspected him of being the Ur-Tugganarong, the Ancestor, who had propelled his outrigger from the Feltham Islands, using only his own paddle-sized hands. In one of these the DA held the smoking digit of a cigarette, cupped on the inside, as a skulking schoolboy would. The contrast between this homely gesture and the giant's sinewy forearms would have been comical, were it not for the belligerent expression on his copper face, and the two aggressive tattoos that spiralled down from his shaven scalp to loop his shark's fin ears.

'Who the hell is he talking to?' Tom blurted out.

'Pipe down!' Swai-Phillips snapped – and Prentice giggled, because the man in conversation with Tancroppollopp was smoking a pipe: a long curved one with a ceramic bowl.

Perhaps the man had chosen this pipe because it conformed to his morphology; for he too was long and curved. An Anglo, almost as tall as the DA but stick-thin like a desert tribesman. The pants of the Anglo's dress kit were cut high, exposing a great length of scrawny thigh. It should have made him look ridiculous – but didn't, for he had the taut watchfulness of a raptor. The pipe-smoker's face was also avian: a sharp beak of veined nose, close-set yellowy eyes and hollow cheeks. He sported a gold pince-nez and a gown the same as Swai-Phillips's – although his ribbons were red and white.

'That's Von Sasser,' Tom's lawyer explained. 'He's the Chief Prosecutor – must be acting as Counsel for the Eastern Province. I'd hoped he'd be down south, yeah. He normally only handles the most serious cases. I'm not in the habit of showing any damn weakness.' Swai-Phillips drew deep on his cheroot, then spoke through a personal thunderhead: 'But he's a formidible bloody antagonist.'

'Von Sasser?' Tom queried. 'I thought he was an anthropologist?'

'The brother,' Swai-Phillips replied. 'This is Hippolyte – the other one's Erich. You'd never catch him up here in Vance, too much civilization for the man to bear, yeah . . .'

It seemed as if the lawyer was going to add to this, but suddenly – as if responding to an ultrasonic whistle audible only to smokers – the men formed a line at the steel dolmen of an ashtray, and one after another shed their butts. Von Sasser carefully knocked out his pipe before replacing it in a leather case. Then they all filed up the steps and into the Central Criminal Court.

The lobby was stygian, even after the sepia gloom of the monsoonal outdoors. There was a tremendous scurrying as clerks, police, court officials and lawyers scuttled over to consult the long lists pinned up on bulletin boards, then hurried back to consult with their clients. Abdul dove into this free-for-all, and, emerging a few minutes later, he went across and whispered to Swai-Phillips.

The lawyer rounded on his clients. 'Good news!' he

boomed. 'You're up this morning, Prentice, and you, Brodzinski, will be dealt with first thing this afternoon.

'You.' He yanked Prentice by his tie. 'Come with me. And you' – he pressed Tom down by his shoulder on to a bench – 'stay here.'

Tom gazed at Prentice being led away like a mangy sheep to the slaughter. He expected some anxiety to show on the abuser's ovine features, yet Prentice appeared altogether unconcerned.

Once the morning sessions had begun, the bustle died away. A few hill people remained in the darkest recess of the lobby, huddling together and chanting their 'bahn-bahn-bahn-boosh' so mutedly that Tom couldn't be certain that it was them and not his own agitated blood pulsing in his ears.

At the main reception desk a cop checked his armaments over in thorough yet listless fashion, removing every bullet from its clip, polishing them with his handkerchief, slotting them back in.

From time to time a lawyer or a court official exited from one of the high double doors ranged across the back of the lobby and scurried outside. There they paced along the sixteen-metre line, snatching smoke from their mouths and yakking on their cellphones, before scurrying back inside.

Tom sat and looked down at the white billow of his thighs. He wondered where Adams had gotten to – and Atalaya Intwennyfortee for that matter. He was missing the Honorary Consul and the plaintiff acutely: as if he were still a smoker and they a pack of cigarettes and a lighter. Once or twice Tom caught himself patting the pockets of his suit jacket, as if in expectation of feeling small bodies tucked inside them: Adams with his seersucker smile, Atalaya with her matt-black skin.

There came more slow hand claps of thunder; then, at last, like a strained-for ejaculation, the hiss of the rains. Tom felt islanded in the lobby, listening to the 'bahn-bahn-bahn-boosh' of the natives, the scrape of a faulty aircon' unit and the measured slap of a large digital clock.

At eleven, scattering raindrops from her plastic poncho, Gloria Swai-Phillips swept in. She scanned the lobby and, spotting Tom on his bench, came across and sat down beside him. Her approximation of Martha's features was at once imperious and consoling: the wide mouth and long top lip writhed as she struggled out of her rainwear. Underneath she wore a cream linen two-piece with a pleated skirt. Tom fixated on the raw pores of her freshly shaven calves.

At first, Gloria said nothing, only leaned over and probed Tom's own leg. Her fingers found the makkata's wound.

'Does it hurt, yeah?' she asked.

'Did you call last—' Tom began, then checked himself. 'Not much,' he answered instead. 'It's like a war wound – aches when the rains are coming.'

Gloria laughed curtly and withdrew her hand. 'I'm leaving this arvo',' she said. 'Flying first to Amherst on the west coast, then heading along Route 2 with a convoy for the Tontine Townships . . .' She paused and looked at Tom. He looked back, wondering what any of this had to do with him. 'Y'know,' she continued, 'the orphanages I run there, they've gotta be supplied, right?'

'Sure,' Tom said. 'Of course – I understand.'

'I – I . . .' She took up his hand in her own, turning it this way and that. Her fingernails were long, sickle-curved and steelily varnished. 'I hope to see you there, yeah?'

Before Tom could think of a response, Gloria struggling back into her poncho. Her heels clacked the stone floor to the main doors. She glanced back at him over her shoulder, then covered her blonde hank of hair with the pointy hood and swept out into the rain.

Tom had no time to analyse this visitation: the doors to Court No. 3 banged open, and Gloria's cousin came striding out. In his train were Abdul, the clerk, and Mulgrene, the attaché. Then came Prentice, together with a huddle of court officials. Mulgrene was saying, very loudly, as if advertising for prospective Swai-Phillips clients: 'That was inspiring, Jethro, absolutely bloody inspiring. I don't think I've ever seen anyone tackle Von Sasser with quite such sheer brio before. You deserve a drink, man.'

The whole posse came across to where Tom was sitting and grouped themselves around him, ignoring him while recounting loudly the feats of advocacy they had just witnessed. Tom tried to catch Prentice's eye, but it was fixed on Swai-Phillips with an expression of nauseating adoration.

Tancroppollopp and Von Sasser came past and straight out into the rain. A clerk came up to the defendants' party and handed a scrap of paper to Mulgrene. The attaché scanned it with goggling eyes, his sad clown's smile turned upside down.

'Four gross of reusable teats, ditto of disposable nappies. Ribavirin – 400 doses in ampoules, amoxycillin, antiseptic wipes–' He broke off and turned to Prentice. 'Nothing here that we weren't expecting. You have the credit available, yes?'

Prentice nodded.

'Then you can load up tomorrow,' Swai-Phillips barked. 'Then get the fuck outta here!'

★   ★   ★

Lunch dragged on for hours. The party sat at Formica-topped tables ranged around a shrubbery that threatened them with its saw-toothed leaves. Swai-Phillips, taking a moment out from the continuous toasting of beer that was celebrating his signal victory, explained to Tom: 'The court won't sit again till at least three, right. They've gotta put up a rood screen so Atalaya and her manager can give evidence to the makkatas. Try not to be so uptight, Brodzinski; it'll play out fine. Have a bloody beer and relax, yeah.'

Tom couldn't. He stepped outside of the food court. Rain hammered down on the glass porch as he hit redial for the twentieth time that day: 'This phone is temporarily unavailable, your call is being answered by AdVance messaging . . .'

When the peep-prompt came, Tom decanted all his pent-up anxiety: 'Jesus-H-Christ, Adams. Are you gonna hang me out to dry, or what?'

Back inside, a wheeled icebox was being pushed from one man to the next. In turn they drew off glasses of beer, then made another toast, to 'Justice!', or 'Rhetoric!', or 'Reason!' Jackets had been slung over chair backs. Bare fore-arms lay among the curry-smeared pannikins, together with a dandruff of coconut flakes.

Swai-Phillips sat at the head of the table, his tie loosened, his globe of hair so beaded with sweat that it resembled a jewelled snood. Yet he was sober compared to Mulgrene and Prentice – both of whom were straightforwardly drunk.

At two thirty, Tom palmed one of the waiters forty bucks to go to the liquor store and get him a fifth of Seagram's. When the man returned, Tom took two swift shots. The whisky slapped him lazily in the face, a knuckle of intoxication catching him beneath one eye. His head spinning, Tom looked up to see the rains smashing through the skylight. Swai-Phillips aimed his painted lens at his client. The lawyer's strong jaw was bearded with bladder clams, his mouth a robotic speaker through which he crackled: 'It's gone two forty-five, Brodzinski. The court'll sit in fifteen minutes; we don't wanna be late, mate.'

Leaving Prentice, Mulgrene and the others, they splashed back through the afternoon downpour. Abdul draped a waxed coat over his boss's broad shoulders. Beneath this, the lawyer's suit and gown remained obstinately crisp; while Tom, who only had a folding umbrella for protection, discovered that his jacket was covered with damp splodges.

As they entered the lobby, they were met by the Honorary Consul, who, taking Tom by the arm, led him directly into the courtroom. Predictably, Adams was sporting a tan seer-sucker suit. Set beside the imposing figures in the court, he looked like an overgrown school boy, an impression enhanced only by the blue sash he wore, which Tom assumed must be the badge of his − mostly specious − office.

The bench was unoccupied, but Hippolyte von Sasser and Tancroppollopp, the DA, were at a table across the aisle from where the defence had seated themselves.

Leaning over, Adams hissed: 'I'm sorry I was late, Brodzinski, but, as you must appreciate, I'm in a, ah, potentially invidious position, given that I've to consider the interests of the, ah, plaintiff as well. I had to go to the hospital early this morning; there have been some, ah, unfortunate developments regarding Mr Lincoln.'

Adams stopped, and Tom, unbridled by whisky, neighed: 'What developments?'

Adams shushed him as the door behind the bench swung open, and a beadle led in the judges.

Staring at the bizarre trio that came in, Tom was flummoxed by how the courtroom had gulled him. On entering, it had seemed so ordinary as to be banal: the rows of plain tables, the railed-off public gallery, the stenographer and the clerks seated at a table below the bench. That the strip lighting seemed harsh and the carpet jaggedly patterned, he put down to the Seagram's. This mental astigmatism perhaps also accounted for the way the escutcheon seemed to be leaning out from the wall above the bench at a precipitous angle.

However, as the native judge, his black body elaborately painted with white stripes, slipped behind the end of the thorny screen that bisected the chamber, Tom realized that he hadn't even noticed this weird organic baffler.

Seeing Tom's consternation, Adams whispered: 'Karroo thorn: it's freshly woven by Tayswengo in from the desert. As I explained, neither Mrs Lincoln nor any of her people may give evidence in open court.'

The beadle banged a gnarled staff on the floor and cried: 'Rise!'

Tom stood and gawped at the two remaining judges: one Anglo, one Tugganarong. Their full-length robes were so bedecked with ribbons of various hues that they resembled raggedy dolls with human heads stuck on them.

There was an awkward pause while the beadle groped for a hidden switch. En masse, the court cleared its several throats. Then came a crackle of static, followed by a fanfare so faithlessly recorded that the trumpets sounded like kazoos. With one tuneless voice the entire company burst into song:

> From shining sea to awesome desert,
> From angry reef to bounteous mine,
> This golden realm of unutterable promise,
> It is thine, O Lord, it is thine . . .

Tom had heard the anthem before – even parodied it for his kids. With its jaunty melody and studious doggerel, it had seemed to him the very essence of the gimcrack national character. Now he was taken aback by the conviction with which it was being belted out, and, when he looked to his right at Swai-Phillips, was amazed to see tears welling in his eyes. Tears that, as Tom watched, swelled and coursed down the lawyer's cheeks.

The court groaned to a crescendo:

> We give it to you, O Lord, our country,
> We give . . . it . . . to . . . you-ooo . . . !

The tape hissed on for a bit, then cut out. 'Sit!' barked the beadle, and they all sat, except for the DA, who, without preamble, began reciting the charges against Tom. 'That on the 26th of August this year, the defendant, Thomas Jefferson Brodzinski, at that time temporarily resident at the Mimosa Apartments on Dundas Boulevard, did wilfully, and with full cognizance of the likely effects of his malicious action, employ a projectile weapon with a toxic payload to assault Mr Reginald Lincoln the Third – hereinafter referred to as the victim – and that the victim, having been grievously injured, now appeals to this court – both through my own office and through his wife's spiritual manager – for the three forms of justice provided for under the linked constitutional and Native Title provisions. To whit: punitive, retributive and corrective.

'Before my esteemed colleague Mr Von Sasser presents the Eastern Provincial Government's case against the defendant, I believe it would be in the court's interest, your honours, for these jurisdictional complexities to be elucidated fully, lest confusion arise at a later stage in the proceedings.'

Belying his monumental and impassive features, the DA spoke with great vivacity. Clearly, he liked the booming of his own voice and was settling in for a protracted oration. Tom, stunned by hearing a flipped cigarette butt referred to as 'a projectile weapon with a toxic payload', had already lapsed into the confusion the DA foresaw.

Then he heard the Anglo judge, who said irritatedly: 'Yes, yes, Mr Tancroppollopp, I think we're all well enough aware of this . . . this *stuff*. Let Von Sasser give us his opening remarks now.'

The judge was elderly and his demeanour mild – pale blue eyes peering over thick bifocals – yet he stopped the massive Tancroppollopp in his tracks. The DA sat down abruptly, and a ripple of amusement passed through the court. The loungers in the public gallery began chatting; the stenographer left off typing and took a swig of water from a plastic bottle.

Swai-Phillips whispered to Tom: 'This is all fencing, Brodzinski. None of the DA's case will be played out in a prelim'; the Intwennyfortee mob's claim takes precedence. All the important action is behind the screen, right.'

The contrast between the sinuous organic curves of the screen and the scuffed wood panelling was total. At the front of the court, where the screen furled into a tube and kinked up to the bench, it was held in place by cables attached to hooks, which were screwed into the ceiling, the floor and even the bench itself.

Through chinks in the tightly woven, thorny sticks, Tom could see the makkata judge sitting cross-legged on his end of the bench, like a spider in a basketwork web. Elsewhere, behind the screen, dark shapes flitted, and there was constant guttural muttering. Tom tried to make out

Atalaya Intwennyfortee's lithe form among the others. He wondered, idly, why it was that he, who had been deemed astande, was none the less behaving as if he were inquivoo, altogether passive in the face of this monstrous inquisition.

Adams nudged him. 'Brodzinski,' he hissed. 'What I meant to say before is that Mr Lincoln has—' But once again he was precluded.

Von Sasser had risen; the public gallery fell silent; the stenographer raised her hands like a concert pianist.

'Your honours, esteemed colleagues.' He nodded to Tancroppollopp. 'Citizens of Vance.' He cast a prosecutorial eye at the defence table before continuing: 'May I proceed by analogy?'

This blunt inquiry seized everyone's attention. The Tugganarong judge, who had been absorbed in some scraps of paper he was rearranging on the bench in front of him, looked up at the Chief Prosecutor and said, 'Why not?'

Von Sasser teased out two of the ribbons from his gown. He held these taut between the thumb and forefinger of each hand, while holding his long back erect.

'I don't need to tell anyone present – except, perhaps, for the defendant himself – the extent to which the introduction of alien elements has contaminated this once pure land.'

Even the native people behind the screen now ceased their muttering. Von Sasser twisted his beak into a smile, then resumed. 'Whether those elements be people, their ways or even the species they bring with them, the results have been almost uniformly disastrous for both our indigenous people and their environment.

'Now.' Von Sasser turned fully to confront Tom, and bore down on him with his raptor's stare. 'Here we have a – a *tourist* – for want of any other appellation – who comes here in ignorance of both our civil and our customary laws. Who both indulges in a filthy alien habit, and who then employs the vile instruments of his addiction to assault – violently assault – an esteemed elder of our community.

'Doubtless, he will soon call upon my colleague, Mr Swai-Phillips, to argue that his action was "an accident"; and, doubtless, the defendant would also argue – as have so many of his compatriots – that the Sangat clam is "an accident", that the tontine is "an accident", that the asbestosis of the Kellippi miners is "an accident", that–'

'Objection, your honours!'

Swai-Phillips was on his feet – Tom was hyperventilating. As calumny had been piled upon lie by the skeletal Chief Prosecutor, he had swooned with the injustice of it all: that this still-smoking Anglo had the hypocrisy to so accuse him.

'You have the floor, counsellor,' the Anglo judge whispered.

'To compare my client to a single invasive element might provide my learned friend with the substance of an analogy . . .' Swai-Phillips paused, vainly patting his wig. Tom was impressed by the clarity of his diction – there was no beer, here. 'But to arrogate to Mr Brodzinski all the ills of colonialism is, I venture to suggest, a false syllogism: all alien species are destructive. Mr Brodzinski is an alien species. QED . . . But I'm sure I don't need to explain the suppressed premise to minds as logical and finely tuned as those of your honours'.'

He abruptly sat down, clearly well pleased with himself.

The bench also appeared taken by Swai-Phillips's reasoning. The Anglo judge turned to his Tugganarong colleague, and they entered into urgent *sotto voce* conversation. Chatter broke out in the rest of the court. Tom turned to Swai-Phillips and asked: 'Exactly how long is this going to go on for?'

'It's in our interests', the lawyer said, 'to curtail it as soon as possible. But, all things being equal, I wouldn't anticipate a conclusion of the prelims in under a week.'

'A week!' Tom gasped.

The $5,000 he had initially deposited with Swai-Phillips had been eaten up by the pre-trial meetings alone; two more had gone on the astande ceremony. Tom had arranged for a further $10,000 to be wired to the lawyer's account, but Swai-Phillips had been blunt about the costs of his representation: 'It's a K a day, every day we're in court. Just 'cause I'm a solicitor-advocate, it doesn't mean I'm not the best, right.'

Seeing Tom's distress, Adams took pity on him. 'Jethro's only fooling with you, Brodzinski. Remember, the Intwennyfortee mob's retributive claim takes precedence. Immediate precedence — especially given that Mr Lincoln has lapsed into a coma.'

'A coma?'

'Yes, a coma, sometime during the night. You'll see: this will cut things short on the prelim' hearing. The Intwennyfortee mob will want to squeeze as much as possible out of you right away, in case—'

'In case of what?' Tom broke in.

Adams sighed wearily. 'In case the old man dies. Because then the charge will change to murder, and their, ah, blood money' — Adams's nose wrinkled with the bad smell of this term — 'will have to be recovered from the state's presumptive bond — and that could take years.'

The Consul swivelled in his seat. 'But, if I'm not mistaken, here comes the doctor from the hospital with the medical bulletin. This will shake things up — you'll see.'

Escorted by two armed police, Vishtar Loman approached

the bench and passed the elderly Anglo judge an envelope. His Tugganarong colleague ignored the exchange; he'd produced a pocket knife from his raggedy-doll robes and was conspicuously cleaning his nails. Loman and the Anglo judge exchanged a few words, and the doctor was then dismissed. The Anglo judge relaxed back into his seat, a relieved expression on his mild features. General hubbub welled up in the court. The Anglo judge passed the envelope to his colleague, who opened and read it. He then shifted along the bench so he could speak through the thorny screen to the painted makkata. The makkata, in turn, relayed the information to a figure that writhed beside him, and who Tom thought must be Atalaya's manager, the Entreati sorceress.

Then, a tremendous ululation went up from behind the screen and dark shapes threw themselves against it. The Anglo judge gestured to the beadle, who thumped his staff on the floor until order was restored.

'This court is prorogued,' the judge said. 'Mr Tancroppollopp, Counsellors Von Sasser and Swai-Phillips, you will all assemble in my chambers in ten minutes. And Mr Swai-Phillips' – Tom's lawyer rose respectfully – 'bring your client with you.'

Tom spent the break sitting, shaking, on the bench he had occupied all morning. Swai-Phillips went out to smoke – and Adams went with him.

The DA and the Chief Prosecutor came sweeping past. Then Von Sasser turned back and approached Tom. 'Mr Brodzinski.' He pecked down with his hawkish beak.

'Y-yes?'

'You will almost certainly be heading over there in the near future. If you chance to encounter my brother, Erich . . .' He paused.

'Yes?' Tom was perplexed. 'What about him? I mean, is it likely? Isn't "over there" a big place?'

'That is correct.' Von Sasser spoke with pernickety precision. 'Never the less, my brother's is a very expansive personality – he takes up a lot of the interior, he . . .' But then Von Sasser broke off, clearly feeling he had said too much, and, turning on his heel, stalked away, without any goodbye.

When Swai-Phillips came back, Tom told him about the encounter.

'Those Von Sassers,' the lawyer snorted. 'They act like it's their personal bloody fiefdom over there. Y'know, it's been years now . . .' But then he too bit his tongue and, together with Adams, began ushering Tom down a corridor that led towards the back of the building.

'I thought Von Sasser and the DA had to come to the judge's chambers as well?' Tom protested.

Swai-Phillips snorted again. 'That? Oh, that was just for show, yeah.'

But whose? Tom thought, as Adams knocked on a nondescript door, and they were admitted by the beadle.

At once, Tom had a strong impression of cloying homeliness. There were lace doilies on occasional tables, muddy watercolours of the cloud forest on the panelled walls, while an electric jug chuckled and spat on a tray.

Then he saw the Intwennyfortee mob. They were sitting on drab easy-chairs around a coffee table slathered with magazines: Atalaya, the Entreati sorceress and two other women Tom recognized from the hospital. With them was the zebra-striped makkata judge. The kettle must have boiled once already, for the natives were all nursing steaming mugs, and, as he watched, the makkata leaned forward to pop two sweeteners in his. Atalaya was chomping on a chocolate-chip cookie.

'Tea, Mr Brodzinski?'

Tom turned abruptly; hovering by his shoulder was a tiny old Anglo man wearing only paisley-patterned boxers and a string undershirt, through which snaggled a few limp chest hairs.

'I – I'm sorry?' he stuttered.

'Tea,' the old man reiterated. 'Would you like some?'

It was only then that Tom noticed the judicial robe, with its hanks of multicoloured ribbons, hanging on a coat stand and realized that he was being addressed by the judge.

'Um, yuh, sure, thanks, your honour,' he floundered.

'Brodzinski.' Swai-Phillips gripped his upper arm. 'This is Chief Justice Hogg.'

'S – Sir.' Tom half bowed to the old man, uncertain whether he should offer his hand. Justice Hogg seemed not in the least put out. He skipped away, and began shooting out remarks as he made tea for the new arrivals.

'Excuse my informality. Bloody robes so uncomfortable – never got used to them, yeah. My colleague, Justice Antollopollollou, skedaddled. You appreciate – restitutional arrangements, interim stuff . . . of no concern to him. Sugar? Milk? Lemon, perhaps?'

Throughout this the Intwennyfortee mob and the makkata judge stolidly chomped cookies. However, once the defence party were seated in their own easy-chairs, and Justice Hogg had perched on the corner of his large knee-hole desk, the makkata loosed off a volley of tooth clacks and palate clicks. Swai-Phillips returned fire, then the two went on, peppering each other with plosives.

Tom looked over at Atalaya. She sat like a teenager, with

her legs over the arm of her chair, and smirked at her cookie. Tom took a sip of his tea. Sweet and milky, it dissolved the whisky crud in his anxious mouth.

Leaning forward to Tom, Justice Hogg explained: 'This'll go on for a while, right.'

'What're they talking about?' Tom asked.

'Well, I suppose your people would call it horse trading, but here such bargaining has a ritual function as well, right. They're negotiating the terms of your restitutional payment to the Intwennyfortee mob.'

'And my lawyer – he's trying to get it, uh, reduced?'

'Not exactly,' Hogg smiled. 'Since you've been deemed astande, it's incumbent on you to offer more than they can rightly accept, yeah. You are the righter of wrongs. The makkata and Mrs Lincoln's spiritual manager will gradually reduce their claims on you to a point at which they are acceptable.'

Acceptable to whom? Tom wanted to ask, but Swai-Phillips, breaking off the negotiations, turned to him, saying, 'We're nearly there, Brodzinski. I don't know why, exactly, but the plaintiff is being most accommodating.' Then he resumed yakking.

Tom couldn't see that Atalaya was being anything much at all. While the other native women hung on to the rapid-fire exchanges, she went on munching, while staring distractedly through the sole window in the room, a tiny glass oblong hung with chintz curtains.

Some kind of conclusion was being reached, for, on a piece of copier paper he'd obtained from the judge, the makkata was laboriously inscribing a list with a felt-tip pen. When he'd finished, he held this up so that everyone present could read it:

TWO GOOD HUNTING RIFFLES
ONE COMPLEAT SET COKING POTS
$10,000.

'That's it?' Tom queried. 'What about medicines? Prentice has to get hold of medicines.'

'Different, ah, strokes for different folks,' Adams said fatuously. 'The mob Prentice has to deal with are mostly in the Tontine Townships; yours are way over there.' He jerked a thumb over his shoulder. 'Out beyond Eyre's Pit in the Tayswengo tribal heartland. These are desert people, Brodzinski, these are the things they most need.'

The Intwennyfortee contingent were getting ready to leave. The makkata stood, stretched languorously and withdrew an engwegge quid from his breechclout. The Tayswengo women, and the frightening apparition that was her neutered spiritual manager, were clucking over the vacant Atalaya. Tom was torn: would it be acceptable for him to ask after the old man – or would he be breaking another taboo? The natives forestalled him by heaving Atalaya upright and quitting the room, without any farewells.

'So,' Tom asked Swai-Phillips, who was standing beside Justice Hogg while the latter pulled some short pants on over his boxers, 'what happens now? Do I simply give them the money, the pots and the rifles, and that's that?'

The big man laughed. 'Ho-ho! Oh, no, Brodzinski, nothing here's ever *that* simple. All restitution has to be made in person. You'll have to rent a car and head out over there – you've gotta lot of driving to to do. There's some good news, though.'

The lawyer and the judge exchanged knowing glances. Nettled, Tom snapped: 'What's that, then?'

'Why,' Swai-Phillips said, grinning, 'Prentice has to head for the Tontines, so the two of you can share costs, and you'll have a road buddy – at least for the first few thousand klicks.'

8

'Have you rented from us before, sir?'

The clerk regarded Tom Brodzinski with professional detachment. Tom inferred from her routine eyes that, while the tourist season may have been over, one Anglo was still much the same to her as another. He took in the purple patches beneath those incurious eyes. Her nappy hair had been severely cut to conform to Western expectations, while her ample, café au lait flesh was scooped into the red A-line skirt and white blouse with red epaulettes that was the company uniform the world over.

Adams had told Tom that many of the hill people resident in Vance had diabetes. They lacked the enzymes necessary to break down the sugar and the other additives in the processed foods they consumed, either out of indolence or economic necessity, or both.

'I – I have.' Tom was flustered. Not only had he rented from the company before, he'd dealt with this very clerk when hiring the MPV the Brodzinski family had taken on their tour of the Highlands.

Tom had spoken with her – on both pick-up and drop-off – for at least twenty minutes. They'd chatted while they checked over the vehicle together. There had also been a couple of phone calls with her concerning the location of the spare tyre, and a dink in the fender. Tom knew her name – which was on her badge, anyway – yet she had forgotten he even existed.

'My name's *Brodzinski*,' he stressed. 'It's gotta be in your system.'

She riffled her keyboard, eyes flicking from screen to paperwork. She made terse remarks without looking at him. 'Collision-damage waiver? Unlimited mileage? Fuel-surcharge waiver? Personal indemnity? Tontine policy?'

Tom grunted affirmatively to all of these save the last. 'I'm sorry,' he asked. 'Tontine policy, what's that?'

'Your personal indemnity won't cover you in the Tontine Townships, sir. So we offer our own tontine policy, right.'

'What does that mean, exactly?'

The clerk sighed deeply. 'If either driver or passenger is rendered non-life-viable in the townships, the basic premium provides between $10,000 and $200,000 to the other party, depending on proximate cause. This is guaranteed by the Company in association with Premium Eagle Assurance. Full details of all tontines are set out in subsection A19 of the rental agreement, right.'

The clerk rattled all this off so fast that, although the oddity of the idea struck Tom, all he said was. 'Is that why they're called that? I mean, the Tontine Townships?'

She looked directly at him for the first time – and it was as if he were stupid. 'Tontine policy?' she pressed him.

Tom glanced behind him, to where Prentice sat on a low chair, his pretentious hat on one of his bony knees, his bald patch sheltered by the waxy leaf of an undistinguished shrub. Prentice nodded.

'Uh, OK, I guess,' Tom said to the clerk.

'In that case' – her chubby fingers flopped on to the keys

and a printer chattered into life. She swivelled, ripped off the printout, swivelled back, slapped it down on the counter. 'Sign here, here and here. Initial here, here, here, here, here and here. Mr Prentice will need to sign here for the tontine.'

Tom wanted to ask her why she knew Prentice's name but not his; especially given that Prentice couldn't drive. However, she was rattling on: 'Here's your driver's licence and credit card. We've deducted a $2,000 deposit, standard for rentals heading over there. Here are the keys; if you'll give me a few seconds to get my rain cape and checklist, I'll meet you in the lot to inspect the vehicle, yeah.'

Tom's and Prentice's respective government envoys were waiting out there. Sir Colm Mulgrene drew Prentice to one side, while Tom asked Adams about the tontine. But the Consul didn't seem to hear him; he was rummaging in a drugstore bag. Tom could imagine the medicaments the older man had been buying: corn plasters, fungicidal powders, pills to relieve the stringy fellow of the bloating engendered by too much rich Handrey cooking.

The cloud cover was very low this morning. So low that the top half of the Metro-Center disappeared in its draggled fringes. There were dashes of rain on the pitted, oily surface of the lot, although the day's serious downpours were still some way off.

Tom prodded Adams: 'C'mon, what is a goddamn tontine?'

But the Consul wouldn't be drawn. 'I daresay you'll discover, ah, en route, Brodzinski. Think of it as adding a little excitement to the journey. Frankly, I envy you. Driving for day after day across that amazing landscape, towering mountains like mere ripples on the horizon . . .

'Y'know, Tom' – the romantic image tilted Adams into

intimacy – 'the desert folks believe the land is always becoming – never, ah, finished. That every time a traveller visits a region it, ah, springs into being for him, taking on the characteristics of his own mind . . .'

As he trailed off, Tom thought back to their first encounter in the breakfast room at the Mimosa Apartments. Then, Adams had seemed the very epitome of buttoned-down, diplomatic rectitude: the kind of Ivy League second-rater who reaches his peak when he makes the right fraternity, and who then finds a niche in the State Department where he can slowly decline. Now, Tom wasn't so sure. Was Adams perhaps a little unhinged?

Perhaps to confirm this – as well as to display his mind-reading abilities – the Honorary Consul lifted his left hand high in the air, then brought it down to truffle in the hair at the back of his head. It was an action Tom had seen him perform before, yet it was too studied to be gestural.

The car-rental clerk rustled up. Drawing Tom's attention to the unusual position of the spare wheel – which was housed beneath the front fender – she said, 'It's only an emergency tyre, yeah, so don't do over forty on it, or go off the hardtop.'

'Isn't that a little dumb?' Tom objected. 'I mean, it's an off-roader, and as I understand it mostly we'll be driving on dirt, with big distances between road stops – hundreds of miles.'

She slapped this down with a hard fact: 'Lissen, this here is the only rental car you'll get for over there – I mean, blokes like you.'

Her eyes slid across to where Mulgrene was unloading plastic-wrapped bales of diapers from the back of his Land-cruiser. Prentice loitered near by, smoking as usual.

'It's not a bad car,' she continued emolliently, as she slid into the front seat. 'You can drive a stick-shift, yeah? Five front, one rear, then this switch here takes you into 4WD, right.'

The SUV looked too short in the wheelbase for rough terrain, and the roof was as high as Tom's head. The front seats were cramped – the back one only a narrow bench, and the trunk was clearly inadequate. Tom began to fret.

'Where am I gonna put my bag? Let alone all the stuff I've gotta take on to Ralladayo?'

Nor did he like the fact that the SUV was a bright white. He'd assumed they would be given one with desert colours – or even a camouflage job.

'Don't get your knickers in a twist,' Prentice said jocularly. 'There's a roof-rack, y'know.'

Ever since Prentice had turned up at the Entreati Experience that morning, he had been the dead soul of bumptiousness. He seemed to think it a fine jaunt to be travelling thousands of miles to make reparation for the sick crimes he had committed. Either that – or his crimes had been so vile that the desert trip *was* judicial leniency.

Tom thrust his flight bag into the cavity behind the driver's seat. There was hardly anything in it anyway: just toiletries, a few T-shirts and pairs of short pants, some underwear, and his copy of the Von Sassers' *Songs of the Tayswengo*. The rest of the pathetic flotsam left behind after the wreck of his family holiday, he had dumped in a cardboard box that the manager of the Experience said he would keep safe.

Then there was the parcel that Gloria Swai-Phillips had left at the hostel for Tom to take to the Tontines. Football-sized and shaped, it was wrapped in layers of newspaper and tied up with string; ready, apparently, for children's hands to tear it apart when the music stopped.

Prentice pointed at his own bag — which was of the squashed, retro-Gladstone type — with the tip of his cigarette. 'I say, Brodzinski, d'you mind?'

'Mind?' Tom snapped. 'Mind what?'

'Mind slinging it in the boot for me. My elbow's playing up.' He flexed it pathetically. 'Beastly gyp — can't seem to shake it.'

Adams came over. 'Commander Squolloppoloppou's men will meet you at the Goods Shed Store; it's at Webley and Frangipani—'

'I know,' Prentice put in.

The Consul ignored him and continued: 'You can get the rifles and such there. Prentice, I believe, needs to obtain his, ah, medications. You'll have to give the police this copy of the Court Mandate, and this one of your original visa-rights waiver; in return they'll give you your laissez-passer. I'm afraid I'll have to take your passport now; you won't, ah, be needing it.'

They exchanged the relevant documentation, Adams neatly tucking Tom's passport away in his floppy briefcase. To Tom, it felt as if they had come full circle, back to the breakfast room of the Mimosa. Adams had retreated from him since the night they had eaten binturang together. The Consul had sealed himself inside the ziplock bag of his professional detachment.

Tom got into the car. Adams leaned down to the window and fixed him with his chilly blue eyes. 'As I've had cause to remark before, the law here works in a roundabout way. Trust me, Brodzinski, deliver the goods to the Intwenny-fortee, come back here, and the situation will have changed — maybe not today or tomorrow, but some day soon, and then it will have changed for the rest of your life.'

By way of an answer, Tom turned the key in the ignition. The SUV spluttered into life. He glanced sideways to check out if Prentice had finished his deliberations with his own diplomat, then said: 'Understood.'

'OK?' Adams probed.

'OK,' Tom reluctantly conceded.

The clerk shouldered Adams aside. 'The law of the car is that it takes diesel, not petrol. Remember that,' she laughed. 'Or you'll be in big shit.'

Tom revved the engine, and it clattered like that of an old prop plane.

'It's possible,' Adams resumed, obviously reluctant to let Tom go, 'that I may, ah, run into you in the Tontine Townships. I have consular business that takes me—'

But Adams's valedictory words were blown away as Tom, tiring of the situation, banged his foot on the gas. The SUV shot across the lot and skidded into the roadway.

'Whoa!' Prentice cried. 'Sir Colm had his hand on the window – you could've hurt him.'

Tom pulled up at a cross street and glared across at him. 'I want one goddamn thing straight with you, Prentice, from the start.'

'W–What's that?'

'No smoking in the fucking car. Got it? No smoking in the fucking car. Do that, and we just might make it through this without me wringing your goddamn neck.'

Tom drove on. The anger felt good – a deep-heat embrocation rubbed into his irritation, which was – he thought – the psychic equivalent of Prentice's increasingly disgusting fungal infection.

'No need to play the giddy ox, old chap.' Prentice said. 'You had only to ask.'

He flipped his butt out the window, then inserted his flat fish hands between his denim thighs, muttering, 'I have the feeling this isn't the start of a wonderful relationship.'

An unmarked car was parked up in the lot at the Goods Shed Store. Even Tom, who knew little of such things, could see that it was armour plated, and that the whiplash aerial was too long for a civilian vehicle. In it, three cops were gollydollying to each other. Their coppery beach-ball faces were impassive, their complicated caps were jammed down on their heads. Beneath their see-through rain capes their side arms were obscenely lethal.

The senior cop – a sergeant – checked Tom's and Prentice's papers. The other two gave them a brusque, pat-down body search, before going to look over their car.

Inside, the Anglo clerks – a couple of nerds with long stringy hair and heavy-metal T-shirts – affected not to notice the police presence. When, eventually, Tom and Prentice approached the counter, the clerks treated them as they might any other customers.

'How may I help you today, sir?' said one to Tom. He looked along the cavernous aisles that stretched beyond the counter. Their racks were stacked with all manner of equipment required 'over there': bales of wire, canvas tarpaulins, water butts, pickaxes, waders, collapsible boats, enormous decoy moai, hanks of rope, stacks of spare tyres and capstans wound with chain.

Further back, the downlights picked out hessian sacks of foodstuffs, and plastic demijohns of chemicals, fuel and potable liquids.

'Uh, well,' Tom said, summoning himself. 'I don't need much.' Involuntarily his hand went to the thick wad of bills he'd concealed in his crotch. 'I need some cooking pots, and, well, a couple of hunting rifles.'

'Okey-dokey, can do, mister, can do.' The clerk wind-milled his skinny arms. 'First things firsty: what kinduv mob are these for, hill? Desert?'

'Desert.'

'Righty-hoo. So, Aval, Inssessitti, Tayswengo, or . . .' He dropped his voice. 'Entreati, maybe?'

'Tayswengo. Look, does it really make a difference?'

'Oh-ho, yes. Yes, indeedy,' the clerk crowed. 'Your Tayswengo are cooking big auraca out there, right, not much else, and that needs a special kinduv pot. It's the same with the guns – they do a very special kinduv hunting way over there.'

His explanation completed, the clerk squeaked across the rubber floor, then swung himself on to a wheeled ladder that scooted off down an aisle.

He was gone for some time. So long, that Prentice's clerk was able to fetch, from a locked pharmaceuticals box up near the rafters of the giant shed, the boxes of ribavirin and amoxycillin that his customer required.

Prentice stood tapping his hat against his leg and clicking the heels of his boots together. He engaged the clerk in knowledgeable banter concerning the drugs. 'This here Apo-Amoxi stuff, is it in 200 or 500 milligram caps?' And when the ribavirin appeared in boxes stencilled SANDOZ, Prentice said, 'Hm, didn't know the generics were available here.'

'Why?' Tom hissed. 'Do your reparations consist of these drugs in particular?'

'Dunno, old chap. I mean, I do know there are plenty of hepatitis cases in the Tontines, but there's as much – if not more – HIV. The amoxycillin will deal with a whole host of infections – chest, ear, urinary . . .' He affected a ruminative expression. 'Look, Brodzinski, I'm not sure how well up you are on the townships – or over there, generally – but don't imagine for a second it's anything like Vance. We're talking Fourth World conditions for the bing . . . for the native people.'

'I know that, Prentice,' Tom said. 'What I don't get is why you've gotta take drugs and I've gotta take guns.'

'Something to do with the nature of our offences, I expect.' Prentice answered blithely; then, turning back to the clerk, he asked him: 'This Apo-Amoxi stuff, suitable for children, is it?'

Tom might have had it out with him there and then, under the very eyes of the cops, who had returned from searching the car and regrouped, gollyfollying by a water cooler. However, his own clerk came squeaking back, dragging behind him a shopping cart cluttered with rifles.

He lifted these out, one by one, and laid them on the counter while spieling: 'This here is an H & K PSG-1. It's a .308, see, five- or twenty-round detachable box. Takes a tripod – and that's a Hendsoldt scope with reticle illumination . . . And this baby is a Parker-Hale M-85.' He nodded at Prentice. 'Which your friend here might be more familiar with. It's another .308, ten-shot detachable box, scope's fine. It's a cool, accurate, long-range firearm. Some say it's a shade too long, shade too heavy – I wouldn't know 'bout that, maybe your friend does?'

Prentice preened. 'I've handled one, certainly,' he said. 'I didn't find it too heavy.'

Tom didn't believe him for a second, but the clerk nodded, hooking his hair behind his ears. Then he took the final weapon from the cart, saying, 'We've got an offer on these, the Galil, er hunting rifle. $355 each, or a thousand bucks for five. It's another .308, this time with a twenty-shot detachable box. This is a neat piece: twenty-inch barrel, and the stock folds down to eleven inches. There's a Nimrod scope and an integrated bipod. At 6.4 kilos it's weighty without being too hefty – a lot of bang for your buck.'

As the clerk detailed each feature of the gun, he ran his boy's hands over it. Now he unfolded the stock and pulled out the two little legs attached to the barrel's housing. He set up the rifle so that it was aiming through the open doors at the afternoon downpour. A barrage of thunder rolled across Vance Bay.

Tom had no interest in firearms. Friends back in Milford hunted, but he himself had only ever gone out for jackrabbits with a .22 when he was a kid. Apart from the ones on cops' hips, he'd only ever seen a handgun, in the flesh, once in his life.

Despite this, as soon as he'd seen the rifles in the cart, Tom knew there was something wrong with them. The Galil was the wrongest of the lot. The barrel was perforated at the end, and its housing was olive-green metal. The stock was heavily grained wood, the long strap khaki canvas, and the magazine – or 'box' as the clerk dubbed it – curved like those on the paramilitary police's assault rifles.

The cops now strolled over and began examining the merchandise. The sergeant – who'd introduced himself to Tom as Elldollopollollou – picked up the Galil and checked the safety. Then he aimed towards the far corner of the store and pulled the trigger.

'Two-stage trigger system,' he said to no one in particular. 'Don't really cut it, so far as I'm told.' He removed the magazine and placed the rifle back on the counter. 'Tell me one time again,' he said to Tom. 'Where you blokes are headed, yeah?'

'We're both going to the Tontine Townships,' Tom told him. 'Then I'm going on into Tayswengo country – all the way down to Ralladayo.'

Elldollopollollou smiled at this, a long, lazy smile. He pointed at the Galil rifle. 'That's your baby, then,' he said. 'It's more like an accurized assault rifle, yeah. The Israelis devised it for' – he smirked – 'suppression in urban contexts. Kinduv hunting the Tayswengo get up to . . . well, pretty much the same damn thing, ain't it.' He turned to his comrades and his voice rose: 'Now, ain't it?'

They all laughed full-throatedly, while Prentice joined in with his snide little snicker.

The sergeant turned back to Tom. 'You'll be needing kecks, boots and such for over there. Thorn scrub'll rip you to shreds. Flake rock an' pummy-stuff'll tear yer feet up 'n' all. Your mate, here' – he thumbed at Prentice – 'he's got the right idea.'

He turned to the clerk. 'Get this bloke here down some desert kecks and the rest of the clobber he'll need. Get some ammo for these rifles while you're at it, yeah, and some eskis for this bloke's pharmaceuticals. There's no aircon' to speak of in that clunker,' he said to Tom and Prentice. 'Drugs'll be perished before you get through cane country.'

'And make it snappy!' he called after the clerk. 'We gotta get these two to city limits and make it back in time for the game.'

This manly admission of dereliction of duty was the most hilarious thing of all; so the cops, the clerks and Prentice began laughing all over again.

★   ★   ★

It was almost four by the time they reached the peculiar juncture where the four-lane blacktop of the City of Vance – complete with its colour-coded kerbs, bright red fire hydrants and fluorescent signage – came to a sudden finish, and was replaced by the single potholed track of Interprovince Route I.

The cops' unmarked car scrunched to a halt on the shoulder, and Tom pulled up behind. They all got out, and Sergeant Elldollopollollou directed his colleagues to get the two Galil rifles, in their olive-green prophylactic sleeves, from the trunk of their car and attach them to the rack on the back of the SUV. The rest of the reparations were already loaded: boxes filled the narrow trunk of the SUV, while the bundles of diapers were strapped to the roof-rack.

'Here are your permits for the Tontines,' he said to the two Anglos. 'And in your case, Brodzinski, for Tayswengo Tribal Land. Remember, you're subject to Provincial Police jurisdiction – that's why your passports are held back here in Vance. This means you have to get these laissez-passers, issued by the Ulterior Deployment Agency, stamped at every checkpoint you reach. If you don't, you'll end up in choky.'

He handed the plastic wallet containing the documents to Tom. 'Now remember, boys,' Elldollopollollou added, 'there's a big bowl of wrong over there.' He jerked his thumb. 'So check it's cooled before you gulp it down.'

He lowered his oil drum of a torso down into the passenger seat of the car. The last bit of him that Tom saw was the deeply creased back of his shaved neck. There, looping down from the speckle of his hairline, were several raised white curlicues: all that was left, Tom assumed, of the Tugganarong's tribal tattooing, lasered away by the police medics when he joined the force.

The cops' car bumped over the hump of Route I, fishtailed back on to the rain-slick boulevard, then nosed through the rainy drapes towards downtown Vance.

Tom stood staring after them, until Prentice called from the car:

'I say, you haven't got a camera, have you? I feel we ought to mark the occasion.'

Through the viewfinder Tom saw the small miracle of three distinct weather systems in the sky simultaneously. The monsoon shaded the gap between the whitish cubes of the civic centre and the maroon cloudbank. A rainbow arced over the Metro-Center itself, the spectrum as neat as an educational diagram. Further north, towards the airport, thunder surged and banged, and as Tom watched a lightning fork plunged into the mudflats of Vance. Yet, in the foreground, Prentice stood, his face illumined by bright afternoon sunlight, the grassy verge at his feet faintly steaming. The shutter caught Prentice in this expansive setting and put him in the tiny aluminium box: another specimen.

A few hundred yards away a cement mixer began to rotate noisily. Observing the piles of cinder-blocks and the bare hilltop fringed by a stockade, Tom suddenly grasped where they were: close to Swai-Phillips's compound.

Tom knew the lawyer had gone 'over there'. The day after the prelim' hearing Swai-Phillips had called Tom. He was sitting in Cap'n Bob's, the kiddie café on the 'nade, eating a hotdog and drinking a Coke.

'You better go and say goodbye,' the lawyer had said without preamble.

'Say goodbye to who?'

'Lincoln, of course.'

'But he's in a coma, he won't even know I'm there.'

The hotdog was ruined now – a bit of medical waste on a wad of of bloodstained sutures.

'How many times have I gotta tellya, Brodzinski, you're the righter of wrongs . . .'

At the hospital Lincoln had been camping alone in an oxygen tent. There was no sign of Atalaya or any of the other Tayswengo. Tom had asked for Vishtar Loman, but the young doctor was on leave, and he too had gone over there.

In daylight Lincoln's room was once again prosaic; terrifying in its anticipation of mundane extinction, human lives switched off like the electrical appliances used to keep it clean.

Tom had stood, together with a monitoring nurse, and observed the old man for a while; all his pep, his busy venality, exhausted. The comatose state, Tom thought, looked worse than death: a provisional finality, the equivalent – in terms of brain states – of one of Adams's 'ahs'.

Now, following Prentice back to the snub-nosed SUV, Tom realized that even at this late stage he had been hoping for a sign – or even a miraculous recovery: the old man sitting bolt upright in bed, laughing merrily, 'Only fooling!' Groping the nurse's crotch, then calling for a beer and a cigarette.

At least Tom had shaken off Prentice that morning. He'd had to see a dentist to get a troubling abscess dealt with. Tom thought this dated dental problem suited Prentice. He hoped the treatment would be commensurately old-fashioned: an extraction, without anaesthetic.

'Damn nuisance, but I suppose it has to be done.' Prentice had held his swollen cheek in his hand as he explained, 'I mean, we're hardly likely to find a competent practitioner over there.'

He reminded Tom of the colonial civil servants that his country had sent out to the wilds, during their brief imperial era. Tom had read somewhere that these men had to undergo appendectomies before they left; pre-emptive strikes against their own redundant organs, lest their inflammation prevent them from putting down tribal risings.

Tom now took one final look at the vista. As the storm moved off to the north, the rain-washed buildings shone in the sunlight. The happy, clean, *rational* city of Vance, with its wide boulevards and its hedges of jacaranda, frangipani and mimosa, where jewel-bright hummingbirds hovered, then vanished.

The marble pyramid of the casino, the hypodermic spire of the Provincial State Assembly building, the bulk of the Central Criminal Court — these were the true actors occupying the proscenium arch of Vance Bay. Naked makkatas and judges in their underwear, kissing consuls and wifely doppelgängers — these were the creatures of mere fancy, with no more substance than the clouds that sailed over the city from the open sea, the lenticular vanguards of which bore a distinct resemblance to the lenses of enormous, wrap-around sunglasses.

Tom shook his head. Behind his own new sunglasses his eyes tiredly wobbled. He hadn't slept well. He thought of the roach motel, which, after much deliberation, he had decided to bring; this, despite the fact that, even with an old chopstick he had found in the grease-spattered kitchen of his apartment at the Experience, he had been unable to remove the corpse of its latest resident.

Getting into the car, Tom scowled at his companion, who was halfway out of the passenger door, blowing smoke.

'I am Astande,' Tom said, mimicking the desert-dwellers' clicks. 'The Righter of Wrongs.'

Prentice discarded his cigarette and slammed the passenger door – another annoying habit. 'And I am Astande Por Mio,' he said. 'The Shifter of Burdens.' He spread over his knees the first of their sectional road maps. It made him look, more than ever, like someone's senile mother.

'Whaddya mean by that?' Tom barked, putting the car into shift.

'Just what I say, Brodzinski – that's the grade of astande that old bing-bong fraud gave me.'

'You've certainly been shifting your goddamn burdens on to me these past few days.'

Tom wanted to accelerate and eat up some road, but from nowhere a dinky hatchback with learner plates had materialized, so they were stuck behind it, bumping along at twenty-five.

'Yes,' Prentice mused. 'Most peculiar, that. I mean, I don't believe in any of that bally juju, yet I do find myself . . . well, I don't quite know how to put this, sort of *compelled*.'

Me too, Tom thought. Me too. And as the rain had started again, he put on the wipers.

They drove in silence for the next three hours. Route 1, after undulating over the outliers of the Great Dividing Range, settled down on to the lowlands plains. On each side of the road there were dense fields of spear-leafed sugar-cane, the rows of which strobed by in a greenish blur. The rain petered out after an hour or so, leaving wraiths of mist clinging to the cane fields. The occasional clapboard shack, raised on stilts, that loomed up had the deathly aspect of a sudden apparition.

Narrow-gauge railtracks crossed the road at intervals, along which clattered locomotives pulling wagonloads of cut cane:

so much sweetness, Tom though, in such a sour place. He had to stop for these trains, but when he saw a road-train, either ahead or in the rear-view, he had to pull right off the blacktop, so as to avoid being crushed as flat as roadkill when the three – or even four – semi-trailers came roaring past.

It was at once tedious and nerve-racking driving for Tom; while, as navigator, Prentice had nothing whatsoever to do. There was only one interprovince highway: this was it, they were on it; and would remain on it through a thousand kilometres of cane country, a thousand of hill country, and a further two thousand of desert before they reached the Tontine Townships. Here Tom would leave Prentice and make a left.

The SUV rollicked down into the broad creek bottoms, and rattled acrosss the bridges of railway ties with a reassuring hum of its tyres. Tom, despite the need for intermittent tricky manouevres, lapsed into that waking dream that is the virtuality of long-distance driving.

Besides, he had driven Route 1 before, with his family, up to the lodge in the cloud forest and then back to Vance. He tried to convince himself that this was merely another jaunt, and that Prentice was only another idiot child. A child Tom was taking white-water rafting or parascending – for the garish signs advertising these attractions reared up along the roadside, their metal tenderized by the shooting practice of passing drivers.

They drove on through rain-washed country towns where the only signs of life were the semicircles of smoking men standing along the sixteen-metre lines outside the bars, and the brightly lit plate-glass windows of agricultural equipment dealerships. Darkness fell on the land, sudden as a cloth dropped on a birdcage. The SUV's headlights carried a runway of bashed bitumen before them, and so they took off into the void, over and over again.

The car had moai bars, but, even so, Tom knew that once they were into the hills, and then the desert, they would have to avoid night driving. He had been warned that the giant flightless birds zeroed in on the lights of moving vehicles; they were damned by their own unevolved psychology to bomb the human occupants with their feathery bulk, and in the process commit suicide.

It was ten thirty when Tom pulled into the forecourt of a lonely motel. The illuminated lozenge of its sign crawled with bugs, and, as he stepped from the car, Tom was perfused with the soupy night-time atmosphere.

Standing in the tacky lobby, while a surly Anglo girl laboriously copied the serial numbers from their laissez-passers into the register, Tom looked in a strip of full-length mirror fixed to the wall and saw the two of them, now dressed identically in elastic-sided boots, jeans and khaki shirts. Like his *bête noire*, Tom had even acquired a broad-brimmed bush hat, complete with a roll of nylon fly screen. He wanted to grab the girl's skinny wrist and cry out: 'I'm not *like* him! I'm only travelling with him because I *have* to.' Instead he put this to her pale face: 'Is there anywhere a guy can score some liquor hereabouts?'

By the time Tom got back, Prentice had retired to his cabin. But, as Tom was unclipping the two Galil rifles from the rack, he re-emerged to ask: 'I say, Brodzinski, would you mind terribly . . .' The request was completed by the tube of ointment he held in his hand, and a tilt of his weak chin that exposed the gooey corruption.

'You want me to put that stuff on your goddamn neck?' Tom took an incredulous swig from the fifth of whisky.

'It's, um, it's . . . well, back in Vance Lady Mulgrene was doing the honours . . .'

Prentice wasn't ashamed; only hesitant, like the moths batting at their heads in the yellowy downlights.

'Is this to do with our respective grades of astande?' Tom said. The whisky was planing away his emotions with bold strokes.

'Oh.' Prentice smiled. 'I hardly think so, old chap. It's just awfully awkward to spread on an even coat. D'you mind?'

Tom took another swig. 'Lissen, Prentice.' He was slurring a bit. 'If I'm gonna do this at all I'll need rubber gloves – I don't wanna *get it*.'

'I hardly think that's possible.' Prentice's clipped tone suggested Tom had committed a dreadful solecism. 'You see, Brodzinski, it's psoriasis – it only flares up like this when I'm bally stressed!'

Tom carefully set the bottle down on the concrete and took the tube. Prentice grunted softly as Tom smoothed on the ointment. His breath was sour. The flesh beneath Tom's fingers felt deeply cracked – fissured, even. When he had finished he said: 'I gotta wash my hands now.'

'Of course, old chap, of course,' Prentice said, yet made no move to thank him or even open the door to Tom's cabin.

Sitting sideways on the bed, Tom sipped his whisky and flipped through the tourist brochures that had been left on the pillow. Should they be so inclined – this being cane country – he and Prentice could visit the Giant Sugar Sachet at Wilmington the following morning, then go on to a hobby ranch at Villeneuve where tame auraca could be ridden.

The lump in his crotch had been bothering Tom all day: $10,000 made a turgid wad of cash. He ungirded himself and got it out: it smelled of his genitals handled by bank tellers' fingers. He would have to find a better hiding place. Casting round, Tom lighted on *Songs of the Tayswengo*. There was no way he was ever going to plough through all of it – even a few pages knocked him out cold. Tom got out nail scissors and spent the next twenty minutes neatly excising the central portion of each of the pages comprising the final chapter of the book; this, he idly noted, was entitled 'Tayswengo Dawnings: A New Future'.

When he had created a big-enough compartment, he put Atalaya Intwennyfortee's blood money in it and closed the book. With the artful application of a few strands of Sellotape, it was possible for anyone to pick up the heavy volume, and even read the front sections of it, without being aware of the small fortune it contained.

As the level in the bottle of whisky fell, so Tom's head sank down on to the book: a moneyed pillow. Gazing woozily at the bedside table, he contemplated his cellphone and digital camera. Unsteadily, Tom aligned the two devices, hoping, blearily, that they might somehow work it out between them during the night.

In that night, Tom found himself with Sergeant Elldollopollollou. The massive Tugganarong cop wore a soiled diaper – he reached his brawny, reddy-brown arms out to Tom. 'Cuddle me!' he cried. 'Cuddle me!'

Tom took it as an order.

9

They did visit the Giant Sugar Sachet at Wilmington. Prentice insisted on Tom photographing him standing on top of it, striking a pose at the railing, which was a steely simulacrum of crinkled paper.

Through the viewfinder, Tom saw Prentice's head, and behind it clouds of white vapour gushing from the refinery's cooling pipes. Prentice also wanted to do the tour, but Tom drew the line at this. The air smelled sweet and burned. Tom, who had a hangover, gagged on it, saying, 'If we're gonna make the Tree Top Lodge before nightfall, we gotta get a move on.'

As the day progressed, the country began to change. The steady beat of the cane rows faltered, became staccato. Smaller fields with arable crops began to appear. The clapboard shacks lost their stilts and grew corrugated-iron hides. Route 1 twisted, turned, shrugged its bitumen shoulders and began to mount the Great Dividing Range in a series of switchback bends. The rainforest, furry with ferns, woven with lianas, tumbled down to meet their puny SUV as it laboured up the inclines.

There were no more road-trains. They came upon trucks, with a single semi-trailer, inching through the hairpins, and forming temporary moving bridges across the churning streams in the upland gullies. The only other traffic consisted of open-topped five-ton police trucks. In the backs of these sat squads of impassive Tugganarong, their hands clenched on their rifles, their eyes vacant.

They stopped for a counter lunch at a bar in Hayden, the hill town where Tom had tried to buy the Gandaro spirit wagon for Tommy Junior. The native craftsmen and trinket sellers were gone from beneath the baobab tree. There were hardly any auraca wagons or rickshaws in the churned-up mud of the streets. Walking past the ATM where he had withdrawn money all those weeks before, Tom half expected to encounter the old wino, but he wasn't around either. Indeed, there were few hill people in Hayden, and, of those that were splashing between the concrete boxes of the stores, a mere smattering were Anglos of any description.

Sitting at the bar, struggling with a burger engorged by eggs, tomatoes, pineapple chunks, cheese slices and bacon rashers, Tom observed: 'I hadn't exactly taken in how few Anglos there are actually living up here. The local people must depend an awful lot on the tourists – what do they do when they're gone?'

'Ah, now, Brodzinski.' Prentice twisted his independent fringe with his nicotine fingers. 'Your bing-bong never does any work, as such. Sits in his longhouse, chews his engwegge, chucks a few seeds out the door. Soil up here's so bloody fertile he doesn't need to even till it. When the taro comes up, he sends out the womenfolk to pull it and pound it.'

Tom yearned for the native barman to come over and slap Prentice, but he was glued to the TV above the bar, which displayed the spark and puff of automatic weapons, and a tanker turned on its side in the desert sand, like a whale stranded on a beach.

The sound was turned down, but in the coloured strip that ran along the bottom of the screen marched the thread: 'Roadside ambush east of the Tontine Townships renders 22 lives non-viable. Insurgents blamed . . .'

'You know what they say, Brodzinski,' Prentice continued. 'The Tugganarong are the ethnics the Anglos wish they'd discovered when they got here, while this lot' – he pointed flagrantly at the barman – 'are the ones they actually did.'

'I don't give a shit about that,' Tom said. Then, calling to the barman, he pleaded, 'Hey, fella, you wouldn't mind switching on that heater of yours, wouldya? I'm freezing here.'

They reached the top of the escarpment an hour or so after lunch. Tom regretted the shot he had taken to warm himself up. No matter how carefully he adjusted the car heater, he was either too warm and sleepy or too shivery to negotiate the potholes that now began to crater the blacktop.

Prentice didn't notice any of this; he was rustling the capacious pages of one of his own national newspapers. Tom couldn't conceive of how he had managed to buy it in Hayden. Prentice insisted on giving him terse, verbal updates on a sports game that was of consuming interest to him: 'Addenley's been bowled out, there's no way we can avoid the follow on now.' Even though back in Vance, Tom had told him that he knew nothing of the game and cared still less for it.

While Tom struggled with the steering wheel, peering through the misted-up windshield, his indolent companion reclined, feet up on the dash, as if he were on a motorized Barcalounger. And if Prentice valued his neck enough not to light up in the car, he never the less asked every few miles, when Tom thought they might stop. Then, in anticipation of his 'fag break', he withdrew a filter-tip from its box and toyed with the miniature white penis, until his chauffeur – gnawed at by attraction and repulsion – pulled over.

At least the landscape was worth stopping for. As Prentice turkey-cocked, gobbling smoke, Tom surveyed the cloud forest. The canopy fell away from the road, dipping into dells, then swirling up in frills and ruffs of greenery, from which surged the petrified waterspouts of volcanic plugs. Cloud snagged on these rocky nodules; while in the deep valleys, where the Handrey's terracing created the contours of an actual-sized topographical map, the mists slowly roiled.

The overall impression was at once homely and fantastical, an effect heightened, once they resumed the drive, by the pasturage of Anglo farmsteads, with its drystone walls and too-green grass, upon which grazed Friesian cattle. Their chocolate and white jigsaw markings were utterly incongruous: kids' stickers, crazily affixed to this alien environment.

Handrey longhouses were set high up on the vertiginous slopes. Some of these were, Tom guessed, enormous, their curved walls of smoothly adzed logs making them appear organic, not man-made.

Wild auraca huddled near the treeline, nuzzling their long necks together: the furry boughs of subsidiary copses. Once, a family group broke across the road in front of the SUV: bull, cow, three or four calves, leaping wall and ditch, their hooves slithering, their necks waggling. Tom braked hard, and Prentice, roused from his paper, said, 'Magnificent beasts.'

Tom cursed, put the car back in shift, drove on.

Shortly before dusk they reached the Tree Top Lodge, where the Brodzinskis had spent the three happiest days of their vacation. Tom had hung on to the prospect of a relaxing break here all the way from Vance. He recalled giggling gaggles of naked brown kids leaping into the pool, and mingling easily with the tourists' paler, pinker children.

Their parents had lain around on the teak decking of the teardrop-shaped pool, while the brown kids' parents brought them chilled drinks and meaty tid-bits on bamboo skewers.

Up in the cloud forest, Tom, Martha and the kids had been at ease. There seemed none of the ethnic tension that otherwise marred this idyllic land. Tommy Junior had emerged from his virtual world, and, wearing skin-tight swiming trunks, he bombed the multiracial pool with his own murky-brown body. The kids had squealed with joy; the adults flinched indulgently.

That night, in their beautiful cabin – a small-scale replica of a Handrey longhouse – Tom and Martha had tenderly embraced. This was enough.

The Handrey mob had gone. Tom dredged up some names and put them to the wet-season manager, a mean-featured old Anglo man who sat behind the reception desk in the darkened lobby.

'Hildegard,' he inquired, 'and is it Harry? I thought they ran the place . . . on behalf of the Tribal Council.'

'Tribal Council!' The old man guffawed. 'Don't make me shit meself. The owner puts them bing-bongs in during high season for local colour.' He was chewing engwegge, and Tom found it difficult to take his eyes off the long bristly hairs that crawled on the old man's Adam's apple.

He missed a spittoon with a stream of juice.

'That mob,' he said, smacking his stained lips. 'They couldn't run a piss-up in a bloody brewery.'

The old Anglo's hands shook as Tom handed over his and Prentice's documents. He glanced cursorily at the laissez-passers, then turned the register so Tom could sign it.

'You can sign for him too,' the old man rasped, and Tom wondered if he had been over here so long that he could tell their respective grades of astande simply by looking.

Prentice stood a way off, behind a rattan divan on which lay the other partner in this dubious enterprise: an obese Tugganarong, who, utterly drunk, was drooling in front of a TV screen that made the lobby surreally cosy, with its close-up picture of the crackling flames from another ambushed convoy of fuel trucks.

Besides this, the only light in the entire compound was shed by the storm lanterns that hung from nails in the walls and the tree trunks lancing up through the boardwalks that connected the cabins. As he limped ahead of them along one of these, the manager chuckled self-indulgently: 'Generator's on the fritz. Only got enough juice in the solar batteries for the telly. Gotta have the telly, yeah?'

He showed them to adjoining cabins; then, before leaving Tom, asked, 'Have you got any firearms in the car?'

When Tom conceded that they had, the manager became obliging. 'I'll get Stephen to bring 'em in and lock 'em up in the gun cabinet. Pissed as he is,' he chuckled, 'he's the same as any other Tuggy when it comes to handling a rifle, yeah.'

Left alone, Tom went straight to the bathroom for a shower. He couldn't find soap or shampoo; instead of the basket packed with toiletries he remembered, it was empty except for a crumpled piece of paper, which, when he smoothed it out, proved to be an IOU for 'sundry bathing requisites', signed in a shaky hand by 'W. F. Turpin, Manager'.

It was the same story with the minibar, only this time there were several IOUs, dated over a period of weeks and reading, 'IOU one miniature gin, London Particular brand', all of them signed with the same Dickensian signature.

Tom didn't have long to think on this, because Prentice tapped on his door to complain: 'How am I supposed to shower after a bally-hard day's driving in a trickle of cold water?'

Taunting him with its own superfluity, the sky chose that moment to gush, and rain hissed into thatch above their heads. Tom pointed out that it was he who had done all the driving, but Prentice wheedled on: 'I say, Brodzinski, you wouldn't happen to have a pair of fresh underpants I could have the loan of?'

Dinner was a morose affair. They sat on the long veranda, looking down at the empty swimming pool choked with dead leaves. In the feeble light from the storm lanterns, the manager limped from the swing doors leading to the kitchens. Behind these, Stephen, the fat Tugganarong, was, he explained, 'cooking up a storm'. A remark confirmed by the loud curses, crashes and bangs that did battle with the thunder rolling overhead.

The appetizer was a grub as pale as Prentice's face slathered in pink, creamy dressing. Tom couldn't even begin to contemplate this; his companion, however, slurped his own down and then, with a curt 'D'you mind, old boy?', took on Tom's as well.

Then, a long wait.

A road-train with two semi-trailers sloshed into the muddy parking lot. In the gloom, the two identical grinning Mediterranean women painted on their sides were sinister: votive icons of ancient goddesses. Beneath their leering faces was inscribed the slogan MAMAS WITH FORESIGHT ALWAYS SERVE SIBYLLINE PIZZA.

The rig's four powerful headlights were lidded with a mascara of bugs, and a still-twitching auraca calf was caught in the mandibles of its steel bars.

With a sharp hiss, the driver applied his air brakes. He cut the engine and leaped down from the cab; a bulky, hairy fellow in a soiled string undershirt. Tom, noting regular features and slanting eyes, as the man clambered stiffly up to the veranda, guessed that he had a dash of Tugganarong blood.

The driver haled the manager with 'Oi! William! Beer!', then sat down at a table as far removed from his fellow guests as possible. He drank his beer and ate his grub cocktail in silence. The auraca calf became still on the grille.

Tom shivered – he was hungry as well as cold. He fixated on the blood-spotted sphincter of an ancient Bandaid that lay on the decking. Beside the pool there was a mouldy pair of cut-off jeans, a perished rubber sandal, a cracked snorkelling mask.

Prentice, detecting a bulletin of interest to him, disappeared into the lobby to watch the TV. Eventually, the manager – or William, as Tom now thought of him – came scuttling from the kitchen, three large platters cradled in his arms. He presented one to Tom with a flourish, intoning, 'Smoked moa collation, Stephen's *pièce de résistance*, yeah.' Then set the second platter down in Prentice's place before scuttling across to the driver.

'Tough drive, Mr McGowan?' he said ingratiatingly.

The driver only grunted: 'More beer, William.' He burped, withdrew a handgun from the waist of his pants and placed it on the table.

The moa collation consisted of thin white slices of the giant flightless bird's flesh laid over two hunks of buttered bread. On the margins of the platter, diced pineapple and star fruit glistened. The unappetizing spectacle was finished off by a slurry of the same pinkish sauce that had coated the appetizer.

Tom groaned and took a long pull on his own beer. William had sententiously informed him that there was no whisky available, and this despite the fact that Stephen had been flagrantly drinking from a bottle of Jack Daniel's.

Prentice came back from the lobby. 'They've followed on,' he told Tom, then tucked into his moa.

Tom still didn't have a clue what he was talking about. He stared down miserably at his own meat-shrouded lumps. Already, the drive had begun to give him constipation, as with each bumpy mile the road impacted his fundament. Tom thought wistfully of the coconut-milk curries that the jolly Handrey women had served on this very veranda in the summer. He poked at his food with his fork, and one of the long chunks wobbled.

Sometime later Mr McGowan stamped over to their table and stood bearing down on them with a confused expression. 'Mind if I join you?' he asked, then, without waiting for a reply, pulled a chair from an adjoining table and slumped down. 'William!' he cried. 'Beers all round!'

Then, nothing.

The trio sat in unconvivial silence for a long while. Tom and McGowan drank; Prentice methodically worked his way through the mound of food. In the kitchen, Stephen was having some kind of mental breakdown. Tom could hear him sobbing, and the whispered imprecations of William, as he tried to shut the temperamental chef up.

Tom felt drunk enough – but unpleasantly so. The beer lay on top of his belly, a subcutaneous demijohn, cold and slopping. Eventually, McGowan gestured at the SUV, which was parked beside his own rig. 'Yours?'

'Yeah,' Tom conceded, and then added, as if to imply that were he to possess such a vehicle, it would be a far better model, 'It's a rental.'

'Figured that.' McGowan shook his head. 'Thing is' – he hooked his thumbs into the straps of his undershirt – 'You'll be needing a bit more fuel capacity if you're headed over there, right.' A thumb jerked. 'At least a ten-gallon can – maybe fifteen, right.'

'I kind of understood', Tom said, 'that there were regular road stops all the way down Route 1 to the Tontines . . .' He paused, then for the first time ever, added the superfluidity: '. . . right.'

McGowan stared at him for about thirty seconds in silence, then burst into uncontrollable laughter. 'Tee-hee! Ho-ho-ho! Oh, yeah.' He gulped back his beery guffaws. 'There're regular road stops, all right. Just don't be too fixed on stopping *at* them, my friend.'

Shortly after this exchange Tom made his excuses and headed for his cabin. When he swung his storm lantern inside the door, its bright whirl caught a shiny rill of roaches, which flowed up the trailing sheet on to the double bed, then snaked across to where a lapping pool of their conspecifics were seeking entry to the motel Tom had brought with him from Vance. Still more roaches flowed over the smooth contours of Gloria Swai-Phillips's parcel, which Tom had also left on the bed.

Tom almost dropped the lantern. Then, hating himself for it, he circled back to the lobby, avoiding Prentice and McGowan, who were smoking studiously in the parking lot, sixteen paces from the veranda and five from each other.

William chuckled when he saw the roaches. 'Kids drop food in these cabins,' he said. 'Their parents do all sorts. I tellya, mate, it's a full, rich environment.'

He'd brought a squeezy bottle with sugared water in it. With this he laid a trail from the bed to the door.

'Leave the door open and they'll soon clear out,' he instructed Tom, then he added, 'Sleep well.'

Tom didn't.

The woman in his convoluted dreamscape was Martha, was Gloria, was both. She sat in the chair in the corner of the cabin and complained of the way the rattan was biting into her bare buttocks. Her stretchmarks were exaggerated – red claw marks on her white belly. She held the parcel Gloria had entrusted to Tom in both hands and pounded her thighs. 'Court is in session,' she announced. 'I am presiding – and I'm spotting, Tom, I'm spotting . . .'

This was minimization, for the teak boards beneath the chair were awash with her blood, blood that fell from the slits in the woven seat as the monsoon fell from the fleshy clouds above the Great Dividing Range.

The nightmare woke him, and, after he had tottered to the bathroom to pee, Tom fell back to sleep and entered another.

He lay in bed smoking; or, rather, he himself was made of dry golden shreds, sheathed in the papery cylinder of his skin. He exhaled, amd his mouth burned terribly as the smoke jetted out.

'You got fever,' Atalaya said. 'Lie still, I bathe your head.'

She leaned over him, pressing her breasts against his face.

'D - Don't,' Tom tried to warn her – but too late. She yelped, jerked away from him.

'Why you fuggin do that?' she spat at him.

Tom's mouth burned terribly; he exhaled another plume of smoke . . .

And awoke with a start. He was lying on his back. Light beams flooded through the blinds, and in them he could see the smoke of his own condensing breath.

Tom climbed on to the veranda to find Prentice already hard at work on an elaborate fried breakfast. 'Heart attack on a plate,' he remarked jovially. 'Best thing for a hangover.' He conducted Tom to the seat opposite with a fork lurid with egg yolk.

There was no sign of McGowan or his rig. Their own mud-splattered SUV had several chickens roosting on the raised cowling of its hood. Lumps of their excrement clung to the windshield. Tom gloomily massaged his sandpapery muzzle, foreseeing that he would have to be the one who cleaned this off.

Stephen, the hysterical chef, deposited a platter in front of him and grunted, 'Coffee?'

Tom sat, nauseated by the foody stench, and stared at the Day-Glo eggs, the rumble strips of bacon, the discs of blood sausage that glistened like oily bitumen.

Prentice cleared his throat. 'Erumph. I hate to say it, but' – he took out the pack of Reds from this breast pocket – 'there's no better way to round off a breakfast like that than with a fag.'

Tom hunched on the commode in the tiny bathroom. He kneaded the folds of his belly, while inventing spells to magic evacuation. It didn't work. The cups of Nescafé with which he had sluiced his brain made him jittery. He might, he thought, do something truly dreadful today: load one of the

Galil's magazines with the long, evil-looking cartridges. Aim lazily at Prentice's denim leg, then shatter it with a burst of fire.

'I say,' said Prentice, looking down at his stump, 'what the devil did you do that for?'

Tom snickered, twirled the toilet paper holder, rasped at the sore skin.

He couldn't find either William or Stephen, although the rifles in their olive-green sleeves had been clipped on the SUV's rack, and the chicken shit was gone from the windshield. Finding a tariff list on reception, Tom counted out the requisite bills. It was high time he and Prentice had a reckoning: so far everything was either on Tom's credit card or he had paid cash. Prentice hadn't even offered to contribute, yet for some reason Tom found it difficult to ask him.

Tom called out, 'Stephen? William?'

Parakeets chattered on the back veranda, but the Lodge was silent – ominously so. Even the TV was switched off. Tom pictured their hosts, loosely entwined on a mattress damp with come. William's ratty brow nestled between the breasts of his Tugganarong friend. Tom tiptoed out of the lobby and down the wooden steps to the parking lot. He was conscious of leaving something irrevocably behind – and had an impulse to return to the cabin and check it again. Prentice was already waiting for him in the SUV, sitting sideways in the passenger seat, blowing cigarette smoke into the golden morning light.

They drove all morning, stopping only to fill up with gas and pick up the can McGowan had recommended.

The landscape was reaching a kind of crescendo: the road

tying itself in knots as it worked its way through a maze of volcanic features. The cloud forest frothed up, so that they drove through dappled tunnels, long, mossy creepers fondling the windshield.

There was hardly any other motor traffic, but from time to time they rounded a bend to find the road ahead filled with a slowly plodding mob of Handrey, the women plump and swathed in brightly patterned togas, the men herding laden auracas, the children naked, skipping along and playing tag.

As the brown mass of humanity parted to allow them passage, Tom wound down his window and exchanged greetings, happy to be enfolded – albeit temporarily – by the jolly hill people.

Prentice was unmoved. He sat stock-still, eyes front, his young-old features twisted in disgust; and when Tom accelerated, he delivered a stream of invective: 'Bloody lazy bing-bongs. The liberals say they're closer to God – but they're hand in paw with the bloody monkeys. I tell you, Brodzinski, the desert mobs are still worse, naked bloody savages. Only your Tugganarong is worth a damn, see, because he's been subjected to a proper colonial power. Trained up, taught to be a servant to his masters. Without the work we put into the Tugganarong who've now come over here, these Anglos would be finished already. Kaput.'

Tom now knew better than to interrupt: to counter whatever Prentice came out with would only call forth still more of the same.

'Down south I've a Tugganarong – well, obviously he's not a friend, but I respect Jonas . . .'

Prentice was wittering on when they entered a clearing, where, in the full glare of the noonday sun, two entire squads of paramilitary police were disporting themselves on the red rocks. Some were brewing up tea on portable stoves; others had stripped off their uniforms and were splashing in the crystal waters of a stream. One group were gathered by a large-calibre machine gun on a tripod. As the SUV caromed past, the Anglo officer who lay prone behind it tracked them with the weapon's vicious muzzle.

This shut Prentice up for a while. They drove on in silence, Tom tormented by Prentice's very proximity – his rotten, cloacal physicality – yet feeling utterly alone. Like a wife, Prentice encroached on Tom the entire time: borrowing nail clippers and shampoo; asking him to lift this, or tote that. And, equally wifely, the other man left Tom alone to be immolated by his own fiery feelings.

The country was changing. The tree cover became sparser, the road un-kinked itself, the volcanic extrusions retreated into the long grass. Up above, the cumulus clouds condensed – then evaporated, leaving behind only cirrus brush strokes on the cobalt-primed canvas. The heat began to build, and build. Then, at some definite – but, for all that, unnoticed – point, the little SUV tipped over the central fulcrum of the Great Dividing Range, and they were propelled down its far side into a new, old world.

'This,' Prentice cried. 'This is the *real* over there, all right. Oh, yes, my friend. Oh, yes.'

Tom gritted his teeth, although he too was overwhelmed by the prospect that opened out before them: a country so wide and vast and old-seeming; a country of beige rock formations, smoothly streamlined like cetaceans, as if they had been beached by the retreat of ancient oceans.

A country of tinder-dry yellow grasses and tall spindly eucalyptus trees, their fire-blackened trunks bare for fifty, sixty feet up to the shimmer of the canopy. The trees were so evenly spaced that they gave the impression of a colossal plantation. Tom stared down avenues miles in length to either side of the road, searching for the habitations of the constant foresters.

The metalled road faltered, stuttered, then the blacktop gave out altogether. Route I was now a red dirt road, heavily corrugated, so that the car's tyres whacked from trough to trough, filling the interior with an insistent thrumming. Tom changed up to prevent skidding, and they bucketed on.

An enormous road sign swam towards them out of the heat-haze – the first they had seen that day. The destinations it listed – TONTINE TOWNSHIPS, KELLIPPI BAUXITE MINES, AMHERST, TRANGADEN – sounded prosaic, while the distances were unthinkable: 2,134 KMS, 2,578 KMS, 5,067 KMS, 5,789 KMS. Tom added on the thousand further kilometres he would have to cover on shifting-desert tracks from Trangaden, to come up with a total that suggested a maritime circumnavigation of a hitherto unknown globe.

Prentice saw them first and barked: 'Pull over!'

Slewing to a halt, Tom leaned across and followed the waxen wand of Prentice's finger to where, a quarter of a mile off, the tightly massed giant birds were tramping through the bush. Tom could make out their pearlescent plumage, and the curious movement of their backwards-jointed legs. There must have been over a hundred moai, and even at this range the men could hear their monstrous gravelly burbling.

'Wouldn't want to be caught out in the open with that lot, old boy,' said Prentice. 'You know they're incredibly aggressive. Down south–'

He was cut off by a black vortex of flies, which spun in

through the open window and corkscrewed into his open mouth. Tom would have laughed – but within seconds the car was a maelstrom of buzzing flakes, shaken up by the two men flailing at them.

'Oh, yes,' Prentice spluttered. 'This is the real over there, godforsaken, flyblown . . . and . . . and y'know who's to blame for it?'

'Who?' Tom gagged.

'The bing-bongs, of course. The bloody bing-bongs.'

Tom drove off as fast he could. With the aircon' blasting and the windows wide open, the suction of the draught extracted most of the flies, but still, entire drifts remained on top of the dash. Prentice put on his hat and rolled down the fly screen, thus completing his transformation into a Victorian spinster missionary. When Tom tried on his own, he discovered that the screen was too opaque for him to see the road. He set his jaw and drove on, determined to become accustomed to the diffident tickling in his nostrils, and at the corners of his eyes and mouth.

The two remained like this – massively stoical in the face of many tiny irritants – for the next two hundred corrugated miles, until Bimple Hot Springs came into view, and Tom suggested they stop to get something to eat.

'It's true,' said Mr Courtney, lazily flicking the flies away from his bulbous grey eyes. 'What your friend says about the bloody flies. It *was* the bing-bongs – and worse, they're still at it, right.'

'At what?' Tom queried. He too was flicking but irritably, and he wondered how long it would be before he could treat the flies with such disdain.

'Oh, yairs.' Mr Courtney tugged up a handful of hot

sludge from the slough they were lying in and applied it to his broad, sun-reddened brow. 'Y'see, yer bing-bong could kill only the odd moa or flipper with his primitive spears, right. Then we pitched up, and we brought rifles, right.

'Well, yer bing-bong, he's a happy little bloke, has no thought for the morrow. He thinks "meat" – now, don't he, so he goes on one bloody almighty killing spree. Been on it for near on eighty years now. Wiped out most of the moai, wiped out the flippers, wiped out the auraca – bloody feral camels and horses in all, yeah. Now yer bing-bong, he only takes the choicest cuts – even his bloody dogs get sweetmeats! All that bloody meat lying around – all these damn flies.'

Mr Courtney allowed his considerable bulk to slide down still further, so that all that was left of him above the mud bath was the top half of his face; his outsized chipmunk teeth gnawed on the sludge.

Mrs Courtney – who was even bulkier than her husband – gave a hippo snort, shifted in her picnic chair and affirmed, 'Bloody bing-bongs, yeah.'

Bloody, thought Tom. Bloody, bloody, bloody.

They had found the Courtneys already comfortably ensconsed at the Hot Springs. Their Winnebago was the only vehicle in the parking lot, and, despite the bullet holes that peppered its rusty sides, its candy-striped canopy, with the picnic chairs and table beneath it, gave their little encampment a gay holiday air. As did Mrs Courtney, who, draped in a tent of a dress patterned with hallucinogenic Van Gogh sunflowers, insisted on serving the new arrivals with tea.

'You'll be lucky if the fat slag in there will dish up for you, yeah,' she had said as she pottered with kettle and tea bags. 'Silly cow's scared of her own shadow.'

To Tom, who was unknotting the muscles that the drive had tied up, this remark was doubly ridiculous: Mrs Courtney was fatter than any cow.

The scarred clearing in the gum trees, with the steaming wound of the hot springs burping sulphurous fumes, had a minatory atmosphere. As did the motel, a ramshackle corrugated-iron building with a warped veranda that was raised up on stubby stilts.

To test Mrs Courtney's hypothesis, Tom walked over, unhooked the screen door and went in. A plump girl with carrot hair and cartoon make-up – a purple Cupid's bow masked her own thin lips – was sitting on a high stool poring over a celebrity-gossip magazine.

Tom was taken aback: apart from a narrow walkway running from the door to the counter, the entire room was behind bars – solid, steel bars that extended from floor to ceiling. In front of the counter there was a slit through which keys or candy bars could be exchanged for money. There were plenty of candy bars on the warped wooden shelves, together with cans of soda and beans, and stacks of Bimple Hot Springs postcards. There was an automatic rifle propped against the wall beside the girl.

Tom remained silent; so did she. He looked first through a blurred windowpane, then at the floor, where between his booted feet flies clustered in neat buttons, each a mutated splash of spilt, sticky fluid.

The girl, very deliberately, licked first her finger and then her thumb. She didn't appear scared of anything. She turned a page.

'We're full,' she said dreamily. 'And there're no take-outs 'cept burgers – bloody bing-bongs hit the last convoy.'

★   ★   ★

Prentice now brought the burgers Tom had ordered across to the springs. When he had seen the name on the map, together with the symbol denoting a road stop, Tom had pictured sylvan glades and clear pools of invigorating, mineral-tangy water. The reality was this smelly mire fringed by ghost gums, the bark peeling from their emaciated trunks. The naiads were these obese Anglo retirees from down south, who were wandering the interior on a permanent vacation.

At least the mephitic stench kept most of the flies off. Tom struggled out of the morass. His torso and limbs were smoothly coated with coffee-coloured mud.

'You look like a bloody bing-bong,' Mrs Courtney laughed, and Prentice snickered through a mouthful of burger.

By the time Tom got back from dousing himself under an outside shower, Prentice had finished his own snack and was gingerly removing his clothes, a towel – which Tom recognized as one of his own – wrapped around his waist like a kilt.

Prentice shifted awkwardly from one leg to the other, struggling out of his jeans. He hunched over to hide his crotch from view. Tom grimaced. But, despite his effortful modesty, as Prentice pulled up his swimming trunks, the towel's flaps parted, exposing white thighs and a pink hairless scrotum.

Tom felt the twinge of the scar the makkata's knife had left in his own thigh. Yet it wasn't until Prentice was on his back in the mud bath that Tom realized what had provoked this: Prentice's own groin had been devoid of marks of any kind.

Once he had reached the mud bath, Prentice lowered himself in and began to flop about in the muck, pushing his whole head under and squirming. Coming up for air, he made arcs for his eyes with fingers-for-wipers, then said: 'I say, Brodzinski. I expect I'm quite a funny sight covered in all this – you wouldn't mind bagging a photo, would you? My lady wife will find this awfully jolly.'

The burger was inedible – burned at the edges, near frozen at its centre. The stale bun flaked away on to the beaten earth beneath the Courtneys' picnic table; the sesame seeds pattered on to Tom's damp lap. He recalled the advertising copy on the billboards; 'The table's set, the silver's polished, we've checked under the table for flippers – so where the hell are you?'

The child molester wallowed in the springs, applying mud to the corruption on his neck.

'That'll help,' Mr Courtney observed. 'Bloody good for eczema and such things, yeah. These springs are the only decent spot left in these parts,' he continued. 'Bloody bing-bongs have done for all the good land 'tween here and the Tontines.'

'What d'you mean?' Tom asked.

'Just what I say.' Mr Courtney lifted another handful of mud and let it plop on to his occiput. 'They've grubbed up all the trees. They get a length of chain, stretch it between two utes and drive through the bush. Once the tree cover's gone, the first few downpours'll wash away the topsoil. But if it ain't turning to desert quick enough to satisfy their black hearts, then they salt it for good measure.

'All this land' – he gestured grandly – 'was bloody bonzer for stock before the bing-bongs crawled in from over there. They did for the game; now they're doing for the bush 'n' all.'

'But why?' Tom interjected.

But Mr Courtney kept right on: 'You wanna know the sickest thing?'

'What?'

'Those sicko liberal pols down south, they're giving the bing-bongs bloody *grants* to do it, yeah.'

'They are! They bloody are!' chimed in Mrs Courtney, who had popped out of the Winnebago's door and now came flapping towards them, a gaudy moa that had somehow managed to escape the natives' hideous decimations.

They were an hour out of Bimple Hot Springs when the country began to change again – change in such a way as to confirm Mr Courtney's description, if not necessarily his analysis.

The gaps between the gums grew greater, while the tinder-dry grasses straggled away, revealing jagged stumps, supine trunks and bone-white fallen boughs. Salt pans fingered their way between the remaining trees, their rims glinting in the burning sun, which beat down mercilessly on their little SUV.

The flies too were merciless. In desperation, Tom said Prentince could smoke in the car; he even asked him to blow smoke into his face. Prentice happily obliged. To Tom, the cigarette smoke smelled unbelievably piquant – as if a filet mignon were being griddled between his companion's fingers. To counteract the dreadful hunger, Tom asked him: 'You don't believe that stuff about the natives getting deser-tification grants, do you?'

'Of course I believe it, old chap,' Prentice exhaled back. 'Because it's absolutely bloody true.'

'But surely it's the Anglos' ranching that did for . . .' He waved at the moribund bush. '. . . all this?'

'So the bleeding hearts would have people think.' Prentice

self-satisfiedly crossed his arms. 'But the truth is they *want* the bing-bongs to have more of their beloved desert. They hand out a thousand bucks for every hectare they clear – that's what my wife's cousin says.

'Some elements', he continued, 'won't rest until all the cultivated land is gone – the cane country up north, even the good pasturage and arable land round Amherst. Bloody all of it.'

Bloody-this, bloody-that, bloody-all-of-it. Why was it, Tom wondered, that this was the entire nation's favoured intensifier? Besides, with this much bloodying going on, there must be a lot of actual blood. This rumination clotted his flyblown mind, and a chant started up in his inner ear: 'Bloody-this, bloody-that, bloody-all-of-it. Bloody-this, bloody-that, bahn-bahn-bahn-bahn-boosh . . .' for mile after mile, as the fireball arced over them and Prentice puffed.

Tom was so mindless in this mantra that he scarcely noticed the first few burned-out vehicles to the side of the road, with bullet holes peppering their bodywork, their windshields smashed and tyres fire-flayed. Then, twin-rotored helicopters began to chatter overhead. These lurched in the hot air, as awkward in flight as roaches.

Then Tom saw the back of the line.

There were Winnebagos and saloons, road-trains with multiple semi-trailers and smaller trucks, pick-ups and SUVS – all crammed with native hunters, their kills lashed to the fenders.

The line was off to one side of the road, and there was room to drive by it. This Tom did for a mile or two, until, with no sign of an end to the procession of vehicles, he pulled up and turned to Prentice: 'How long to the next road stop?'

Prentice examined the map. 'Maybe another five klicks.'

Tom hailed a native, who sat erect behind the wheel of an ancient Ford pick-up. 'What're you guys in line for?'

The man turned red-veined engwegge eyes towards Tom; his face was masked with indifference. 'Gas,' he clicked. 'Then road block. Only gas fer a thousan' klicks – plenny road blocks.'

He snorted derisively, then spat a stream of brown juice through the window on to the rusty roadway.

10

The motel was a blockhouse of blue-grey cinder-blocks with a corrugated-iron roof. It looked like a latrine built by intelligent horses. Each of the stall doors was equipped with a coin-operated lock, into which the 'guest' was obliged to feed twenty dollar-pieces in order to obtain his key. There were no staff in evidence.

Tom, having left Prentice at the wheel of the car with strict instructions to pull forward if the line moved – 'No matter what your degree of fucking astande is' – now worked his way back along the scores of stalled vehicles, gathering the required change as he went.

Most of the drivers were indifferent to his plea. They sat in their hot boxes, oblivious to the flies dancing on their faces, and listening – Anglos, Tugganarong and natives alike – to the radio commentary on the same interminable sports fixture that Prentice was obsessed by.

As he moved from fan to fan, Tom gathered that this was being played at the Capital City Oval, between the national side and a team from Prentice's homeland. The commentators spewed the usual trivia, but Tom did learn – with considerable pleasure – that Prentice's team were losing by many points.

This explained the sulky expression on his face when Tom

eventually rejoined him. Tom dumped the forty bucks' worth of coin into his cupped hands.

'Go along to the motel and check us in,' he ordered. 'You can at least do that, can't you?'

Prentice stubbed his cigarette out in the car ashtray with unnecessary violence. 'Only so long as I don't have to carry anything, Brodzinski.'

'Anything?'

'Anything.' Then Prentice tried to be emollient; it didn't suit him. 'Look, y'know I don't hold with this bing-bong rubbish, but I feel, well, *forced* to obey it. And . . .' He turned in his seat, eyes flicking to the boxes of medical supplies. 'Well, if I don't get this stuff to the Tontines, things could go very badly for me.'

It was the first time Prentice had referred directly to his own crime. Tom again felt the urge arise to force the foul man to reveal exactly what he had done. He pictured a summary execution out in the desert sunset: Prentice kneeling beside a shallow grave he had, in a break with taboo, dug himself. His face was a study in contrition; 'Goodbye, old chap,' he was saying. 'Sorry for any inconvenience I may've caused you . . .'

'Whatever.' Tom snapped back to the present. 'I'll wait here; if we don't fill up with gas now, things will go badly for both of us.'

The sun swelled, grew darker, its ripe bulk squashed against the horizon. The stony bled, so unlovely in full daylight, transited rapidly through a bewildering succession of poignant shades: roseate red, early-spring violet, silvery-grey – until night empurpled the gigantic mesas in the far distance, and bunches of stars dangled down from the empyrean.

The gas line had barely moved.

Prentice's game had long since been abandoned for the night, and the radio station had ceased transmission soon afterwards. Tom twiddled the dial, but he could find no other. They sat, not talking, and Tom ruminated: would it go as Swai-Phillips had suggested? Once the rifles, the cooking pots and the cash had been delivered, would the constipated legal process back in Vance loosen up? Maybe he would be at home in Milford in time for Thanksgiving. The candles modelled like effigies of the Pilgrim Fathers would be burning on the sideboard in the dining room, wax dripping from the brims of their black hats.

'Look,' Tom said eventually, 'I gotta get some sleep. I'm gonna drive the car off the road a ways, then we can take the valuable stuff and head for the motel. We'll have to get the gas in the morning.'

'Are you sure that's wise, old chap?'

Tom was only grateful he couldn't see Prentice's superior expression, and the idiotic lappet of his dyed hair. Tom turned the key in the ignition and pulled off Route 1. With headlights off, they bumped a few hundred yards into the desert. Then, humping the rifles, their ammunition and the boxes of Prentice's ribavirin and amoxycillin, Tom followed him towards the blazing lights of the road stop.

Later, they stood at the motel's sixteen-metre line while Prentice smoked and Tom applied the ointment to his psoriasis.

'The hot springs seem to've cleared this up,' he said. Then, hating his own note of wifely concern, he added: 'You should've stayed there.'

Prentice only grunted.

They were both tired and hungry. There was no hot food available, except for meat pies from the gas station: sad pastry sacks containing a disgusting purée of minced meat and potato. Even Prentice hadn't been able to finish his.

Besides, rank exhaust and gasoline fumes hung over the whole area, while the heavily armed paramilitary police manning the checkpoint introduced a nervy tension to the soiled atmosphere.

'I'm gonna bunk down,' Tom said, and handed Prentice the tube of ointment.

For a few seconds the macho remark sustained him, then Tom found himself alone in the neon light of his rental cubicle, with its blue insecutor fizzing and popping as the night bugs committed unpremeditated self-murder.

Tom woke in the utter darkness. He could hear the wheezing and trickling of the aircon', a generator pounded, a helicopter chattered overhead. He had fallen asleep reading the Von Sassers, and the weighty tome still sat on his chest, pinning him down, a somnolent lover spent by coitus. Shreds of dream whirled behind his eyes. He had been reading of the engwegge ceremony before he slept: how the women chewed the seared shoots, then passed the wad from their mouths to those of the men. He had dreamed of Gloria doing the same to him, her assiduous tongue pushing the bitter cud.

Tom groped for the cord and yanked it. The tube flickered, then slammed the cinder-block walls, the concrete floor and the rifles propped in the corner into stagy existence. The Gloria succubus flew towards the insecutor, then fizzed and popped out of the playlet. Tom groped for the bottle of mineral water and drank deep of its warm, brackish contents. He felt like a cigarette; felt that deep and visceral need for nicotine that had long been absent. Felt it as if it were a banal mode of lust.

Outside the arc lights blazed down on the checkpoint. The long gas line had evaporated, and the only vehicles Tom could see were a couple of police half-tracks parked in front of the steel bar lowered across Route 1.

He wandered on to the garage forecourt. Behind the plate-glass windows a clerk was sitting by the cash register, drinking a can of Coke. It could have been somewhere on the outskirts of Tom's own home town – the building was that international, that dull. The oval sign bearing the corporation's logo was an a priori category: this was how creatures like Tom viewed the world.

He found himself inside, fondling the crackling balloon of a bag of potato chips. The clerk looked up at the sound.

'Forty Greens,' Tom said.

The clerk pulled an ectomorphic pack from the rack. 'We only got fifties, mate,' he explained, holding it aloft.

Tom pulled limp bills from his jeans pocket. Together with the cigarettes he received a promotional lighter with the legend EYRE'S PIT: EXPERIENCE THE DEPTHS OF PROFUNDITY printed on it.

Back in the night, Tom stalked to the edge of the forecourt, then took sixteen careful paces. Peering at the gravel between his boots, he could make out the expected line of butts, tidal wrack left behind by the great perturbation of human need, its empty troughs and satiated peaks.

He fumbled with his fingertips for the little cellophane ripcord, desperate now for the smoky parachute to open over his head.

Then stopped.

What would be the point? It wasn't as if he would only have one – he'd have another twenty or thirty thousand, a world-girdling belt of braided tobacco strands . . .

Gloria. The dream. The engwegge – her parcel. Tom remembered he'd left the damn thing in the car. He put the unopened pack in his shirt pocket and strode off into the desert. With every step the pride rose up in him: he *was* Astande, the Swift One; he was the righter, of his own wrongs at least.

If Prentice was grateful to find the car filled up with gas and parked outside the motel block when he emerged the following morning, he did a good job of hiding it. His eyes were like raw eggs in the monochrome dawn: greyish albumen that he rubbed with his ugly fingers.

'Bloody awful night's sleep,' he groaned. 'Bitten to buggery. I'd swear those insecutor things just ginger up the mozzies.'

'See here, Prentice.' Tom was resolute. 'Last night's motel was twenty bucks, Tree Top Lodge was sixty-five. The car rental is on my fucking Amex. There's been gas, counter meals . . . How much longer d'you expect me to pick up the goddamn tab?'

'I say, old chap.' Prentice was insouciant, as Tom stomped in and out of his motel room, loading the car. 'You certainly got out of bed on the wrong side this morning.

'Brodzinski,' he said, his tone becoming conciliatory, 'I'm fully intending to pay my way, it's just that I'm suffering a temporary financial embarrassment – the ribavirin cleaned me out.'

'Oh, really?' Tom snidely mimicked Prentice's accent. 'How have you been paying our mutual friend, Mr Swai-Phillips, then, old chap?'

'Well, um, to tell you the truth,' Prentice said, flustered, 'he's handling my case on a no win–no fee basis. But look here.' He ran on, clearly not wanting this to sink in too deeply. 'My wife's cousin promised me he'd wire some funds to the Tontines; we'll settle up there.'

Tom barely registered this; he was thinking about Swai-Phillips, recalling the lawyer's brusque assertion: 'I don't do no win-no fee personal-injury cases.' Surely this was further confirmation – if any were needed – that from the outset, Prentice's offence had been far more serious than his own?

After they had negotiated the maze of blast walls wreathed with razor wire, then sat – mute but tense – while the bored Tugganarong cops checked the underside of the SUV with telescopic mirrors, Tom was surprised by the cursory inspection of their laissez-passers. The officer leaned in through the window and slung the papers on to Tom's lap.

'You headed to the Tontines?' he asked.

'Sure am,' Tom replied.

'You blokes have a good trip, then.' He waved them on with the muzzle of his sub-machine gun.

Beyond the checkpoint Route I stretched out ahead, a dirty tongue already flexing in the building heat. The surface alternated between metalled and dirt, so Tom concentrated on his driving, changing up when they came off the blacktop to avoid wheelspin.

Apart from the agitation of the flies and the soughing of the wind through the windows, there was silence in the car. After an hour or so, Prentice turned on the radio. There was a faint whoop of joy. 'Yes! He's had him! He's clean-bowled – and he's not going to like that one little bit, he's . . .' which then faded into static. With a tortured expression, Prentice hunched forward and dickered with the radio controls as if he were a blind piano-tuner. Then, deflated, he sat back.

Tom wondered: where has all the traffic gone? The road-trains, the pick-ups and the retirees' Winnebagos that had been in line for gas the night before had all evaporated. The highway was empty, and the hurting blue sky devoid of the twin-rotored helicopters that had clattered overhead the previous day.

Towards mid morning, Tom saw a burned-out car beside the road. He slowed to assess whether this was a recent happening; but then, seeing the rust streaking the buckled panels, and the interior choked with sand, he accelerated.

Soon there were other abandoned vehicles. Some were more or less intact, with perhaps only a rumpled fender, starred windows and a few bullet holes in their side panels. Others had been wrung-out by awesome forces, their body-work twisted and crushed, as if a giant child, tiring of his toy cars, had had a destructive tantrum. There were SUVs, pick-ups – even the trucks used by the paramilitary police. Every sort of vehicle Tom had seen on Route I was present in this edge city of hulks. Further away from the road, he saw a gasoline tanker, its tank opened out in petals of blackened metal.

Prentice, normally keen to sermonize on the basis of this or that wayside attraction, remained silent, rocking and rolling as the car bucketed along.

Then there came a quite ordinary sedan – ornamental tissue box still intact on its rear-window shelf – that was still alight. Vivid flames licked the mashed hood, dense billows of black smoke clotted in the air. Prentice roused himself a little as they drove by – then relapsed into torpor. Not knowing what else to do, Tom kept driving.

But a few miles further on he had to stop.

The first indication that something was seriously amiss

came when a clutch of helicopters roared low over the car. These were single-rotor aircraft with bulbous plastic canopies. Even though they were gone in moments, Tom saw the missiles mounted beneath them. Where the helicopters disappeared over the horizon a column of smoke was visible; although whether this had been caused by them or was an effect they were seeking to dispel, he could not be certain.

Tom slowed to a crawl as two cops approached the SUV. With fluorescent batons, they directed him into a lane formed by striped cones. They also held signs. One read NO WEAPONS, the other GET IN LANE. Beyond the cops, stubbed out in a crater by an inky finger of smoke, was McGowan's road-train.

Further off on the bled, the helicopters stood, shiny visages facing one another in a conversational grouping. Slow-turning rotors idly chit-chatted, as if these were bored guests at a party, the centre-piece of which was this enormous barbecue.

'What's the problem?' Prentice asked the sergeant who came up to his window.

Tom thought this a deranged denial of the obvious, but the Tugganarong took it in his stride.

'Bing-bong buggers stuck another IED under the highway, sir,' he said, taking the sheaf of papers Prentice handed him. 'No worries, Aval mob, they'll be way over there by now, yeah.' He jerked a thumb over his shoulder, then tucked his baton between his thick thighs so he could check through the permits and the laissez-passers.

'Are those your rifles on the back rack, sir?' asked the second cop, who had come up to the driver's window.

'Uh, yeah. I mean, of course they are,' Tom replied nervily.

'Have to take 'em off of you, I'm afraid. Purely routine safety – and your ammo. I'll hand 'em back to you a half-klick on, where you rejoin the road, OK?'

'Yeah, fine. I guess.'

Tom handed over the boxes of ammunition, then waited while the cop took the green-sleeved Galils from the rack. When the sergeant handed Prentice their papers and rapped on the roof, Tom pulled away.

The lane of cones took them on a neat diversion across the bled, circumventing the burning road-train. Prentice made to light a cigarette, but Tom snapped at him, 'Are you fucking crazy, man! Why d'you think they took the guns? There's spilled fuel all over the place.'

Globs, dashes and even pools of thick black viscosity smirched the sable. One of McGowan's semi-trailers had been thrown up in the air by the explosion, and come down on top of the other. Both were burning. From a hundred yards off Tom could feel the angry pulse of the flames. Flames that licked the ruptured faces of the giant Neapolitan mamas. Crates smashed by the blast had disgorged their contents: the doughy discs lay scattered on the ground – fast-food fallout, cooked to a turn. The aroma of melting mozzarella mixed weirdly with the gas fumes.

The rig, however, was hardly damaged. It stood on the crown of the highway, only a few detached slats of fairing to suggest that it wasn't idling for a moment before roaring away. There were these, and there was also McGowan's corpse, which, as the car bumped back on to the road, they both got a good sight of.

The driver's face was composed, his posture relaxed, his hair smoothed against his rounded head – all of which was strange, because McGowan was tilted backwards out of the window of the cab, as if he had attempted a Fosbury Flop to safety at the very moment of his expiry. His chest had also been liquidized, so that through each hole in his string undershirt squirmed a worm of tomato purée.

The cone lane terminated in a makeshift roadblock. Cops lounged about, accessorized by their carbines and flying helmets. The sergeant drove up in a jeep and offloaded Tom's rifles.

Tom got out of the car and went to help him clip them to the rack. 'Is there any . . .' He decided to change tack: 'What would your assessment be of the security situation between here and the Tontines, officer?'

Tom hoped this sounded authoritative – brave, even. The sergeant didn't seem taken in; he looked sceptically at Tom.

'No worries out here, sir,' he said. 'Insurgents'll only hit fuel or other supply trains – stuff headed for the bauxite mines at Kellippi. This is a basic law and order problem for us – no big drama. And no offence, but these crims couldn't give a rat's arse about a couple of stray Anglos.'

'None taken,' Tom muttered.

'Mind you,' the sergeant continued, 'that only goes so far as the next thou' clicks – after that you'll be in striking distance of the Tontines.' He laughed bitterly. 'Anything can go down there. Bloody anything.'

Tom laughed as well, in a manner that he hoped suggested shrewd understanding.

The sergeant patted one of the rifles. 'Galil,' he remarked. 'Nice piece. Bing-bongs down south favour them – we've got a few too. Two-stage trigger's a bit of a non-starter; still, whack in a box, put it on fully auto', and you can take out those black bastards before they get in too close, yeah.'

The sergeant flicked a finger to his shiny origami cap and sidled away to join his colleagues at the checkpoint. Then he turned back. ' 'Course, you've gotta handgun, yeah?'

'You heard that, did you?' Tom asked Prentice, after they had been waved through, and the SUV was rollicking once more along Route 1.

'Oh, yes, old chap,' he replied.

Struck by Prentice's self-satisfied tone, Tom glanced over at him. He was holding an automatic pistol. Agitated, Tom looked at the highway, then back at the gun. It appeared quite alien in Prentice's soft hand: a space-blaster hefted by a clerk. The automatic had crude, functional lines: rectangular barrel, larger rectangle for the stock. His yellow finger rubbed the trigger guard, then poked inside it and flicked the steel curlicue of the trigger itself.

'I hope that fucking thing is on safety,' Tom snapped.

' 'Course it is, old chap.' Prentice spoke with dreamy self-absorption. 'D'you take me for a moron?'

'Where'd you get it from? D'you know how to use it properly? Why didn't you tell me you had it? You could've gotten us arrested.'

These remarks ricocheted in the smoky interior of the car. As Tom understood it, handguns were an anathema to Prentice's countrymen; it hardly seemed likely that he could handle one competently.

Prentice went on titillating the trigger, and when he replied it was with an air of erotic reverie. 'Honestly, Brodzinski, I didn't take you for such a nervous ninny. There's nothing illegal about carrying a handgun in these parts – anyone with any sense does. If you weren't quite so wrapped up in yourself, you'd've taken the trouble to assess the security situation a little more thoroughly.'

'Fuck that,' Tom spat. 'Do you know how to use the thing?'

'It's my wife's cousin's.' Prentice raised the automatic to

his furtive mouth; for a second it seemed he was going to kiss the barrel. 'I brought it with me from down south; even in Vance you never know when some buck bing-bong might run amok, try and rape your lady.'

Tom yanked the wheel and jabbed the brake pedal. The SUV slewed, then jumped over the ridge of earth at the side of the highway. They came to a halt. Tom rounded on Prentice: 'Do you know how to use it? By which I mean to say: have you ever actually fired that gun, you fucking poseur?'

For moments there was shocked silence, then the flies, which had been hypnotized by the thrust of glassy hardness against their hairy feet, began to flit.

Prentice cleared his throat. 'Eurgh-ahem, well, now you come to mention it, Brodzinski, no, I haven't fired it, as such, although I do have a perfectly good understanding of it as a weapon. It's a Browning BDM. It has a fifteen-shot magazine, nine-millimetre calibre. This toggle here' – he fiddled with the stock – 'switches it to "revolver mode" . . .'

Tom wasn't listening. He slammed the SUV into gear, and it scrambled back on to the blacktop. He didn't speak until they were humming along.

'Put it away, Prentice,' he said. 'Put it away. Till we know how to fire the thing it's just another fucking liability. Put it away, and then . . .' he said, groping for conciliation, 'when we've put some distance between us and that, um, incident, we'll find a quiet spot where we can practise with it and the rifles. OK by you?'

Prentice signalled his assent by withdrawing the magazine from the automatic. With great deliberation he placed it, together with the gun, in the glove compartment.

*　　*　　*

The SUV hummed on across the interminable desert. The heat spiralled; the men sweated. Prentice rolled down his fly screen. The landscape, which, since they left the road stop that morning had been intimidatingly featureless, now began imperceptibly to alter, slowly becoming threatening, and then downright scary.

The wavering silhouettes of the mesas on the far northern horizon declined. The bled, absorbing their bulk, buckled and then broke up. Deep furrows appeared in its surface, gathered, then consolidated into severe wadis. The colours went from bright to lurid: rusty reds flared scarlet, subtle sable sands became wastes of pus-yellow dirt. The salt pans' mineral glitter intensified, bluer and bluer.

With each cigarette Prentice lit, Tom felt his own desire for nicotine rise up his gorge. He swallowed it down with pride. In his self-denial lay his strength, his probity, his – Tom blanched at the phrase, yet embraced it – moral fibre.

The glare lasered through Tom's Polaroid sunglasses. He could feel his skin tighten, his blistering lips flake. He resolved to buy better glasses, more sun block and moisturizer, as soon as they reached a decent drugstore.

At least the badlands hid the burned-out vehicles. Route 1 maintained its arrow-straight westerly flight, over embankments and through cuttings, while the car carrion was hidden in hollows: ragged metal obscured by ragged rocks, its paintwork camouflaged by the desert's own deceptive bends. Tom knew that they would never see the ragged rascals coming.

They drove fast for fifty, a hundred, three hundred klicks. It was well after noon, when Prentice – adopting the wheedling, infantile tone that made his requests sound like 'Are we nearly there, yet?' – broke the silence. 'Um,' he ventured. 'I'm awfully peckish, Brodzinski, what say we pull over for a picnic?'

'Sure,' Tom replied. 'Why not? Picnic and pot-shots, eh, Prentice? Just the ticket, *old boy*.'

They made camp in the bed of a deep, angular wadi that Tom had negotiated the SUV carefully into. They were only a few hundred yards off the road, yet completely hidden from it by bluffs streaked purple with glittering mineral deposits.

Prentice fussed about like an old maid. From the pile of trash that had accumulated on the back seat of the SUV he retrieved a square of whitish cotton that he spread on a flat rock. He found the sandwiches Tom had bought during his night-time provisioning and arranged them, together with two bottles of mineral water, on top of the cloth.

Tom said listlessly: 'Shrimp cocktail or coriander chicken, Prentice? The choice is yours.'

Prentice unsealed the cellophane pouch of the shrimp cocktail sandwich and recoiled from the smell. Then he dutifully commenced chomping.

Tom took his time, feigning picnicking leisure. He raised one of the hot water bottles to his chapped lips, then held it away so he could scrutinize its label. 'Deep in the desert wastes of the Western Province,' the copywriter had written, shivering in a smoked-glass fridgidaire in Capital City, 'Lake Mulgrene stretches for a thousand kilometres across the land, a crystalline expanse of health, purity and hydrolytic balance.

'Here, the Entreati people make their winter encampments, on the shores of what they call "The Great Mirror of God's Face". And, employing technology perfected throughout millennia, they refine and distil the precious fluid you are about to imbibe. They call it *entw'yo-na-heemo*, "The Tears of Paradise". We call it, quite simply, Mulgrene Mineral Water − because we know you like it straight.'

Tom laughed sourly and took a swig of the brackish water. Prentice left off his chomping. 'You ought to watch that, Brodzinski. We've only got two or three more litres.'

'I got,' Tom said, and took another long, defiant swig. He wiped his sore mouth with the back of his hand. 'I got, Prentice − you don't got nothing, feller. You wrong grade of astande, yeah. You ain't got nothing but fiddling about, fiddling about.' He sang: 'Tra-la-la, fi-fi-fiddling about!'

A vacuum opened up inside Prentice's head, and his features prolapsed into it. 'What're you implying?' he bellowed. 'What're you bloody well implying?' Then, recovering himself, he added, 'Old chap.'

'Nothing.' Tom was appalled by the way he backed down. 'Nothing at all. Calm down, Prentice. Eat your fucking shrimp sandwich.'

The rest of the repast passed in silence. They sheltered in the sharp shadow beneath the bank of the wadi. Could it, Tom wondered, get any hotter? Unlike tropical Vance, this was a dry heat. He yearned to sweat more freely − but only leaked. He felt his organs boiling in their own salts.

Prentice finished his sandwich. With vulgar fastidiousness he applied a soiled handkerchief to the deep dimples in his neotenous face.

'There's one thing I can do,' he said.

'Oh, and what's that?'

'Fire a gun − Jethro said that would be fine.'

Tom laughed, but Prentice was already up from the rock where he had been sitting and waddling over to the SUV. Tom scooped up the picnic litter and joined him. Together, they took down the rifles, got out the automatic pistol and found the ammunition.

Hefting the naked Galil rifle in his bare arms, Tom felt right and whole. He lifted the warm stock to his cheek: it smelled, suggestively, of oil. He peered into the telescopic sights. Through a notch in the wadi's bank a patch of bled 500 yards distant sprang into thrilling proximity: a flipper lizard's neck wattles shook as it panted in silent congress with its own rightness and wholeness. Tom wanted to touch the wattles with his finger. He slowly crooked it, feeling first a solid click, then a firm shove to his shoulder.

'GEDDAWAAYWITHYOUeeeeeeouuuuu!' the rifle sang. The lizard was on its back, hind legs bicycling, claws snatching dirt.

'Excellent shot, old boy!' Prentice cried in delight. 'Excellent bloody shot!'

'Your turn,' Tom said modestly, and Prentice took up a stance.

If the Galil sang, the handgun roared: a shuddering boom that echoed through the dry river bed. Arms and knees flexing, Prentice rode out the big Browning's recoil. The mineral-water bottle he had aimed at was obliterated: plastic shreds lay in the Tears of Paradise.

'Didya see that? Didya? Didya?' Prentice was cock-a-hoop. He snatched the bush hat from his head and slapped it against his leg. He hoed down on the sandy ground, his boots kicking up little dust devils that the breeze waltzed away.

A whoop sprang unbidden from Tom's own chapped lips: 'Woo-hoo! Way to go, Prentice!'

Suddenly, Prentice was serious, the steely automatic aiming at the ground in front of Tom's boots.

'Brian,' he said. 'Please, Tom, call me Brian.'

'Uh, OK.' Tom was inveigled by the informality of their mutual gunfire. 'Brian it is, then, uh, Brian.' And he completed the outbreak of peace by taking the pack of fifty Greens from his shirt pocket and handing it to Prentice.

Tom was utterly seduced by firing the Galil: it all came so easily to him. Taking the shells from their cardboard boxes, slotting them into the magazine, fitting the magazine to the breech, lifting the stock to his cheek – these were rousingly instinctual actions, as, with his pulse quickening, Tom manipulated himself towards ballistic consummation. The two men resumed their stances, and soon the evidence of their lust lay smoking on the rumpled rocks – yet they continued to blast away.

Tom shuffled up a rubbly mound and fired into the mid distance, aiming for rocks that flaked and whined. Prentice assaulted the foreground, loosing off shots with total abandon. The automatic's magazine emptied before the rifle's and he called out: 'I say, Tom, whoa!'

Tom ceased fire. His cheekbone burned where the Galil had delivered an uppercut.

'How about a photo?' Prentice was giddy with excitement. 'My lady wife will get a real kick out of seeing me like this.'

Reluctantly, Tom fetched his camera from the car, and, as Prentice did a macho dumb show, he shuffled more images into its memory card, where they interleaved with Prentice at Bimple Hot Springs, Prentice in the cloud forest, Prentice on top of the Giant Sugar Sachet.

Then Tom's cellphone rang. He hadn't even realized it was switched on. How, he stupidly wondered, could its battery not have drained away, as they drove for day after day into the interior?

Tom thumbed the button and the puny carillon cut out. Hand shaking, he brought the clam shell to his ear. Nothing – or, rather, a foamy hiss on the sands of a terminal beach. He slid it back into his pocket.

Prentice's mouth hung open. 'What the–' he began, but was cut off as the cellphone began trilling again. Tom took it out, hit the button, listened to the hiss. Then he held the cellphone away from his face, interrogating it with his stare.

'Must be a glitch of some kind,' he said to his companion. 'I mean, there's no network coverage out here, is there? Look, I'm gonna switch it off.'

Prentice resumed his stance and loosed off a shot at a sandstone pinnacle. It crumbled.

Then the phone rang yet again.

'What the fuck! What the fuck!' Bellowing, Tom wrenched it out and dropped it. It lay on the ground at his feet, peeping like a wounded bird. Prentice walked over and, picking up the cellphone, switched it off again.

'I don't know what all this means, Tom,' said, handing over the cell. 'But I don't like it. I think we'd better strike camp.'

Tom walked over to the SUV. He was about to open the door when an unfamiliar voice said – distinctly, although not loudly – 'G'day, mate.'

The owner of the voice was standing a few feet from the car's fender. He must, Tom realized with adrenalized clarity, have worked his way along one of the gulleys that led down into the wadi. He was a very tall, very muscular Anglo. He held a rifle so as to suggest he had Tom and Prentice covered, even though he wasn't pointing it directly at them.

There was silence for a few moments. The plume of flies that had trailed behind Tom dallied down to enfold his head in their humming atomic diagram. The Anglo, despite his sudden materialization, his bulk and his weapon, was hardly a threatening figure. He had a round babyish face; his short pants were so short, and the sleeves of his matching skyblue shirt so truncated, that they resembled a baby's one-piece garment.

The Anglo saluted Prentice: 'And g'day to you too, mate.'

Flicking the flies from his eyes, Prentice replied, 'Was that you? On the mobile phone, I mean.'

The big Anglo chuckled. 'Oh, yairs, that's right, mate. Gotta transmitter on the rig, see. We sent out a signal every now and then, right.'

'But why?' Tom asked.

The man regarded him as if he were very stupid. 'IEDs, mate, IE-bloody-Ds. Bing-bongs – yer sophisticated mobs, that is – use cellphones to set 'em off, not just guide wires. If we think there're insurgents on our patch, we give 'em a little surprise, maybe set off their booby-trap a bit early – or at least screw with their timing. We triangulate our signal with a transmitter way over on Mount Parnassus.' He jerked a sausage finger over his shoulder. 'Then we get a position fix, come and check things out, maybe do a little' – he ratcheted the bolt of his rifle – 'mopping up.'

To confirm that he had checked things out to his satisfaction, the baby-faced man propped his rifle against the car.

Prentice, perversely, objected to no longer being covered. Keeping his hands up by his shoulders, he said, 'But don't you want to see our papers? Don't you want to know what we're doing here? Where we're headed?'

'I couldn't give a rat's arse, mate.' For the first time, the Anglo was aggrieved. 'I'm not some jumped-up fucking Tuggy copper, now, am I.'

'W-What,' Prentice said, havering between bravado and cowardice, 'what if we were armed? I mean, we are, y'know.'

Getting himself out a cigarette and lighting it, the Anglo threw back his head and chortled. 'Gentlemen,' he said, pointing behind them, 'meet the wife.'

Prentice spun round. Tom swivelled, squinting into the sun, which was now dropping down from its zenith. Splitting the low-angled rays, arms like the wings of an avenging angel, was a figure spreadeagled behind a machine gun on top of the bluffs. It rose, and called over: 'Seems like introductions are in order. I'm Daphne Hufferman, and this is my hubby, Dave.'

It was a woman's voice, although her body was as big and muscular as her husband's.

'Look, you two,' she continued, 'I dunno what your plans are, but if you were thinking of stopping at the eighty-mile bore roadhouse, then forget it. Bing-bongs took it out a couple of weeks ago. Unless you're gonna swag down – which I wouldn't advise – you're best off coming back to camp with Dave an' me.'

While she was speaking, the woman lofted the machine gun on to her shoulder and descended towards them. As she drew nearer, Tom saw that, as well as having the same physique as her husband, she also had the same tight pants and shirt. In her case they were bright pink. The full breasts that pushed up into the open vee, strangely, only enhanced the debatability of her sex.

'Well.' She stopped in front of Prentice and sceptically eyed him up and down. 'Whaddya say, sport?'

Like a nervous, comedic suitor, Prentice quailed beneath her steady gaze. 'Um . . . If . . . If you, er, folks aren't cops, then who are you?' he managed to squeeze out at last.

It was Daphne's turn to guffaw. 'Us? Us? We're pet-food shooters, mate. Bloody pet-food shooters. Now get in yer rig, you blokes. Camp's a fair haul, and we want to be there before the night's as black as a bing-bong's black heart.'

11

The pet-food shooters' camp consisted of a demountable motorhome and a refrigerated container. The container sat beneath a stand of gum trees, gurgling. Leaking coolant dripped between its steel ribs, ribs that were warty with paint blisters. The demountable was a silvery aluminium capsule, humanized – if that was the right word – by net curtains in its portholes, and a striped awning staked out in front of the door.

Tom stopped the car by the Huffermans' pick-up and got out.

Behind the camp a network of dry watercourses scored the land: veins on the palm of a giant hand. In the mid distance, the fingers of this hand twisted into the spurs of a rocky mountain that rose some 5,000 feet above the desert floor. Mount Parnassus. A hot, gritty zephyr came scooting down from its peak, stinging Tom's sore lips.

'Not a lot, but we call it home,' said Dave Hufferman, clambering down from his pick-up. He was altogether relaxed – at home, in fact – but his wife bolted to the back of the demountable and began to take down what appeared to be enormous towelling diapers from a clothesline.

Dave Hufferman got out folding chairs for his guests and lit the barbecue. Next, he went over to the container, unbolted it and pulled the tailgate down. A thick white cloud of condensation rushed out to meet him. He emerged clutching an armful of beer cans. Tom hurried across to help him close the tailgate.

The container was stacked high with the jointed portions of scores of moai. The outsized wings, legs and breasts were laquered with ice, and fitted tightly together, pieces of a bizarre three-dimensional puzzle. The few square feet in front of this rampart of frozen fowl were scattered with the Huffermans' frosty provisions: boxes of pizzas and TV dinners, tubs of vanilla ice cream and plastic bags full of steaks.

'I put these in here before we left to check you out,' Hufferman explained – assuming the question uppermost in his guest's mind would be why the beer wasn't frozen solid.

It wasn't. There had also been a box of babies' feeding bottles in the container. Could the pet-food shooters have a kid out here? If so, it was a very large infant – the bottles were three or four times the size Tom remembered. He thought of Tommy Junior, but asked: 'What happens when the container's full?'

'Well, mate,' Dave Hufferman continued as they strolled back to where Prentice was sitting smoking, 'we slow our work rate down towards the end of the month when the road-train's due, yeah.' He tossed a can to Prentice, handed one to Tom, and all three men snapped the ring pulls and took swigs. 'Trouble is – Oi, mate,' he barked at Prentice. 'You're inside the bloody line!'

'Line?' Prentice was bemused.

'The sixteen-metre line, mate. Shift your arse over there, yeah.' Hufferman indicated an arc of cigarette butts pressed into the red dirt. 'I like a smoke-o myself, but the container is classed as a workplace, and rules is rules.'

Prentice shuffled his picnic chair over the invisible line. Hufferman snorted. Then, judging that Tom was interested, led him away from the camp.

After a hundred yards they passed through a screen of eucalyptus. The sight that met Tom's eyes was extreme: an al fresco abattoir. There were heavy trestle tables with chopping boards on them and a steel rack hung with cleavers and butchers' knives. A winch dangled from the trunk of a dead tree, bloody feathers caught in its links. There were drifts of feathers trapped in the wiry grass, while bits of bone and shreds of flesh were scattered on the bare earth. The flies were clustered so densely on the large scabs of dried blood that they transformed them into glinting black rugs.

Hufferman said: 'The missus and I can bring down ten moai a day, load 'em on the ute, get 'em back here, joint 'em and bung 'em in the freezer. But, as I was saying, only prob' is the truck ain't so regular nowadays on account of the bing-bongs hitting the convoys. So, we don't like to fill it right up till we're sure they're through, right. It's piece work, see, and if the container ain't packed as tight as a fag's strides we don't get our full whack.'

But Tom didn't see this at all – he saw McGowan, the road-train driver, strung up on the winch. An enraged insurgent was sawing away at one of his jerking arms. The beating heat from McGowan's burning semi-trailers crumpled the evening into Hades.

Tom took another metallic draught of the cold beer and turned to his host. 'I hate to say it,' he said, 'but aren't you worried by the, uh, insurgents?'

'Us?' He was incredulous. 'We've gotta motion-senser system right round the camp, yeah, rigged up to thermite bombs. If the black bastards aren't burnt to a crisp, Daphne an' me 'll take 'em out. We've got night goggles, and we're pros, ferchrissakes. Bloody pros. Daphne' − Hufferman's honk muted with tenderness − 'she's only the finest bloody shot in the Eastern Province.'

Later, the odd couples ate moa breast under the silvery horns of the risen moon. The beers kept coming. The gum trees whispered in the wind, one that carried with it an oddly appealing, astringent smell. Tom asked Hufferman what this was, and the pet-food shooter said: 'Engwegge, 'course. Where there's engwegge, there's moai, right. There's bing-bongs too, I'll grant you that − but not yer real head cases.'

The moa was dark, powerful meat. Tom slumped low in his picnic chair, slurping the gamy juices from his paper plate. After a while he ventured: 'Are there really enough moai here to, uh, make it worth while? I mean, given the secur . . . the security situation.'

The euphemism sounded ridiculous, a kitten's miaow in this terrible fastness.

'It's not only worth it financially,' Daphne Hufferman said, 'it's worth it morally, right.'

'Morally?'

The big woman, who had barbecued the meat and served up re-fried beans and thawed-out coleslaw with hardly a word, now grew animated. 'Down south, in the cities, yeah, a little boy or girl loves their little darlin' pussy or puppy. Loves it, yeah. I tellya, Tom, that's what we're fighting for − that love. That's what we're living for − and that's what we're shooting the bloody moai for, right.'

'I − I didn't mean to offend . . .'

'None taken, mate, none taken,' Daphne said, then relapsed back into contemplative, beer-sucking silence.

Prentice had been silent throughout the meal, his scant hair plastered on his brow, his scrawny neck pale and flaky, his thin torso kinked. To Tom, he appeared more than ever to be at once weak – and dangerous. He found himself repeating his companion's name over and over in his mind: Prentice, Prentice, Prentice ... Until consonants were ground down, and Tom was thinking: penis, penis, penis ...

Prentice chose this point to break his silence. 'Look, er, Dave, you wouldn't happen to know the score in the Test, would you, old chap?'

Dave Hufferman laughed. 'Your lot got creamed, mate. All out for two-two-nine in their second innings – it's done and bloody dusted.'

'H-How did you know that?' Prentice was outraged but managed to keep it in check. Tom, jerked out of his reverie, sat up.

'There's not a lot we don't hear about over here,' Daphne put in. 'There's the short-wave radio, and people like to use it.'

'And the Tontines?' Tom inquired. 'What are people saying at the moment? Are they bad?'

Before answering, Dave Hufferman drained his beer, then crumpled the can in his ham fist and chucked it on the growing pile of empties.

'For blokes with your grades of astande? Well, tricky I'd say.'

It was Tom's turn to splutter: 'How did you know that?'

'Well,' Hufferman drawled, 'like Daphne said, in these parts a man's deeds go before him.' He looked significantly at Prentice. 'But that can change, mate – your respective grades, that is. It's all up for grabs in the Tontines. You signed the rider, yeah?'

'The rider?'

'The tontine rider on the car-rental agreement.'

Tom thought back to the rental company in Vance, the bored hillwoman rattling through the paperwork. The tontine policy she'd outlined, the oddity of which had stayed with Tom for a while, only to be supplanted by other oddities along the way.

'Yeah,' he conceded. 'Yeah, I did sign for the policy, the woman said it was in place of personal cover.'

Hufferman laughed again. 'Oh, yairs, they always say that – and overseas tourists always sign.

'Thing is, mate, the tontine kinda loops you in, right. Yer tontine *is* a special kind of insurance policy, yeah – a collective one. It's taken out by a group, yeah, a family, a mob, a bunch of work mates, whoever. Now, whenever one of yer tontine holders karks it – and it don't matter if it's natural causes or a machete – then the principal derives on to the remaining blokes, and so on, until there's only one of 'em left and he gets the lot!'

It took a while for Tom to absorb this – because he was saturated with beer.

Prentice grasped it first: 'B–But, if all the money goes to the last policy holder left, then there's every motive for them to–'

'Do fer each other,' Hufferman laughed. 'Bang-on, mate. You ain't so dusty.'

He leaned forward and chucked a handful of dry bark on to the still smouldering barbecue. It flared up, licks of flame that illuminated the pet-food shooter's babyish bulk. Hufferman went on intoning: a witch doctor over a crucible.

' 'Course, guvvie banned tontines for Anglos down south ages ago – caused way too much agg. But over here . . .

well, some say the whole point of introducing them was to get the bing-bongs to think, er, constructively – invest for the future. Others – yer bleedin' hearts – they figure the tontines were a cynical move, a way of finishing off the desert tribes altogether.

'These mobs believe nothing happens by accident – but there's plenty of accidents over here. Plenty – specially in the bauxite mines, where a lot of 'em work. Feller gets crushed by a slag heap, truck drives over him – his mob go after the other tontine holders – stands to reason, right. Then their mobs go after his mob, and so-bloody-on. The tontine's like a virus – goes straight into their brains, drives 'em haywire. They can't stop. They take out more tontines, do more killing, take out more. Round and bloody round it goes.'

'And the Tontine Townships? How do they relate to it all?'

Tom couldn't take his eyes from Daphne Hufferman's bovine face, as, in answer to his question she uttered these dreadful moos: 'The Tontines suck the bing-bongs in, yeah. Nothing there to begin with but a road stop and the guvvie sector. Now there's a whole heap of brokers flogging tontines, and the killings are 24/7, yeah.'

'Thing is,' Dave Hufferman said, sounding almost sympathetic, 'once you've gotta tontine yerself, well . . . Like I say, it kinda loops you in, right. Even the best of mates can fall out in those circs', and a bing-bong hitman'll cost yer no more that a pack of bloody cigs.'

'So what can we do?' Tom hated the drunken, hysterical edge to his voice. 'Can we cancel our tontine?'

'Ha–ha, no way, mate. It's a Catch-22 sitch, see. You can't travel this way without one – it's on your laissez-passer.

No, your best shot is to head straight for the guvvie sector; you'll be safe there. Then you'll have to negotiate for a rabia.'

'A rabia – what's that?'

But this was one question too many for the pet-food shooters. Husband and wife both stood and stretched, quite unselfconsciously pulling at the sweat-soaked towelling of their crotches.

'Reckon that's enough jawing for one night,' Dave said. 'We'll give you the rest of the gen come dawn. The missus'll show you blokes where you can sack down. Dunny's over by the container if you need it, right. Take a torch, though, there can be stingers at night.'

Tom's head swam. He struggled to rise, his boots rattling the discarded cans. Then there were hands in his pulling him up, gently but firmly. Tom realized it was Prentice.

He led Tom to the latrine, then waited while Tom swayed and gushed. Prentice guided him to the demountable, then into the cubicle where Hufferman had said they could sleep. Narrow steel bunks were bolted to the curving wall; on them, flowery coverlets were stretched tight.

Tom was too drunk to protest that Prentice was helping him to undress, but, as he unbuckled his belt, Tom said: 'Whassup? You wrong kinduv . . . astande . . .'

The aircon' in the demountable was blissfully efficient. Lying stretched out in the cot, Tom was almost chilly. This sobered him up. Over the unit's rhythmic clunking he could hear voices coming from the pet-food shooters' cubicle. He tried to ignore them. Prentice was already asleep, his smoker's snore sawing through the bunk above.

Then Daphne Hufferman lowed: 'You're a big bad baby boy.'

'Ma-Ma. Goo-goo,' her husband rumbled.

'Mummy's gonna have to change you before bye-byes,' Daphen cooed, then came the loud 'pop-pop-pop' of the big man's babygro.

'Want bottle. Want powder,' he whined.

'You'll get a good old wipe, right, before you have bottle, or powder, or cuddle, young man.'

After that, Tom blocked his ears to the increasingly rambunctious horseplay of the adult baby and his carer.

The familiar flashback took possession of him: the leafy balcony at the Mimosa, the aerial view of Atalaya's perfect breasts, the moonscape off Lincoln's scalp – then the final fervent pulls on the terminal cigarette.

Where had his thoughts gone? Tom thought back to his own thinking back. He had been up in the hills, yes. In the dust beneath the banyan tree, where the hillman refused to sell him the spirit wagon. Had it been in that reverie itself that his own culpability had incubated? Could Tom now locate – with numb, drunk mental fingers – the precise point where his inattention had become a form of intent? The grey roll of ash lying in his palm, the butt pinched between his fingers, the smoke drawn into blue loops. The butt shifted to gather tension, as index finger strained against thumb pad. Then . . . the flip.

Tom slept. And came to in a room bright with chilly winter light. He could see the bare branches of northern trees through cold windowpanes. Directly in front of him there was the icy finality of a perfectly made bed. Tom sensed sterile hospital corners beneath the brightly patterned patchwork quilt.

On the far side of the bed stood his mother. She was

erect, dressed in dark slacks and a dark sweater, and smoking. One arm was crossed beneath the 1950s jut of her breasts; the other was crooked up, so that the cigarette was poised before her sharply inscrutable face. Yes, she stood upright, yet her thin frame hung in the room: a shroud dangling from smoky hooks. It was the discarded clothing of her humanity, rather than the woman herself.

'It's time for you to go now, Tom,' she said with characteristic asperity.

He found himself unable to answer – although he yearned to. This, she seemed to understand: 'It's time for you to go now,' she reiterated. 'I'm married – so are you.'

Tom's mother, grimacing with the vulgarity of it, morphed into Martha, then back again. Tom shook with horror ague. The transmogrifications continued: mother to wife, wife to mother – back and forth with increasing velocity.

He awoke; the sheet suckered on to him with sweat, the phrase *pia mater* sticking, a shard of meaning, deep in his hurting brain.

Breakfast was last night's beans – fried up yet again – and reconstituted orange juice. Tom could manage only the juice.

'We bin thinking,' Dave Hufferman said, poking through the grille at the nuggets of burned charcoal in the barbecue. 'It's still a fortnight till the road-train's due, and we've gotta bust part in our main generator – bin on auxiliary for a while now. Daphne'll ride into the Tontines with you and pick the spare up.'

Tom stuttered: 'B–But how will she get back?'

'No worries there, mate,' Hufferman said. 'She can grab a ride with the cops. Ain't that right, me little darlin'?'

'Right enough,' she said, snuggling in under his ham of

an arm. 'And I'll be in the right place to help these blokes if the shit hits the fan.'

The Huffermans were both wearing canary-yellow baby-gros this morning, and the sloppy expressions of large animals that were sensually replete.

'It's really . . . it's good – I mean . . .' Tom skidded on the glassy surface of his hangover.

Prentice – who was applying ointment to his psoriasis himself – oozed into the breach: 'We're jolly grateful for everything you've done for us already – and now this. Thank you *so* much.'

The Huffermans, who, Tom had felt certain, shared his own instinctive repugnance towards Prentice, seemed to have had a change of heart during the night. Dave Hufferman punched Prentice lightly on the shoulder, while grunting: 'Good on yer, mate.'

Then, limping back from the latrine, where Tom had vomited into the flyblown trench, he was amazed to hear Hufferman holding forth: 'Y'see, most Anglos have got the bing-bongs all wrong, yeah. After all, they only see the scum that pitch up in the cities ruined by the grog.'

He was striking a pose, with one hand on his towelling hip. It should have been ridiculous – but for some reason wasn't.

'Now,' he continued, 'don't get me wrong, yeah, I've no time for the black bastards that shoot up convoys or plant IEDs – they deserve every damn thing we throw at 'em – but yer natural bing-bong, yer bing-bong in his own environment, well, he's a different proposition.'

'Meaning?' Tom croaked.

'Meaning, my friend' – Hufferman put a sceptical eye on his returned guest – 'that I've never met any bloke more generous than a bing-bong. Why, he'll give yer the last swallow of his canteen when you're way over there.' He jerked his thumb. 'But, by the same token, I've never met any bastard more greedy than a bastardly bing-bong – that's why they go troppo over the tontines. No, there's no one more humble – or more arrogant, more restrained – he'll go for months in the desert without even thinking of a root – or more bloody sex-crazed when the oppo' presents itself.'

He looked over at his wife, who was hanging out damp sheets on the washing line, and the machine-gunner simpered. 'There's no bastard braver or more cowardly than a bing-bong. Before all this shit got going, Daph' 'n' me used 'em as trackers – best there bloody are. They could smell out moai twenty clicks upwind. The guvvie – the Tuggy coppers, they'll never get the better of 'em. They don't understand the bing-bong – and they don't understand his politics, 'cause yer bing-bong is a highly political bloke. These desert mobs, they've got all their own internal conflicts going on, and they hate each other even more than they hate us Anglos and our foot soldiers.'

Tom roused himself: 'There's one thing that confuses me, and that's why they don't make it clearer what a mess things are, uh, over here. I mean' – he was gabbling, yet couldn't prevent himself – 'there's TV footage of firefights and that kinduv thing, but the media – the government – they never say outright how dangerous it is – why's that?'

The pet-food shooter ignored Tom and called across to his wife, 'Daph', you leave those things, my pet. These blokes'll haveta hit the road straight away if you wanna make it through.' Then he answered his guest. 'That's easy, mate, yeah. The security situation' – he put on a portentous, official voice – 'cannot be reported for security reasons.' Then he laughed and threw the dregs of his orange juice on the parched earth. 'C'mon,' he said. 'I reckon your mate's got the right idea.'

Prentice was already fetching Tom's rifles from the freezer container. He emerged in a vaporous cloak that was torn off at once. The day was hotting up. Mount Parnassus was bleached bone white in the sun, and the radio mast the pet-food shooters had used to locate Tom and Prentice was an alien space module, touched down on its scarred summit.

'You wanna make sure the action on those is working,' Daphne Hufferman called to Prentice. 'And keep one of 'em in the car,' she added.

The big woman had left the laundry and was slinging a cartridge belt around her neck as she plodded towards them. She held the machine gun itself in her free hand as casually as any other housewife might tote a shopping bag.

Tom went into the demountable and gathered up his effects, which had been considerately placed there by his companion the night before. He had intended asking the Huffermans if they'd let him have some sun block – moisturizer, even. But the strangeness of seeing Prentice active and helpful distressed him. Was it true, Tom wondered, that their respective grades of astande were changing in relation to one another?

When Tom got back, Prentice was attaching one of the Galils to the rack on the SUV. He fed the other through the back window. He was, Tom noticed, wearing his own automatic in a shoulder holster, and couldn't forbear from regarding himself in the dusty side mirrors of the shoddy little vehicle.

Dave Hufferman came puffing up with a large trash bag full of empty beer cans. These he proceeded to shove in through the back window.

'Look out when you drop the recycling off at the eighty-mile bore, Daph',' he said.

She replied: 'Will do, poppet,' then crunched herself inside with them.

Next, Hufferman tossed a canvas bag in through the front window and on to Tom's lap. Tom recoiled.

'Whoa, mate.' The pet-food shooter grinned. 'It's only the bust part – there'll be plenty of oppos along the way to sharpen yer reflexes.

'Look,' he continued, his breath smiting Tom's face, 'I'm not gonna put down a fellow Anglo, right, but I sometimes wonder if you blokes from overseas even pay attention to your dicks when you piss . . .'

'Steady on,' said Prentice.

But Hufferman silenced him with a menacing look, then said: 'Everyone knows the security situation is shit over here – any bloody idiot who reads a paper or squints at the TV can see it in a sec'. Daph' 'n' me have dug you out of this–'

'We're awfully grateful . . .'

Another hard stare. 'I'm not interested in yer gratitude, right.' Hufferman sighed deeply. 'But what I would like is a bit of respect, yeah. A bit of respect for the bloody bing-bongs, yeah.'

With this curious remark, the pet-food shooter straightened up and banged on the SUV's roof. Tom wrestled the car into a wide turn, and they bumped away from the camp, following the ravelled tracks that twisted away across the desert.

He hoisted up a bottle of mineral water from the compartment under the dash and took a swig. The water of life! In his ruined mouth it tasted like the water of death.

★   ★   ★

They drove until the sun was at its zenith: a coruscating rivet hammered into the gunmetal sky. All the stress of the preceding days had gathered in Tom's shoulders, forming a hard yoke of pain.

Prentice had rearranged the stuff in the back so that the hefty woman was able to sit, bare legs akimbo, with her machine gun cradled in her lap. Whenever Tom chanced to glance in the rear-view, there she was, her pink face gibbous beneath a pink sweat band.

The uplands in the vicinity of Mount Parnassus had declined into blazing white sands and harshly iridescent salt pans. Route 1 stretched ahead, an arrow-straight strip marbled with veins of wind-borne dust. The only life to be seen in all this baking void were carrion birds, their plumage as tattered and oily as the roadkill they pecked at, before the approaching hum of the car startled them, tardily, into ungainly flight.

Tom stayed silent, the deathly aftertaste of the mineral water still in his mouth. His mother continued to reject him with the tip of her cigarette, a brand that, like her, had long since been discontinued.

Insensitive to the atmosphere in the car, Daphne Hufferman chattered away, while Prentice smoked. Each time he brought the flame to the end of one of his successive filter-tips, Tom awaited the swelling of his own need; and each time Prentice flipped a butt out the window, Tom basked in his own radiant pride.

'I'm confident, right,' Daphne said, 'that the security situation is improving. The army is drawing down, right, and most of the patrols over here are conducted by the police.'

This bizarre statement came only minutes after the pet-food

shooter had casually remarked: 'Y'know, the only real economic activity between here and the Tontines is the systematic robbing of travellers, right.'

Then, sounding as if she had memorized her lines from a fourth-rate documentary on an educational cable channel, Daphne came out with: 'In time, right, the insurgents will tire of their activities and gratefully abandon them for careers in industry, the arts or teaching, right.'

It was while Tom was stuck in the mental groove that these multitudinous affirmations were scoring in his brain – 'Right, right, right . . .' – that the insurgents ambushed them.

The IED must have been prematurely detonated, because the flash, then crash, of the charge was a fair way off. Through the fly-smeared windshield Tom saw a small bonfire suddenly lit beside the highway. He thought of delinquent kids chucking firecrackers in a trash can.

One second Daphne Hufferman had a mouthful of nuttiness, the next she was screaming orders: 'Pull the bloody car off the road, man! Grab yer guns, geddout and geddown on the bloody floor!'

Later, Tom had found it hard to believe the alacrity and efficiency with which they had all acted: a tight little squad marching in the lock-step of adrenalin.

Tom wrenched the wheel, and the SUV skidded off the blacktop and stopped. He reached behind and yanked up the Galil rifle. Prentice was already out of the car, taking cover behind the door. His pistol in his hand, he sighted through the open window.

Daphne Hufferman, despite her size, had somehow managed to twist round in the jump seat, unlatch the tailgate and burst out of the boxes of medical supplies. She now came sidewinding on her belly through the sand, to where Tom and Prentice were quaking on their knees.

The crack of the explosion was still echoing, and grit pattered down on the bundles of diapers strapped to the roof-rack.

'Down! Down!' Daphne urged them, and when all three were supine beneath the SUV she pointed south to where a deep gully snaked away into the desert. 'That's where they laid the charge, yeah, in the culvert. They're gonna come up outta there any sec'.'

She was right.

Four figures sprang on to the roadway and, zigzagging crazily in the absence of any cover, came towards them firing staccato bursts from their assault rifles.

Daphne snorted: 'They've screwed up royally, right. They've got 300 metres to get across. Chill out, pick your man. If you don't drop him – I will.'

She commenced firing in concentrated bursts, systematically traversing the road. The cacophony of the gunfire boxed Tom's ears. He fumbled for the safety and eased it off. He placed the stock to his shoulder, the sights to his eye and crooked his index finger on the trigger. The crazy thought came unbidden: at all costs he must protect not himself . . . but Gloria Swai-Phillips's parcel, which was under the seat in the car.

The insurgent running directly towards him sprang into view. Tom wasn't expecting this tubby youth, with doe eyes under the brim of his baseball cap; rather, some fearsome male version of the Entreati sorceress. A scarred apparition with an erect penis sheath, bellowing a death chant: 'In-twakka-lakka-twakka-ka-ka-la!' In time with his rifle fire.

The advancing figure swelled in the telescopic sights. The

cross hairs wavered across the bulbous letters and figures on his green nylon football shirt: GREEN BAY PACKERS 69. The clumps of nappy hair pushed out by his cap were Mickey Mouse ears, his mouth was agape.

Tom felt the first stage of the Galil's trigger action snap – then the youth tried to perform a backflip in the road, a ridiculously ambitious gymnastic feat for somebody so over-weight. No wonder he failed, and instead ended up sprawled on his behind, a maroon loser's badge pinned to his chest.

As soon as it was done, Tom returned from the murderous realm he had bolted into. Jittery, he rose to his feet and lurched away from the SUV. From a long way off in the mental fog, he was aware of the gunfire having ceased, and three other losers recuperating on the ground.

But one of the insurgents must have been lying in wait to the north of Route 1, because, as Tom stumbled into the desert, he reared up from behind a ridge. The boom of the heavy Browning automatic fused with the gory hole punched in his shoulder. He went down bellowing, 'Ya-yaaa! Ya-yaaa!'

Tom turned to see Prentice, who first blew the wisps of cordite smoke from the barrel of the gun, then broke down in sobs.

And was still sobbing – albeit muffled by the cigarettes he held to his lips – as they trundled on towards the Tontines.

Tom was only relieved that he, personally, hadn't killed anyone. After the dust had settled, Daphne Hufferman pointed out that the Green Bay Packers kid had her bullets in his chest. 'I dunno where your shot went, Tom,' she told him. 'But you were game for a rookie – I'll give you that.'

Then she went from corpse to corpse and, taking them by the ankles with workwomanly efficiency, dragged them off Route 1. As for the insurgent Prentice had shot in the shoulder, she gave him a hefty shot of morphine from the medical emergency pack she carried with her. Then she and Tom got the man on his feet and led him into the shade of a rocky overhang.

At first the Aval tribesman had been shocked – latterly he was stoned. Tom had sat with him, while Daphne walked away into the desert, found the insurgents' pick-up and used their short-wave radio to call the grid reference into the police.

'What will the cops do to him?' Tom asked as he drove.

'Shit knows, yeah,' Daphne replied. 'Might drag him into choky in the Tontines, yeah. Might just do him there and dig a pit.' She chuckled. 'That might seem a little harsh to you, right, but that one ain't gonna abandon killing for a career in industry. You should've seen the bumper sticker on his ute: WE SHALL KNOCK ON THE GATES OF HEAVEN WITH ANGLO SKULLS. Makes yer think, right.'

Tom wasn't thinking much at all. His tongue curled back and probed the dry gulches of his mouth, then extended into his psyche and explored its numbness. So, he thought, this is what real shock feels like: nothing at all. Self-defence was moral dentistry, accompanied by a whole-conscience shot of Novocaine.

He tried to thank Prentice for what he had done – but the gratitude fizzled out on his parched tongue. Besides, Prentice was engaged in some peculiar introspection of his own: as the sobs died down, the tempo of his smoking increased. He began, once more, to toy with his automatic, taking out the magazine, ramming it back home, then aiming at the lengthening shadows out in the desert.

Daphne instructed Tom to stop at the buckled steel skeleton of the eighty-mile bore. While the two men covered her, she bolted over and deposited the bag full of beer empties in the recycling bin. When Prentice, at long last, tucked the Browning away in its shoulder holster, he wasn't himself again – he was more than himself: an anthropoid mosquito full of sucked-up blood. Tom could make out the words in his ultrasonic whine: 'I am the Swift One, I am the Righter of Wrongs . . .' While from time to time, Prentice muttered aloud, 'It's just not cricket.'

Twenty kilometres before the Tontines the ghostly cavalcade of burned-out vehicles began. Ten kilometres later they saw a perfectly ordinary grader working on the road and were waved through by gangers in fluorescent safety jackets. Then they reached the city limits.

The sign was as stark as a gibbet in the desert twilight: WELCOME TO THE TONTINE TOWNSHIPS, it read. TWINNED WITH OENDERMONDE, BELGIUM. The three vertical stripes of the Belgian flag – black, yellow, red – were set beside the shield of the Republic. Next to the sign's rusty posts lay a bloated body with greyish patches on the dark skin of its outstretched arms. They were travelling at too great a speed for Tom to be able to tell if it was a corpse or a drunk.

He pushed the SUV on down a long, dusty boulevard with outsized concrete flowerpots on its dividing strip. To either side there were street after street of identically shaped bungalows, each one a steel shoebox with a veranda tacked on one side and an aircon' unit on the other. On top of the bungalows were sloping aluminium roofs, painted tile-red.

'They're modified freight containers,' Daphne explained. 'Guvvie ships 'em in and plonks 'em down. If one of 'em gets whacked by the insurgents, or the bing-bongs that live in it have a party and burn it out, they ship in another one.'

There wasn't anyone much on the streets, only the occasional skulking figure that recoiled from the vehicle's approach, and disappeared into one of the identical bungalows. A police checkpoint hove into view: a series of blast walls and a chain-link fence twenty-five feet high, topped by angle-irons strung with razor wire. The Tugganarong police stamped the trio's papers while exchanging desultory chit-chat with Daphne about the ambush. Then they waved them on.

They turned into another wide boulevard. This one had fat-trunked baobab trees with whitewashed trunks planted along its dividing strip. Here, the containers had been installed side-on, and there were paved sidewalks. The containers lacked roofs, but windows had been cut in their sides. These were covered with security grilles. Each of these commercial premises had a large electric sign on top of it, and, with darkness fast falling, a robotic finger pressed a button. Slogans cascaded along the blank façades, racing the little SUV: APEX ASSURANCE, COVENTRY REAL ASSURANCE, PERSONAL FIDELITY, AMHERST LIFE, TIP-TOP TONTINES . . . Tom wondered who these were aimed at, for there was still hardly anyone on the streets.

They reached another checkpoint with more bored cops, more blast walls, more razor wire. The cops checked under the car with their mirrors-on-poles. Then there was a third checkpoint, a fourth and even a fifth. Each necessitated the same laborious procedures, the same routine interrogations.

Prentice had come down from his maiming high, and in the short transits between the checkpoints he nodded out. His forehead, pressed against the window, looked in the sodium glare of the spotlights as brittle as glass.

Rousing himself, at what it transpired was the final check-point, Prentice reached for his cigarettes, only to have a flat-faced Tugganarong non-com' snap at him, 'You better not spark that one, yeah,' and gesture to a sign that was bolted to the blast wall. The sign shouted: NO IFS, NO BUTTS, STUB IT OUT!

'If I were you, yeah, I'd take your stay in the TGS as an opportunity to kick the habit. Perhaps it's the Lord's way of persuading you to stop.' Then he slung the sheaf of their papers back into Prentice's lap and waved them through the raised barrier with a negligent flick of his rifle barrel.

It was the first time Tom had heard the Lord referred to since the courtroom had lustily sung the National Anthem, back in Vance.

There was no time to dwell on this. Daphne Hufferman's hand was on Tom's shoulder, tending him this way and that, along driveways as smooth and dark as chocolate cake. Minia-ture office blocks with mirrored-glass walls were set in pocket-sized lawns upon which sprinklers played. Apart from the swishing caress of these, and the tired grumble of the SUV's engine, the Sector was unnaturally silent: a man-made oasis, where interloping blossoms skulked in the moist beds at the foot of the buildings.

A perfect little Hilton emerged from the orangey gloom. It was exact in every way, from its pseudo-Hellenic portico to its ornamental ponds dappled with water lilies, but maybe one fifth the size of any other Hilton Tom had ever seen.

And there, standing by the main doors, apparently fore-warned of their arrival, a swirl of black-winged moths fluttering round his fastidious form, stood Adams, the Honorary Consul. While beside him was the morphed version of Tom's own wife: Gloria Swai-Phillips, wearing a floral-print cotton dress.

12

The following morning, Tom had just returned from the concession stand and was at the sink in the bathroom, applying arnica ointment to his cheek – which had been badly bruised by the rifle's recoil – when there was a knock on the door.

He admitted Adams, who walked past him and crossed at once to the far side of the room. Tom moved his discarded clothes from the easy-chair to the floor and invited the Consul to sit.

'Good trip?' Adams asked, crossing one thin shank over the other. He wore his habitual tan seersucker suit, and Tom was underwhelmed by the clocks on his red socks.

'Don't be facetious,' Tom replied, and, heading back to the bathroom, called over his shoulder, 'How the hell did *you* get here?'

Adams took a while answering. Then Tom heard the flat chink of hotel china and the bubbling of the dwarf kettle. Adams was making himself a cup of Nescafé. Tom concentrated on flossing his teeth, then pulling the hairs from his nostrils with a pair of tweezers. The sharp little twinges were reminders: You're here! You're here!

Eventually, he heard a slurping intake, followed by: 'Don't get snippy with me.'

'I'm sorry?' Tom went back into the bedroom. Adams was bent over the three-panelled mirror on the vanity table, examining the back of his head. He looked round. 'I said, don't get snippy with me. I've had a, ah, hard-enough morning already.'

The Consul set his coffee cup down on the carpet and peered at Tom through his increasingly pellucid spectacles. Clearly, like a batty old hypochondriac, he was soliciting sympathy.

Tom obliged. 'Oh, why's that?'

'Fellow countryman of ours called Weiss – he was caught smoking in the john of a flight coming into Amherst–'

'My, my. That *does* sound serious.'

'Serious enough.' Adams glared at him with eyes now entirely visible. 'He's doing ninety days at Kellippi, and even after a month he's not in very good, ah, shape.

'Have you ever seen a bauxite mine, Brodzinski? The convicts get the worst jobs. It's very brutal, ah, extraction – huge machines, a lot of highly toxic dust. The Belgian outfit that operates the mine isn't overly concerned with safety, given that the workforce consists of convict labour, native, desperate, or all three.'

'What're you trying to say, Adams? That I've gotten off lightly? And anyway' – Tom sat down opposite him on the end of the bed – 'how *did* you get here?'

The Consul took another slurp of his Nescafé before answering. 'Miss Swai-Phillips and I flew to Amherst, then drove along Route 2. The mine people did offer us a light aircraft, but, as I'm sure you, ah, appreciate, I have to keep my distance . . .'

He fell silent. He was staring past Tom's shoulder – not at the Andrew Wyeth reproduction that hung above the bed, but the fifth of whisky that stood, half empty, on the beside table.

'I kinduv assumed your, uh, jurisdiction wouldn't extend this far,' Tom said. He was trying deliberately to nettle the Consul. 'I mean, isn't this the Western Province?'

Adams was unperturbed. 'Yes, but I'm a servant not of the national government, Brodzinski, but of our own. It's in that capacity that I've driven another thousand kilometres through the Tontines to come and, ah, liaise with you.'

'I'm not sure who it is you goddam serve, Adams,' Tom said bemusedly. 'But tell me this much: if you could fly clear across to Amherst, then drive *only* a thousand klicks – why the hell did I have to come overland for three and a half, nearly getting my goddamn ass shot to pieces in the process?'

'I can see you're upset,' Adams said, and Tom had the gnawing insight that this was all diplomacy ever consisted of: the understatement of the obvious. 'Have you spoken to your family yet? You'll find that you can dial them direct from here without the country code – a little, ah, quirk of the Tontine Governmental Sector.'

He stood up and set his stained cup down on the vanity table. 'Paradoxically,' he added, 'if you want to phone someone in the actual Tontines, it's an international call.'

'What about Gloria?' Tom had meant to say 'Martha' – the two women were, once again, confused in his mind.

'I'm sorry?' Adams fastidiously detached Tom's hand from his arm – a hand Tom hadn't been aware of laying on him.

'W–What's she doing here?'

'I thought Miss Swai-Phillips explained that to you back in Vance? She's responsible for running orphanages here in the Tontines; she's a well-respected charity worker and philanthropist. I believe her charity is holding a function this evening, here in the hotel. No doubt you can be invited if you'd like to find out more.'

Adams was making for the door when Tom had a sudden intuition: 'That's bullshit, Winnie.' He hadn't used this intimacy since the night they had eaten the binturang together at Adams's house. It pulled the Consul up short, and, when he turned, Tom saw he had lost some of his aloofness. 'It's to do with Prentice, isn't it? It's to do with . . . his . . . With what he did. I mean, she looks after kids – and he . . .' Tom left the insinuation hanging there: an ugly odour that the hotel's aircon' could never dispel.

Adams's voice softened. 'You know perfectly well that I can't discuss that with you, Tom.'

'But you're not denying it, are you? Those drugs – the baby stuff, it's for her orphanages, isn't it? Jesus! I dunno what's worse, carrying the can for my own dumb mistakes or chauffeuring that sicko.'

'As I understand it, Tom, you have every reason to be grateful to Brian Prentice. Mrs Hufferman told me that whole story yesterday evening. I believe the technical term for what he did' – the Consul's long face warped into sarcasm – 'is saving your life.'

Tom stood, cowed, as Adams reached for the door handle. Then the Consul detonated one of his deadpan devices: 'Incidentally, Brodzinski, I think you should know this. Shortly before I left Vance I had a call from the DA's office. Mrs Lincoln has instructed the medical staff at Vance Hospital not to resuscitate her husband if he should have a, ah, crisis. Bluntly, this means you probably haven't got long to get down to Ralladayo and make your reparations. As I'm sure

Jethro Swai-Phillips explained, all bets are off if this becomes a capital offence.'

With that, he quit the room.

Tom found Prentice smoking behind the Hilton parking lot. The sixth sense by which the local smokers always knew exactly where the sixteen-metre demarcation line ran never failed to amaze Tom. There were so many public buildings clustered in the TGS that the intersection of several lines allowed smokers only a small curvilinear plot, within which to stand, sucking and blowing.

Clustered with Prentice were seven other Anglos. Their short-pants suits, pressed shirts and flamboyant ties gave them the look of insurance salesmen – which is precisely what they were. It was tragicomic the way these men were compelled to stand, shoulder to shoulder, steeped in their own fumes, while on all sides there was the cool play of sprinkler systems on beautifully manicured lawns.

Tom stood off to one side, grinning and swinging his free hands. One after another the insurance men finished their cigarettes. They carefully extinguished them on the ground, then picked up the butts. Pocketing these, they walked over to a couple of beaten-up Japanese hatchbacks, which they piled into.

'They're going into the townships to work,' Prentice explained. 'That's why they don't drive anything flashy.'

'Selling tontines to poor bastards who're gonna kill each other for the pay-out,' Tom spat back. 'You call that work?'

'Really, Tom,' Prentice replied equably, 'everyone's got to make a living.'

Tom gulped. 'And you, uh, Brian, what's your occupation nowadays – still the Swift One, the Righter of Wrongs?'

Prentice shifted uncomfortably from one boot to the other. 'Ah, well . . . I don't know, old chap,' he muttered.

'Don't you?' Try as he might, Tom's voice crept up the register. 'What exactly went on back there in the desert, Prentice? D'you understand it? Because I sure as hell don't. And what's it got to do with this?' He waved the tissuey paper of the car-rental agreement that he had dug out from his document wallet. 'I've read through all this goddamn corporate legalese. Turns out, that if either one of us gets killed, the other guy's his legal heir and comes into' – he examined the small print again – 'a cool two hundred Gs.

'I never figured you for such an altruist, Prentice. I mean, you could've hesitated for one tiny second back there and you'd've come outta that ambush one very wealthy man.'

Prentice puffed up his sunken chest. 'I don't know what you're implying, Tom,' 'he blustered. 'Whatever you may believe about me, old chap, I hope you wouldn't think for a moment that I'd let a fellow Anglo be shot in cold blood by one of those black bastards.'

'Black bastards – black bastards. Sheeeooo!' Tom shook his head in disbelief. 'You certainly do know how to coin a phrase, my friend. Oh, yes.' Then he decided to change tack: 'Your wife's cousin come through for you, did he?'

'Come through?'

'I mean, did he wire you your funds? Seems to me a man with your high moral standards would be anxious to pay his debts.'

Suddenly, Tom felt drained by the effort of it all. The Sector may have been well irrigated, yet the air still crumpled with the desert heat. He sank down into a squat, his head spinning.

The previous night's dream came to him. Some kind of cookout or camping trip. His daughter, Dixie, still sporting the ridiculous disc of greased hair that he had last seen heading through security at Vance Airport, but otherwise completely naked and lying in the long grass.

Tom had looked wonderingly at her. She was supporting herself on one slim arm, her long legs bent sideways. It was the same posture – he had realized on waking – as that of the girl in the Wyeth reproduction over the bed. But, unlike Wyeth's Appalachian waif, flopping on to Dixie's lower thigh – resting there justly and weightily – was a large, perfectly formed penis.

I better not tell her, Tom had reasoned in his swoon. I better not tell her she's gotta dick – it'll be upsetting for a teenage girl.

'Are you all right, Tom?' Prentice was bending over him blowing smoke into his face.

Tom coughed. 'Eugh – yeah, yeah, sure. It's . . .' He pulled himself together and rose. 'It's just I feel so goddamn weak. It started back at the Huffermans' camp – that's when you started to, like, *do* stuff. You unloaded the car – then there was the ambush. Come to think of it, you even put your own psoriasis stuff on the night before, didn't you?'

Tom sank back down into his squat. Grit pricked his palms. He looked up: the dark halo of Prentice's hat eclipsed the hurtful sun. Tom said, 'D'you believe what Hufferman said: that it's changing between us? And what about the tontine – do the two things kind of gear into each other?'

Prentice shook his head. 'I don't know, Tom, but I'm keeping an open mind.'

He stubbed out his cigarette and pocketed the butt. 'Now,

if you'll excuse me, I have to meet with Ms Swai-Phillips. After that' – he adopted a pained expression – 'I shall visit the bank.

'Incidentally, Tom,' Prentice said, hurrying on – the mention of the bank had been an indelicacy – 'Gloria told me you've got a package for her; perhaps you should give it to me?'

This reanimated Tom. He stood. 'I don't think so,' he said. 'She entrusted that package to me, alone.'

He stalked towards the doors of the Hilton: their photo-electric cells acknowledged, then admitted him to a shushed lobby, where silk scarves, long unsold, were creatively pinned to velvet cushions. Rubbing the edge of his key card with his callused thumb, Tom rode the elevator up to the fourth floor and the peace of his room.

Which was no peace at all. The key card when he swiped it in the lock; the debris left by Adams when he had made his coffee; Tom's own paisley-patterned washbag – all of it struck him as horribly grotesque: the corpses of objects rather than the objects themselves. Was it that the TGS was real, while he had become robotic? Or were its pocket office blocks and neat lawns only a zone of reality imposed on the ruggedly anarchic Tontines? Then again, perhaps it was the Tontines that were the mirage, and only the desert truly existed at all?

Concentric rings of mind-bending illusion rippled out from where Tom lay, stretched out like a water boatman on the surface tension of the bed. His legs weakly spasmed, his cordite-coarsened fingers felt gross against the smooth nap of the coverlet. He could hear his own breathing, the ceaseless shushing of the aircon', the intwakka-lakka-twakka of a helicopter landing in the military base beyond the parking lot.

He was very close now to the hysteria that had courted him, politely opening door after door as he ventured further into his ordained nightmare. He was saved – by the red eye of the message light, blinking on the phone.

Tom picked up the handset and pressed it to his ear. 'One. New. Message . . . Hi, yeah . . . It's Gloria Swai-Phillips here, Mr Brod – Tom. Lissen, that package of mine. Thing is, I've had a frantic day, so we'll have to meet up later, right? I'm hosting a little reception thing – soirée I s'pose you'd say . . .' She giggled girlishly. Soirée, Tom thought. No one says that, not even Adams. 'Anyway, maybe you could drop by, yeah? It's downstairs at around six. It'll be full of dull charity and guvvie types, but there'll be a raw bar.'

Tom replaced the handset, then roused himself. Now she had called, now that he had a liaison with Gloria, he could entertain the thought of further intimacy. After all, why not? He was a free man.

He looked over at her parcel, which was sitting on the easy-chair. Caught in the beams that shone through the blinds, the columns of the newsprint it was wrapped in seemed to form the contours of a face. A desert tribesman's face. Tom broke from its hollow stare and called the concierge. 'I, uh, wondered . . .'

'Sir?'

'I'd like to go out – out of the Sector, that is, and have a look round. Is this possible?'

'There's a walking tour at three this afternoon, sir. Shall I put your name down for it?'

'Walking? You mean, like, a hike?'

'Oh, no,' the concierge laughed. 'It's more of a stroll – even our elderly guests manage it, so no worries there.'

* * *

Promptly at three, Tom went down to the lobby, only to discover that he was the sole taker for the excursion. A massive Tugganarong man, wearing a bullet-proof vest and holding a sign with BRODZINSKI written on it, was standing by the concierge's desk. His name, he informed Tom with great solemnity, was Valldolloppollou – although he was happy to be addressed as Val.

Val went with Tom to get one of his rifles from the hotel armoury. Here, Tom was also issued with his own vest and a helmet with the Hilton logo on it.

'Is all this strictly necessary?' he asked.

'Not really, sir,' Val replied. 'There's no real action, yeah, until the end of the week, when the miners, yeah, come in from Kellippi. Then all kinds of shit happens.

'Besides,' he continued, snapping a magazine into his own rifle as they strolled towards the first of the checkpoints, 'when you checked in, you signed a tontine transfer.'

'Meaning?'

'That if some pissed bing-bong drops you while we're out, the balance of your tontine is assigned to Hilton International. So the flak jacket and helmet are only a courtesy, yeah.'

Tom reflected on this as the cop at the barrier stamped his laissez-passer, then waved them through. Perhaps this was why, with each step he took out of the TGS, Tom felt his strength returning: he was no longer in thrall to Prentice.

By the time they had negotiated the third checkpoint the fresh greens of the TGS had been filmed over: the atmosphere was saturated with gritty particles, and Tom could taste the ferrous crud. Then there were the flies. How could he, even for a few short hours, have abandoned them? They made straight for the corners of his mouth and clustered there to engage in interspecific French kissing.

Outside the final blast wall, Val quartered the empty, dusty maidan with his rifle. Tom, not wanting to appear a wuss, did the same.

'Sir, yeah, I'd keep your safety on – if you shoot someone, the paperwork's a nightmare, yeah,' the tour guide gently advised him.

Tom was digesting this when they were mobbed by a crowd of native women who materialized from nowhere. They wore dirty shift dresses and T-shirts with cartoon characters on them: Hello Kitty. They crowded round Tom and Val – yet didn't touch them. The women's hands jerked up and down in front of their faces, while their cheeks bulged spasmodically. It took a few moments, then Tom realized: they were miming fellatio.

As the two men proceeded across the maidan, then down the main bouleward, still more prostitutes debouched from the trash-choked alleys, skipping over open drains running with raw sewage. They all importuned Tom and his guide with this obscene pantomime, but they never touched them. It was too eerie to comment on; so it was in silence that the men moved from window to window of the container-ized offices that Tom had noticed the previous evening. Inside they were kitted out with desks, chairs and plexiglas holders full of brightly coloured leaflets.

Tom halted outside Endeavour Surety. 'Can we go in?' he asked.

'Sure,' said the big Tugganarong. 'Press the buzzer – all the tourists check it out, yeah.'

Responding to the rasp, an armed guard rose up from behind a seating area. He unlocked the door, and, as he ushered them in, a thin, harried-looking Anglo came out from the back office, then carefully shut and locked the door behind him.

'Are you selling, buying or only bloody gawping?' was his salutation, and, when Tom failed to reply immediately, he went on: 'I see, another bloody gawper, right.'

'I'm sorry,' Tom said. 'I didn't mean to—'

'It's OK, mate.' The insurance salesman waved away the apology. 'I understand, you've blown into town and you wanna know what's what, right. Well, here's the listing.'

He reached under the counter and pulled up a pegboard with rows of letters and numbers stuck to it. 'If you've gotta car-rental policy rider, I can give you 12.2 percent on it, seeing that it's midweek. If you're buying outright, there's not a lot happening, though this here is interesting.' He indicated a quotation with a nicotine-stained finger. 'These blokes, right, they're down to seven now; tontine's been running for twenty-two months, pay-out's in the region of eighty-eight K, and' – he paused for emphasis – 'they bought right at the bottom of the market, so the premiums are low. There are two blokes who want to sell right now, or the entire tontine is offering a randomized spread bet of threes.'

The Anglo may have been grumpy to begin with, but he started to be taken in by his own spiel. 'These blokes,' he laughed, rubbing his crew cut with the knuckles of one hand, 'they're miners out at Kellippi, Inssessitti mob – never thought they'd last this long, right. Sold 'em the policy myself.'

The salesman finished his pitch, and, with a note of child-like wonderment, Tom asked him: 'You mean I can buy someone else's tontine, and if the other policy holders . . .'

'Kark it, you get the lot. That's right, mate. You're from

overseas, aren't you? I s'pose you don't have tontines in your neck of the woods. Yeah.' He warmed still more, his pinched nostrils flared, sniffing out the prospect of a sale. 'We'll sell you a tontine. We'll sell you tontine options or futures. We can even sell you a weighted basket of high-performing tontines. You may've been gawping, my friend, but it so happens that here at Endeavour we specialize in tontine derivatives. A lot of the fancier ones are designed by our financial engineers down south.'

'When you say high performing,' Tom said, choosing his words carefully, 'you mean that the original tontine holders are, uh, dying pretty . . . fast?'

The salesman was delighted. 'That's bang-on. 'Course, the beauty of it is that the longer the tontine runs, the less able these blokes are to keep up their premiums. They start out thinking it'll all be cushty, right.' He shook his head amusedly. 'That once a few of their mates've been done in, they'll have the incentive to keep off the grog – but it never happens that way. Your tontine holder – specially your bing-bong – basically comes in two types: killer or be killed. Once the tontine's up and running, both types give in to paranoia; they're always looking over their shoulder to see who's creeping up on them. Can't stand the tension – so they drink. Then they can't keep up the payments – so they sell out.'

Despite the salesman's sly face, Tom had to admit to himself that he *was* becoming a prospect.

'But if I buy out only some of the policy holders,' he said, 'what's to stop the rest of them coming after me?'

The salesman laughed. 'Ha! Do you think they'll get it together, my friend? You're a blow-through – they're stuck right here. All you gotta do is make it home, then you can sit by the pool with a tinnie and wait for your investment to mature, yeah.'

Tom leaned forward and placed his sunburned arms on the counter. He glanced over his shoulder to see if Val was listening, but he was over by the window chatting with the guard.

'What about my, uh, tontine? I thought that was only valid while I and my, er, fellow policy holder were actually here, in the Tontines?'

The salesman gave a broad grin; gold crowns gleamed in the cave of his mouth. He picked up the phone and punched a button. 'Darlin',' he drawled, 'would you bring me out a couple of glasses of that Volsted Pinot Noir?' He replaced the handset and said to Tom: 'That's true, but not a lot of carpet-baggers know what I'm about to tell you, my friend. You can convert the car-rental tontine to a standard one, then there's no limit on its territory. You can be bushed in the middle of Aval country, you can be at the bottom of Eyre's-bloody-Pit; hell, you can be boogying the night away at a disco in Capital City, but if your fellow policy holder gets it, you're his beneficiary.'

He stopped, while a desert tribeswoman, incongruous in a neat navy two-piece, emerged from the back office and handed them both glasses of white wine filmed with condensation. The salesman took a sip, put his glass down, listened for the click of the door closing, then added with a wink: 'Or hers.'

Later, Tom dressed for Gloria Swai-Phillips's charity reception.

'I am the Swift One,' he said aloud, as he used the tiny hotel iron to press the short pants of his absurd suit. 'I am the Righter of Wrongs.'

He checked himself in the mirror. The tie he had worn in court was speckled with stains; never the less, he dutifully knotted it. He looked, he thought, OK. Was it his imagination or had the long journey with its violent incidents mysteriously agreed with him? The Tom Brodzinski in the mirror was fitter and leaner – younger even.

There was a knock at the door. Prentice stood in the dimly lit corridor, his head tilted back, his scrawny neck exposed. 'It's a beastly fag, Tom.' He held up the tube of psoriasis ointment. 'But I just don't seem able to do this again. I was all right last night and this morning . . . Would you mind awfully?'

Tom said: 'It'll be my pleasure.'

Then, after it was done and Tom had washed his hands, they took the elevator together down to the lobby. Tom carried Gloria's parcel, and, of course, the muzak never stopped.

It wasn't until they were almost in the function room, and level with a sign on an easel that said, THE THREE RIVERS CHILDHOOD DEVELOPMENT AGENCY WELCOMES TGS EMPLOYEES, that Prentice hurriedly excused himself, claiming he had to 'buy some fags'. Tom, who had noticed the usual oblong bulge in his shirt pocket, snorted and turned on his heel.

Gloria had been right – the reception was insufferably dull. Shortie-suited bureaucrats stood here and there on the pinkish carpet, holding plates with wine glasses clipped to them – a buffet accessory Tom hadn't seen in decades. The conversations he overheard as he made his way across the large room, with its oppressively low polystyrene ceiling, were banal to the point of being surreal. One man's gutters were choked with leaves; a second was having difficulty getting his car serviced. A woman in a frumpy dress with puffed sleeves was telling another woman – in an equally frumpy outfit – that she suspected the super' in her apartment building of having 'a tiddly prob' with the grog'.

The only person Tom recognized was Daphne Hufferman, who was over by the raw bar, defiantly out of place in her canary-yellow towelling babygro, and with a hessian sack lying on the carpet by her big booted feet.

'Wow,' Tom exclaimed as he joined her. 'What's all this?'

'Yeah,' Daphne replied, then paused to suck up a large shelled shrimp, as a child might a spaghetti string, before adding, 'It's quite a thing, right enough.'

The raw bar stretched the entire length of the room: a vast trough of galvanized zinc heaped with ice chips, upon which were piled shrimp, clams, crayfish, lobster tails, whole softshell crabs, oysters and still more Crustacea that Tom didn't recognize – spidery arthropods, the spindly basketry of their legs as big as a football; tiger-striped shellfish with the flat, coiled aspect of ammonites; and some sort of sea bug like a giant woodlouse. This dead reef was fringed with bowls of salad, sauces, and tumblers stuffed with celery stalks and whole carrots.

'Tom,' Daphne said, 'this is Jean Lejeune. He's the child protection officer for Tontine 901, out towards Kellippi. Jean – Tom.'

Tom turned to this man, muttering an apology for having interrupted, then recoiled. Lejeune was a six-footer with a bear-like build. He wore spectacles with round frames and combed his black hair straight back; yet this was all beside the point – mere details, because surrounding Lejeune's full-lipped mouth was a lustrous goatee of Sangat clams.

Tom's eyes involuntarily slid to the raw bar, then back

to this extraordinary sight. Lejeune was unperturbed. 'You're taken by my infestation, yeah,' he stated.

'Uh, yeah, well . . .' Tom demurred.

'Don't be embarrassed – it's in yer face, yeah.'

Daphne Hufferman snorted with merriment and, grasping Lejeune's arm, bent to pick up the sack. 'Got the part, right,' she said, hefting it. 'Soon as this is done I'm back over there.' A jerk of her thumb. 'Gotta seat with a Tuggie patrol.'

Lejeune pursed his lips, and the clams crepitated. Tom wondered if the man had been making a move on Daphne; it wouldn't have been a bad bet, given her own interest in child protection. He addressed Tom: 'The lady here tells me you're from overseas; some of you blokes are a bit critical of the way we do things here.'

'No, not really – not at all.'

He felt awkward with the newspaper-wrapped parcel in his arms, but there was nowhere he could set it down.

Lejeune resumed at an odd tangent: 'I'm from Amherst myself, yeah – so's the rest of the seafood here. You might think it a waste of resources, freighting all this stuff thousands of clicks over here, but lemme tellya, yeah' – he crowded Tom with his clams – 'the interior of the entire bloody continent was once under water. That's right, mate, if we were standing here millions of years ago there'd be sea over our bloody heads. So what I say is . . .' He leaned in still further, and Tom could see rotting kelp between the shells. 'What goes around bloody comes around. It's a measure of Anglo civilization, yeah, that we can do such marvellous things.'

Tom was struggling to digest this when the man offered him another tid-bit: 'Besides, I was going to grow a beard anyway, yeah. Can't stand bloody shaving.'

Searching for a pretext to break from this repellent fellow, Tom spotted Adams skulking behind a trough of shrubbery. Tom was making his excuses, when there was a sudden 'thwock-thwock-thwock!' Gloria Swai-Phillips was standing on a small rostrum tapping a mic'. The desultory hubbub died away altogether, and she addressed the throng. 'TRCDA is pleased to welcome you all to this gala reception, right?' she began. 'It's a great honour to have such distinguished company here to meet our staff and field workers, yeah? I'd like to extend an especial welcome to the Proconsul' – she inclined her head towards a hefty blond man in a Mao tunic – 'Mr Fabien Renard, CEO of Endeavour Surety' – this one had salt-and-pepper hair, a shiny suit – 'and, of course, Commander Ellanoppolloppolou, for without the cooperation of him and his men, our work here would be impossible, yeah?'

The police commander's hair was so sharply sculpted that it sat on his round head like one of the angular caps worn by his men. He withdrew a swagger stick from under his arm and conducted himself in a curt bow.

'As you all know,' Gloria resumed, 'this is the fifth anniversary of our project being up and running in the Tontine Townships, yeah? During that time, we've helped some 700 tontine orphans to find new domiciles, yeah? These can be state facilities or private institutions, yeah? Other children stay in our own homes, and in several cases we've even managed to secure adoptions, yeah?'

Tom heard everything that Gloria said as a question. For weeks now he had ignored the locals' nonsensical interrogatives – but she seemed genuinely to be querying reality, rather than simply affirming it.

There was a polite scattering of applause, and Gloria

blushed. When she began speaking again, Tom found he couldn't concentrate on her words. He stared at the flapping red slot of her mouth. It was no longer her resemblance to Martha that made him feel he knew Gloria intimately; it was an overpowering sense of déjà vu. He had been in this function room before, with these people and those chairs. He had been with a woman exactly like Gloria, who nurtured him, cuddled him, loved him as a mother loves her child.

She was saying. 'There are real signs of change and progress, yeah?' when Tom began to cry. The tears ran down the inside of his eyes, smearing this commonplace: the middle-aged woman giving a halting speech.

Adams sidled up. 'We need to have a chat,' he said in an undertone. 'I'm afraid we got off on the wrong, ah, foot this morning. My apologies.'

He turned and discreetly worked his way towards the exit. Tom followed.

He found the Consul in the lobby. He was sitting on a leather divan, beside a smoked-glass coffee table with a large ashtray on it. Tom sat down. There was a NO SMOKING sign *inside* the ashtray. There was the iconic red roundel, with its oblique bar anulling a stylized cigarette. The slogan below this read: NO IFS, NO BUTTS, STUB IT OUT.

'Tell me,' Adams asked, 'have you ever heard the term "rabia"?'

Tom thought for a moment, then said: 'Yeah, I have – the Huffermans, Dave, Daphne's husband. He said I'd need one if I was heading down to Ralladayo, but he never told me what it was.'

'Who it is, rather.' Adams pulled up a fold of seersucker over each knee. He rested his elbows on these pads, then pressed his palms together and brought his fingertips up to

243

his horsy chin in a prayerful gesture. 'A rabia', he intoned, 'is an individual who can guarantee a traveller safe passage through the territories of hostile tribes, or tribal subgroups.'

Jesus! The man's insufferable, Tom thought, while to Adams he played the good student: 'How do they manage that?'

'The concept is, ah, simple enough. The rabia will belong either to a tribe that isn't enemies with the tribe whose land you wish to cross, or – and this is where it gets complex – to an allied tribe. You see' – the Consul squirmed with enthusiasm – 'even if this more distant tribe is, technically, at, ah, loggerheads with the local mob, it doesn't matter – it's the proximate relationship that counts.'

'And I need one of these rabia guys?'

Adams ignored the interruption. 'The disputations concerning whether a given rabia can frank through a given traveller often become, ah, byzantine – especially where you're headed, into the very heart of the native lands. I've witnessed this myself: scores of tribespeople, big men and women, powerful makkatas – all of them gathered in the remote desert for days, debating like learned statesmen!'

Adams's face was flushed. One of his hands went up high, then came down to pat the back of his head.

Tom persisted with the practicalities. 'How do I get the right one, then?'

Adams recovered himself. 'Ordinarily, an Anglo traveller has to advertise here in the Tontines – there's a message board. But it can take time, and even when you have the right rabia, they can prove costly. I should imagine your, ah, resources are rather depleted by now.'

Tom ruefully considered the Amex bill that had been forwarded to him in the TGS, Dixie's girlish handwriting looping across the cellophane window. Tom was within a few hundred dollars of his credit limit. Prentice, naturally, had yet to pay back what he owed. Perhaps, Tom thought, I should raise this with Adams? But then he dismissed the idea. Instead, he grunted affirmatively.

Adams resumed. 'However, I've managed to secure a rabia for you who doesn't require payment, someone who urgently needs a ride down to Ralladayo.'

'Oh, and who is this guy?'

'Not a *guy*,' the Consul said pedantically. 'A, ah . . . *girl*. Miss Swai–Phillips.'

'Gloria? How so? I mean, she doesn't exactly look like a . . .'

'Be that as it may, Miss Swai–Phillips has all the main kinship lines – Entreati, Aval and Tayswengo, the latter through her mother's great-uncle. She can get you through, and she's happy to do so without charge–'

'OK,' Tom said, cutting him off. 'But what's the reason she's going there?'

Adams's Polaroids were clear enough; even so, he removed them, imposing – as Tom understood it – still more transparency on his next remark: 'She wishes to help you in what you have to do – and make sure that you, ah . . . do it. There's also a small orphanage at Ralladayo; I believe she's been called in for, ah . . . consultancy. There is one other thing, though . . .'

To punish Tom for his own interruptions, Adams now broke off and beckoned to a lurking waiter. 'Nescafé, please,' he instructed the flat-faced Tugganarong. 'No milk or sugar. D'you want anything?' he asked Tom, who only waved the waiter away irritatedly, before interrogating the Consul: 'What one thing? Goddamnit, Adams!'

'Brian Prentice,' Adams said airily. 'He'll be going with you as well. Seems his business here in the Tontines hasn't been, ah . . . successfully concluded; so he will have to accompany Miss Swai-Phillips, and you, to Ralladayo.'

For a while Tom said nothing. He was getting used to the Consul's penchant for such theatricality. Besides, he was also struck by the Consul's 'ahs'. These hiatuses were increasing in length, and during them the intent expression on Adams's face suggested he was attuning himself to an inner voice.

The waiter deposited Adams's bitter gloop on the coffee table and withdrew. Adams sipped it as if it were nectar.

It was plain that the Consul was telling Tom something that it was impossible to state directly. Tom followed a poisonous thread of speculation back along the corrugations of Route 1, across the desert, looping up and over the Great Dividing Range, threading through the cane fields, until it reached the complicated knot tied up in Vance. Could Adams even be aware that Tom had visited Endeavour Surety that very afternoon? That, unsure of his own moral outrage, he had provided himself with a baser, more legible motivation?

Tom meditated on how grossly intrusive it would be to kill another man. Even at half a mile's distance, with a high-velocity rifle bullet, he knew it would feel as if he were slowly dabbling his hands in Prentice's intestines. Yet it was blatantly obvious that this was what was expected of him – had been expected all along, by both Swai-Phillipses, by Adams – even by Justice Hogg. Prentice had to be terminated: his perverted consciousness stubbed out like one of his own filthy 'fags'. And, although nothing could be said – and never would be – Tom's own debt was to be paid in this coin:

two rifles, a nest of cooking pots, $10,000 in cash and a man's life.

Tom took a deep, shuddering breath. 'I noticed', he said, 'that Prentice couldn't bring himself to attend Gloria's charity reception.'

'Really?' Adams was unconcerned. 'I expect he had to get some help to bring his stuff back to the TGS; apparently only half of it is required here; the ribavirin will go south, with you.'

Tom stood up. 'If it's all the same to you, Adams, I think I'll start getting my own stuff together. I've gotta gas up the car, check the mechanics. I've also . . .' He paused and gave the Consul a meaningful look. 'I've also got to get a signature off Prentice, then finalize some paperwork with a guy outside the Sector.'

For the first time that Tom could recall, Adams smiled broadly, his normally pursed lips drawing back to reveal large and sharp teeth. 'That's excellent, Tom,' he grinned. 'I'm glad to see you're adopting such a, ah . . . practical attitude. Miss Swai-Phillips asked me to tell you that unless she hears otherwise, she'll meet you here in the lobby at six tomorrow morning, so you can get an early start.'

Adams stood, and they shook hands formally, concluding the deal.

'And Tom . . .' Adams seemed on the verge of saying something incriminating. He shuffled his suede lace-ups, glancing round to see if anyone was within earshot. Tom assumed it would be the quid pro quo: how even if Lincoln were to die while Tom was over there, the conclusion of this other business would result in the charges against him being summarily dropped. But the Consul wasn't such a fool. 'That parcel Miss Swai-Phillips gave you. She said please not to forget it, whatever you do. It's contents are most, ah . . . important – vital, even.'

'Sure,' Tom replied. 'Absolutely, uh, Winnie. She can rely on me.'

And they parted.

Back up in his room, Tom began packing his stuff. The flimsy clothing designed for walking from poolside to lounger, the tubes of scientifically formulated skin unguents, his digital camera, cellphone and the roach motel, to which he had become sentimentally attached – all these he reverently slotted into his battered and filthy flight bag.

Once, he sat down on the bed and started to dial the familiar digits of his home phone, but halfway through he stopped, then replaced the femoral handset on its pelvic cradle. Tom put his elbows on his knees, his face in his hands. He peeked out between his fingers. Gloria's head-shaped parcel sat on the plinth of the Von Sassers' *Songs of the Tayswengo*, watching him with its newsprint eyes.

13

They missed the left turn that Route 1 made for Trangaden and the south. Missed it, and didn't even realize that they had until they reached an enormous 'Route 2' waymark, and a sign saying that Kellippi was a mere 807 kilometres further.

Tom pulled up abruptly and began manhandling the SUV into a three-point turn.

'Better not,' Gloria said, laying a hand on his arm. 'Look up ahead.'

Low-flying helicopters were circling over the blast walls of a checkpoint. Even from several hundred yards off, Tom could see the coils of razor wire flaring in the evening sun.

'They'll've seen us,' Gloria went on. 'Better go through, yeah?'

By the time they had negotiated the checkpoint, it was twilight – too late to go back through and resume the right road. The sergeant on duty told them there was a decent motel a few klicks on, so Tom, close to collapsing with the frustration of it all, drove there.

It had been a long day, most of which had been taken up with having their papers checked. The 300 kilometres of Route 1 that ran through the Tontine Townships had more checkpoints than the previous 4,000.

The townships were at once desultory and threatening: the plantation settlements, each with its paramilitary block-house, dusty maidan and empty boulevards lined with converted containers, were identical to each other. As Route 1 turned into yet another central boulevard, to either side of which were ranged the same insurance offices, so another flock of prostitutes rose up and flapped after them, their wings beating invisible meat, their throats gobbling.

Stopping at the fifth checkpoint of the morning, and noting the paramilitaries' Humvees, equipped with steel skirting to prevent hand grenades being tossed under them, Tom asked Gloria: 'Why don't the authorities stop the selling of tontines if it's fuelling the violence?'

'It's the economy, stupid,' she explained, employing the sing-song voice patronizing people use for children – or idiots. 'The financial-services industry down south would have an absolute bloody fit if the guvvie messed with them, yeah? No pol who wants to hang on to office could risk *that*.'

Now, Tom waited while Gloria showed her ID card to the security camera, then pulled the SUV in through the motel's steel gates. Prentice – who had been banished to the jump seat – took his time getting out. He had been forbidden to smoke by Gloria, who, like most of the native Anglos, seemed untroubled by the flies. Tom waited for him to make his usual lame excuses, before skulking off for a 'fag'. But instead, Prentice stretched, clapped his hands together and said, 'Right. You must be worn out after that drive, Tom. You go get a sundowner while I unload the gear and check the firearms into the motel armoury.'

Tom's hand went to the tontine conversion certificate concealed in his pocket – was its juju not working? Were his and Prentice's grades of astande shifting once more? Certainly, Tom felt worryingly debilitated, and as he shuffled into the motel he heard Gloria saying, 'Mind you check that parcel into the motel safe as well, Brian.'

The motel bar was full of fleshy red-faced men who stood drinking outsized wineglasses full of dark Belgian beer. Equally fleshy women, with peroxide hair, sat at the small tables eating dishes of what appeared to be cooked chicory. Obnoxious fleshy kids charged across the tiled floor from the reception desk and flung themselves into a small swimming pool that stank of chlorine. The bored Belgian barmaid explained to Tom that it had been built inside on account of the security situation.

'I should think things'll be easier tomorrow on the driving front, right?' Gloria speculated, perching on the bar stool next to Tom's.

He looked at his badly drawn wife. Gone was the hesitant charity worker recounting statistics in the function room of the Hilton. Gloria had been acting all day as if Tom and Prentice were annoying boys and she their competent elder sister. Tom wanted to reconnect with a still other Gloria: the woman who had swabbed the makkata's gash on his inner thigh, then caressed him at the law courts. But, while his longing had grown through the long, flyblown day, she had became steadily more distant.

Tom was so weary that once he'd had a couple of beers and tottered to his cabin, he didn't have the energy to rejoin his companions for supper. Instead, he fell asleep, fully clothed, on the bed, the sanitary strip he had removed from the toilet bowl twined in his fingers.

This time giant fingers pinched his waist, then rolled him back and forth. Tom heard a rib crack — yet couldn't cry out. Next, violent acceleration. Tom flew end over end, his mind smouldering with the effort of trying to alter his course: a bullet in dread of its own trajectory. If only, he smouldered, if only I can twist myself this way and hold my arms out, then I can go that much further, and fall harmlessly into the flower bed at the front of the apartment block . . . But he had no arms.

He reached the zenith of his parabola and, screaming, plummeted back down into the tangled and hairy mess of the bedding, where he burned.

In the morning Prentice had the SUV loaded up by the time Tom managed to drag himself along from his cabin. He felt terrible, and Gloria greeted him with 'You look bloody terrible.' It was a nagging enervation that reminded Tom of the aftermath of flu.

What was Gloria wearing? She stood in the colourless void of the pre-dawn desert entirely swathed in a black toga, the complicated drapes of which covered her face, her hands and even her feet. Her costume was creepily completed by green-tinted goggles.

'It's gonna be hot where we're headed, yeah?' Gloria said as Tom drove the SUV out of the motel compound and they set off back along Route 2.

He snorted, 'And what's it been here? This is the desert, isn't it?'

'Strictly speaking,' said Prentice, pushing his face forward between the seats, 'this is only the channel country, the River Mulgrene Delta. That's why there's so much gravel, and so many wadis — which are the dried-up tributaries.

When it rains here – which only happens once or twice a decade – all this floods.'

'What is this? A fucking geography class?'

Prentice, aggrieved, sat back, but Gloria said: 'You'd do well to pay attention to geography, read the land – that's how the traditional people survive here, right?

'Take this Tayswengo toga,' she continued. 'It's perfectly adapted to handle fifty-degree heat, yeah? The black cloth absorbs the sun's rays, you sweat, then the folds hold and cool that sweat, so that you've gotta kinduv sleeve of coolness, yeah?'

As ever, Tom reflected, Gloria didn't sound that sure of what she was saying.

This time they made the right turn to the south. The blacktop that had carried them through the Tontines, on towards Kellippi and now back again gave out after a few kilometres. There was a last road sign – TRANGADEN 1,570 KMS, LAKE MULGRENE NATURE PARK 876 KMS – then the impacted dirt corrugations began, the constant judder making further conversation, or even thought, an effort.

The trio were abandoned, each to his or her own discomfort. The flies infiltrated themselves into the rotten environment of the little vehicle. The heat built – then built some more. The stony bled crumpled up – then disappeared, subsumed by sand dunes that came flowing in from the east and the west.

At first these were low swells, then gradually they whipped up and up, until the rutted track was plunging through a mountainous sea of eighty-foot-high dunes. The SUV, never the easiest car to control, twisted and slid on the uncertain surface.

Tom couldn't suspend disbelief in his own driving: it felt

as if he was being rolled over and over through the desert. The lack of low-flying helicopters, checkpoints and even the threat of ambush, far from being a relief, was a further oppression; for without tension he couldn't prevent himself from lapsing into a stupor.

After five draining hours, two signs staggered towards them out of the heat-haze. The first read TIREDNESS KILLS – TAKE A BREAK, the second YOU ARE NOW ENTERING ENTREATI TRIBAL LAND, SMOKING PERMITTED.

'Smoking permitted,' Tom croaked. 'What the hell does that mean?'

'Exactly what it says, right?' Gloria replied sententiously. 'The desert tribes – the Entreati in particular – have never been fully subjugated. They live, for the most part, as they've always done. Not, you understand, that smoking is wide-spread, for the most part the mobs use–'

'Engwegge, yeah, I know that.'

Prentice was gurgling with suppressed laughter. In the rear-view, Tom saw that he had one of his fat packs of Reds out and was fondling it suggestively, sweaty fingers slipping on the cellophane.

Two oil drums sprang up in the road, and, as Tom brought the car to a halt, two toga-swathed figures came from behind a dune and strolled towards them. They carried long hunting spears in one hand, automatic rifles in the other.

'Entreati checkpoint, yeah?' Gloria said superfluously. 'Let me do all the talking – I'm the rabia. And remember,' she preened, 'don't worry – you are my companions and your safety – both of your blood and your possessions – is in my face.'

'Mind if I get out, old chap?' Prentice ventured. 'I need to stretch my legs.'

Tom got out and tipped his seat forward. Prentice emerged blinking into the harsh sunlight. He immediately scrabbled open his cigarettes, ostentatiously lit one, then paced up and down beside the Entreati tribesmen, taking exaggerated puffs.

Tom observed him with clinical loathing.

Gloria spoke to the men in a pidgin of clicks, clucks, tooth clacks, rights and yeahs. She indicated her companions, then led the Entreati to the rear of the SUV so she could point out the rifles and the ribavirin boxes in the trunk.

The Entreati were interested in all this. As they bobbed along with Gloria, their black garb and fast-nodding heads made them seem not threatening but pantomimic: children's TV presenters taking part in an ethnological playlet.

Eventually, Gloria came over to where Tom was slumped in the shadow of a dune, sipping tepid water from his bottle.

'There's not exactly a problem,' she began. 'More of . . . an issue.'

'Issue?'

'It's a ceremonial thing, yeah? These blokes' makkata needs to examine you and Brian – your cuts, that is.'

'I'm sorry?'

Tom knew full well what Gloria meant; he just didn't want to know. The Entreati were leaning on the SUV, smoking. Gloria had presented them both with cartons of cigarettes. Snaggle-toothed grins unzipped in the hoods of their black robes as they drew on them.

There was a rustling on the face of the dune, and, glancing round, Tom saw the spidery figure of a makkata surfing down it, hanging ten on an invisible board.

The ceremony – if that's what it was – was mercifully short. Tom was first: he followed the makkata a few paces from the road and dropped his pants. Feeling the light inquisition of the makkata's fingers on his inner thigh, Tom flashed back to Bimple Hot Springs. Surely Prentice would fail this test? He had no scar. He would be unmasked while half naked. But Prentice showed no apprehension when it was his turn to go with the wizard.

When the makkata returned, he entered into muttered conference with the two other Entreati. This lasted a long time, many cigarettes were smoked, and the sand at the makkata's feet was dashed by the long streams of engwegge juice he had ejected. Eventually, one of the robed men approached the three travellers, who were squatting in the ditch beside the road. He squatted as well and consulted with Gloria.

This is it, Tom thought, scrutinizing Prentice's venal features. It's the end of the road for you, kiddie-fiddler.

The clicking stopped and Gloria said, 'Uh, OK, that figures.'

'What?' Tom said. 'What figures?'

'This bloke says the makkata has determined that your degrees of astande have been swapped over. We're allowed to proceed, yeah? But since Brian is now astande vel dyav and you, Tom, are astande por mio, you can't drive the car any more, right?'

'What?' Tom cried.

'You heard me.' Gloria was adamant. 'Brian will have to drive – if he can, that is.'

'Of course I can bloody drive,' Prentice said huffily.

'Why can't *you* drive?' Tom asked Gloria. He was unwilling to trust his safety to Prentice, even though he doubted his own ability to drive the car any further.

'I can't drive because I'm a rabia, yeah? I'm only along for the ride – if I drive I compromise my status. It's obvious, yeah?'

Prentice tamped his latest butt into the sand with a fussy motion of his boot. 'Well,' he said, 'that's settled, then.' He marched over to the SUV, a resolute expression on his face.

His face? Clambering into the SUV, where he then sat awkwardly pinioned, knees tucked up to his chest, Tom took surreptitious peeps at the hateful countenance. In the rear-view he confirmed his suspicion: 'It's cleared up.'

'Whassat?' Prentice was yanking at the stick shift.

'Your psoriasis – it's gone.' Tom leaned forward between the front seats. 'Yesterday it was as bad as ever – don't you remember, I had to smear your fucking cream on? Now it's gone.'

'Yes, well, it does clear up like that sometimes; it could be the desert air, y'know.' He had managed to get the SUV going and was piloting them along the track – it was barely a road any more – with hesitant pumps of the gas pedal.

'Bullshit,' Tom said succinctly. 'It's to do with the astande stuff; your skin has righted its own goddamn wrongs.'

'Don't bicker, you two,' their big sister intervened.

Tom fell back. The jump seat was savagely uncomfortable. If he sat sideways, he got cramp in his legs; if he faced to the front, his back ached. The boxes stacked in the tiny trunk kept sliding forward and jabbing Tom in the neck. Then there was Gloria's package, which she insisted on having in the back so whoever was sitting there could 'Keep an eye on it, right?'

Tom kept an eye on it – and it eyed him. The *trompe l'œil* effect he had noticed in his room at the Hilton was no illusion: the package really did have eyes – and a nose and mouth. It was a severed head, Tom realized with mounting horror, its putrefying skin legible with coded messages: '600-Horsepower Chrysler Marine Engines . . . Premium

Aluminium Siding . . . Bovine Spongiform Encephalopathy . . . Would like to meet M 45–50, GSOH . . .' He read the enigma of its features as, uncomfortably lulled by the bumps in the track, he began to slide in and out of consciousness.

The package was on Tom's lap and he was chatting to it. 'Sorry I had to take you out like that, old chap,' he said, undoing the string and pulling away the newspaper to reveal Prentice's ancient foetal features. 'Nothing I could do to prevent it. You shouldn't have fucked with the kiddies, man; no one likes that.'

Tom groped out a tube of psoriasis ointment from his shirt pocket, uncapped it and spread the oily gunk on to the squamous severed neck. 'Like I say,' he burbled on, 'I had to do it. I'm, like . . .' He snickered. 'The *butt* of this situation as much as you are – more, even. They were all on to me, fucking riding me, man – Adams, Swai-Phillips, Squolly, the judge, even Gloria here.'

Gloria swivelled in the passenger seat and showed Tom her face – which was Martha's. He took this in his stride, resumed his soliloquy. 'They all wanted to be rid of you – I happened to be in the wrong place at the wrong time. Uh-oh!' He lifted the head to his lips and reverently kissed it. 'Uh-oh, poor Yorick, I fucking hated you, man . . .'

'Tom! Tom! Wake up, right?' It was Gloria, shaking him. He came to, fumbling to check that his tontine was still where he had put it, then immediately examined her face to see whether he'd been talking in his sleep. But if he had, she made no sign.

They were at another checkpoint. Prentice was already out of the SUV and strutting up and down the road, puffing away. Struggling out, Tom saw that he had been asleep long enough for the desert's character to have changed. Previously, the sand dunes had been rolling downs; now they had closed up and grown in height. To either side of Route 1 they marched away: vast, pyramidical hills, 500, 600 feet high, with steep slopes, soaring arêtes and summits from which the wind unwound long ribbons of sand.

It was an awesome sight. Gloria stretched and took a deep breath, then exhaled: 'Aaaah! The erg!' As any proud suburbanite might hymn the praises of her garden.

Again Tom was summoned by a leathery-skinned, leather-aproned makkata. Again he went along meekly, this time behind the spur of a dune. Again the meaty breath, and the brown engwegge flecks on his pale thigh, as the makkata's fingers sought out the scar. He dragged himself back to where Gloria was squatting and remarked: 'I guess it's gonna be like this the whole way – I mean, these guys having to, uh, examine us.'

'Well, they aren't exactly examining you, yeah?' Gloria had acquired the pedantic tone Tom associated with Adams. 'They know what grade of astande you are – the guys at the last checkpoint will have told them.'

'But how?'

She shrugged. 'I couldn't say. The point is, the desert is a crowded place, yeah? Here, everyone knows everyone's business, and if a man does something noteworthy, right? It's at least with the hope that his deed will be sung of, yeah? In the camps of the Entreati and the settlements of the Tayswengo. In the cliff-cut houses of the Aval, and among the vagabond miners of Eyre's Pit – from the Feltham coast to the Great Divide.

'The desert people are tremendously proud, Tom, you must understand this. Proud and fierce and just and terrible, yeah? They would rather see a man dead, yeah? Than humiliated.' She stopped perorating and gave Tom a significant look. It struck him that it was his own future deed – the homicide that was hardening in his heart – that she meant.

These bare-buttocked makkatas – they knew. They knew that Prentice had no grade of astande at all, that he had never had the cut. They realized exactly who and what he was. Now they were simply confirming it: ushering him towards the death seat.

'So, why the exam?' Tom asked Gloria, as Prentice returned, buckling his belt.

'That's easy, old chap,' he butted in. 'As Ms Swai-Phillips was saying, no one wants to be left out. I expect these chaps will still want to jaw for a while, have a good old powwow before they decide whether we have the right rabia to go on.'

'And if we don't, smarty-pants?'

But that was the limit of Prentice's desert lore, and he only shrugged.

The Entreati did want to jaw – at length. They chewed it over with their makkata; they talked with Gloria. They went back to the makkata, then they talked among themselves. Tom drowsed in the lea of a dune. It was unbearably hot: a fierce, dry heat. Frazzling hair – frying skin. Tom couldn't believe the flies were still able to get aloft – but they were.

Eventually, the deliberations were concluded. Gloria came to report: 'They want us to spend the night at their settlement. It's only seventy clicks from here, down at the shore of Lake Mulgrene, right? Frankly, it's a good idea. I'd been hoping to stop with a different mob, but that's at least another 200, and it's too late now.'

As he inserted himself into the hot-box-on-wheels, Tom was appalled by his own lack of foresight. He had never given a thought to where they were going to stay on this leg of the journey. He hadn't asked if there were road stops, he hadn't considered the availability of fuel. He hadn't even checked if there was enough water in the ten-gallon hessian bag that hung on the back rack beside the rifles.

Yet it transpired that Prentice had done all of this – and more; because when they were under way, following the Entreati's fish tailing, sand-spewing pick-up, he produced an aerosol and, passing it back to Tom, said, 'Spray some of that thingamajig on your face and hands, old chap, it'll cool you down.'

It did, deliciously so, and Tom was applying it liberally when Gloria barked, 'Watch out for the bloody package!' Cowed, Tom went back to his tortured introspection.

This alternation between childlike yearning and murderous repulsion was familiar; so too was the lust that now flushed through him with a desperate intensity. This was not to do with mere coupling with another human body; it was an urge to universally propagate in defiance of both space and time: tumescence that might raise up from the dead the innumerable creatures lost in the great extinctions . . . Then he collapsed back into a torpor that was equally global: the world was balled up in his palsied hand, yet he hadn't the strength to chuck it in the trash can.

It was, he decided, nicotine withdrawal – but grown gargantuan; nicotine withdrawal experienced as a full-blown mental illness. Nicotine craving that no quantity of actual nicotine could ever assuage, even if he were to smoke all day long, then pace all night, chaining furiously.

★   ★   ★

The rough track they were following began to dip towards the west, where the white-hot iron sun was puddling into molten fire. The parcel head nuzzled against Tom's thigh, and he pushed it away. From some memory cranny crawled the following words: 'Deep in the desert wastes of the Western Province, Lake Mulgnene stretches for a thousand kilometres across the land, a crystalline expanse of health, purity and hydrolytic balance. Here the Entreati people make their winter encampments ... And employing technology perfected throughout millennia, they refine and distil the precious fluid–'

'That's all gammon, that is!' Gloria expostulated.

'Gammon?'

'Gammon – bloody bullshit; the lake's crystalline all right, but only 'cause of the salt and all the run-off from the mines.'

'So, no swimming, then?'

Gloria almost spat. 'No, no bloody swimming at all, yeah?'

She was growing coarser, Tom felt, as they journeyed into the interior. The floral-patterned charity worker who had hesitantly addressed the reception in the Tontines had been returned to a closet full of hanging personae; then this tough, capable identity had been slipped on.

'You don't know how these people live at all, do you, yeah?' she said.

'Well, I've read the Von Sassers,' he blustered, but then conceded: 'I did find it tough going.'

Tom remembered the nights at the Entreati Experience in Vance and then on the road: the enormous anthropology book pinning him to the bed, crouching malevolently on his chest, almost as if it were aware of the blood money he had hidden in its papery belly.

'The important thing to grasp, yeah?' Gloria hectored

Tom as Prentice pulled up behind the pick-up. 'Is that these people have never been subjugated, right? They live now as they always have, beautifully and harmoniously. Respect their harmony – and they'll respect you.'

If the copywriter's screed on the bottle of Lake Mulgrene mineral water had been hyperbole, then so was the term 'settlement' when applied to the Entreati camp. It was a dump. Fifty or sixty men, women and children grovelled in the dirt, dragging themselves from beneath corrugated-iron sheets that had been laid over pits to sit chewing engwegge around smoky fires.

Then there were the dogs: slinking, squirming, yapping curs. There were chunks missing out of their mangy fur, their tails were twisted, their legs seized up. It struck Tom how few dogs he had seen – either over here or back on the coast. The dogs smelled, and they came dallying in – canine flies – to thrust their proboscises against his bare legs.

At the first moist contact, Tom's own nose unblocked and a crowd of stenches – human and animal waste, rotting meat, wood smoke, singed hair, gasoline fumes – jostled for admission. Smell, the most ancient and canny of the senses. Apart from the very strongest, the most rank of odours, he had for a long time now been smell-blind, the white lines of his cigarettes blocking them out indiscriminately. Tom's nose backtracked along Route 1, sniffing sweat, perfume, eucalyptus tang and foody bouquet. Back and back to Vance, where Tom had snuffled in the hollow of one of his twin's neck, unaware that it – and he – were both redolent of ashtray.

In the midden the Entreati tenanted, shit, trash and broken glass were scattered everywhere. The pot-bellied children's eyes were filled with pus from untreated trachoma, while fully a third of the adults were completely blind. All of them, except for the active young men, had streptococcal infections. Tom also saw the spavined legs of rickets sufferers, and heard the popping wheeze of tuberculosis.

Shortly before they had arrived a dead auraca had been thrown on a fire. It lay there, its coat smouldering, with a startled expression on its lama-like features. 'It's a great honour,' Gloria explained. 'They're welcoming us to their cosmos, right?'

She seemed not to notice the disease, the malnutrition, the trash or the dogs. She strode from one humpy to the next in her black robes, a ministering nun handing out cartons of cigarettes and packets of bubble gum.

Soon, everyone over the age of seven was holding a fat packet of Reds and puffing away – some, preposterously, on more than one cigarette at a time. Meanwhile, the little kids blew blue bubbles that burst on their pinched black faces. Soon the dump became yet more littered, with butts and the slick films of the cellophane wrappers.

One thing that wasn't hyperbole was Gloria's estimation of their welcome. The Entreati were warm towards them, effusively so. Tom sat by the fire, torn between shame and disgust, as toothless old men and leprous children embraced him with their diseases. At last he managed to drag himself away and set off towards the unearthly limelight that played about the lake shore.

'Don't even touch the water,' Gloria called after him.

Night was encroaching. Away to the east, back in the direction of Route 1, enormous crescent-shaped dunes marched along the horizon, each like the cast of a giant worm that was boring beneath the sands. The wind was soughing in off the lake, laden with mephitic fumes. There could be no question of even attempting to dabble in its celebrated waters, for the shoreline consisted of hundreds of yards of crusted salt and cracked mud. Oily fluid oozed between these platelets, streaking them cobalt, viridian and carmine – colours that belonged in a nail parlour, not the natural world.

As the last rays of the setting sun fingered the limpid surface of the immense depression, they caught on strange-looking rafts of some bubbly excrescence – like enormous frogspawn – that were floating perhaps a mile offshore.

Tom stood, swaying slightly, staring out over this desolate scene. After a while he realized he was not alone. One of the young Entreati men from the checkpoint had followed him down, and stood a way off, smoking, and apparently lost in his own thoughts.

Tom approached him: 'Do you – can you speak–?'

'English, mate? Yairs, 'course I bloody can. Did elementary in Trangaden – we all have, right.'

The Entreati was younger than Tom had supposed – little more than a boy, despite his height. Although he had directly contradicted Gloria's insistence on the cultural isolation of the tribe, it wasn't this that Tom wished to pursue.

'Those' – he pointed – 'um, like, *rafts* out there – d'you know what they are?'

The Entreati lad laughed bitterly. 'Them? They're corpses, mate, big bloody mobs of corpses.'

'Corpses? Have they been there long, I mean, shouldn't you . . .'

'Some of 'em', the lad said philosophically, 'must be bloody historic – they've been out there all my life. See, here's how it is,' he went on, becoming animated. 'When a bloke gets karked up in the Tontines, they dump his body in a wadi. Come the rains, they get washed down here, yeah. But the water in the lake – well, you can see what it's like. It doesn't matter if the bodies are rotting when they're chucked in, yeah, when they get to Mulgrene they're pickled for-bloody-ever.

'Weird thing is' – the young man poked meditatively at the crusted salt with the barrel of his gun – 'the way they cluster together like that into those rafts. There's no current out there, but they still do it. Bloody big bunk-ups – it's like they're keeping each other company, yeah.'

When they returned to camp the auraca had been buried in the ground and the fire raked over it, then built up.

'It's a traditional earth oven,' Prentice told him.

'Where do they get the fuel?' Tom asked.

'There's mulga scrub south of here, apparently. Devilish stuff when it's living – burns like billy-o once it's dead.'

There was a bustling purposiveness about Prentice as he unloaded the SUV, taking three fat canvas bundles down from the roof-rack. Tom rubbed his sore eyes – he hadn't noticed them before.

'Got these in the Tontines, together with the other gear,' the newly Swift One said, unrolling one of these. 'Swags – you can't sleep out in the desert without one.'

He left off his preparations and took a sheaf of receipts and bills from his jeans pocket. 'The swags, a water bag, emergency flares, medical kit, gifts for the native mobs – it's all here. I've added it up, old chap, and here's the balance of what I owe you in cash.' He gave Tom an affable smile and passed the money and papers over. 'Thanks for the loans; we should be even now.'

Tom spyed another difference in Prentice as the other man readied the swags. He looked leaner and more ascetic – altogether less ridiculous. Then it struck Tom what it was: 'Prentice – Brian. You've – you've . . .' he tailed off, stupidly embarrassed.

'It's my thatch, isn't it, old chap?' Prentice patted his bare forehead. 'Ye-es, I shaved that daft fringe off – dunno why I hung on to it for so long.' He laughed. 'Nostalgia, I suppose. Better to face up to the fact that I'm going bald. It's most peculiar . . .' He tilted his face up and his clear complexion glowed in the firelight. 'I don't think I could've, y'know, accepted that, without coming out here and being with the bing . . . with these people.'

He stopped, clearly feeling that he had said rather too much, and busied himself with setting up their little subcamp for the night.

The following day Tom was even weaker. They set off from the Entreati camp at dawn, and until mid afternoon were still in the tribal lands, stopping at checkpoints approximately every fifty kilometres, so the the rabia debate could be rejoined.

Then, at the point when Tom felt he could stand the constant lurching over the impacted sand no more, and the newspaper head was, once again, assuming a slack-mouthed, garrulous appearance, they came to an enormous billboard erected on the side of a dune. It showed a muscle-bound man wrestling with a giant cigarette butt. The caption to this bizarre cartoon was: 'Wrestle that filthy addiction to the ground and swim away from it!'

'Swim where?' Tom muttered to himself. 'Lake Mulgrene?'

A few yards on a second sign appeared: YOU ARE

ENTERING THE TRANGADEN REGIONAL ADMINISTRATIVE ZONE. ALL TOBACCO AND ENGWEGGE CONSUMPTION IS ILLEGAL. DEPOSIT ANY SUCH MATERIALS IN BIN PROVIDED BEFORE PROCEEDING. POSSESSION IS A FELONY. MINIMUM PENALTY: 3 MONTHS' HARD LABOUR AT EYRE'S PIT AND $5,000 FINE.

'Y'know,' Gloria said wistfully. 'it's funny, but whenever I see that sign it's almost like I'm coming home, yeah?'

Prentice pulled over and began fussing around. He tipped up the seat, rootled in the glove compartments, the side pockets of the doors and the trunk, pulling out cigarette packs, disposable lighters – even turning clothes pockets inside out so that the tobacco residue could be scattered by the sirocco. The transformation from the tough character who had been driving the SUV with dash and competence was immediate and complete. Furtive, old–maidish, lubricious Prentice had returned. Prentice the kiddie-fiddler, Prentice who was in search of a 'little company' – preferably black – and who now, to Tom, seemed to be rehearsing just such an outrage, as he nervously fed his paper tubes into the slot of the bin provided. What made the sight absurd was that Prentice was standing in a slag heap of discarded cigarettes, cigars, pipes, loose tobacco and engwegge quids.

Tom found he was laughing: deep guffaws that expanded his ribcage, so that he sucked in gouts of healthy, arid, desert air.

Gloria ignored him: 'I did my social work training in Trangaden, yeah?'

Yeah, Tom thought. Like fuck you did.

'It's a backward kinduv place, and the people are total bloody wowsers, but I still have a great affection for it, right?'

Tom thought: whatever.

Prentice's gait was crabbed as he returned to the car; with his new olfactory powers Tom smelled fear and sweat and need. Prentice put one chicken wing on the steering wheel, while with the other he groped out a blisterpack of nicotine gum. As he tucked one in his ugly mouth, Tom snidely observed: 'Isn't that a tobacco product?'

'Strictly speaking, old chap.' Prentice put the SUV in gear, and they drove away. 'It is, but so long as it's on prescription you're allowed it in the TRAZ.'

'And yours is?'

'Absolutely. I fixed it up before we left the Tontines – you have to look ahead.'

But when he said this Prentice hadn't been looking ahead: there was an auraca on the highway – the first live one they had seen since the badlands before the Tontines. He had to swerve violently at the last second to avoid hitting it. The car stopped on the very edge of the road, teetering. Prentice was draped over the steering wheel, shaking, his jaw working his nicotine gum; a jaw that bore the unmistakable marks – pink, lumpy, scaly – of fast-returning psoriasis.

'Lissen, Prentice, you goddamn nearly got us all killed!' Tom said. 'You know the auraca bars on this heap are as flimsy as fucking paperclips! We better swap over. I'll drive for a while – you can concentrate on your dumb addiction.'

They changed places. As soon as Tom was holding the wheel, he felt a surge of energy coming through it: the transmission directly connected to his nervous system.

The linked chains of mighty dunes that had marched away to either side of Route 1 slowly collapsed in on themselves, dumping out into a dull and featureless bled. A road-train came barrelling towards them, and Tom expertly took evasive action. It thundered past: four semi-trailers, their double sets of wheels throwing out cannonades of grit and pebbles.

A gas station loomed up out of the rumpled atmosphere, the first they had seen for 2,000 kilometres. Parked cars were ranged on its pristine blacktop apron. Leaning on the open doors, fiddling with the sound systems that blasted out rap music, were Anglo teenagers. They were drinking sodas as the wind riffled their T-shirts and sweatpants.

'Y'know,' Tom observed to Gloria, 'I'm not completely ignorant, I did absorb some of what the Von Sassers wrote.' He reeled off a few of the prosaic field notes he had internalized: the Tayswengo's traditional range was between Ralladayo and the foothills of the Great Divide; they subsisted on hunting moai and digging succulent tubers called effel; their kinship system was matrilineal, with children raised by their maternal uncles; they believed that the desert – which was their entire world – rested on a massive flipper lizard, which they called Engeddii, meaning 'Back of the World'.

Gloria kept nodding her head to all of this, although when she voiced her 'yeahs' and 'rights' they remained questions rather than affirmations. They drove over a wide, empty watercourse on a long box girder bridge. The SUV's tyres thwacked the concrete. Finally she interrupted him: 'Thing is, yeah? All that has some truth in it, but what stands out about the Intwennyfortee is that, unlike most other Tayswengo mobs, they have a remarkable . . . Well, I wouldn't exactly call him a leader, yeah? Such a status would be incompatible with their profound democratizing spirit, yeah?'

Profound democratizing spirit? Tom withered internally,

recalling the flyblown Entreati 'settlement' that Gloria had hymned the praises of. 'Who is this guy?' he said aloud. 'And how does it affect me?'

'Well, you'll see,' Gloria said enigmatically. 'I felt you oughta know, right?'

Trangaden shimmered towards them, the chlorophyl city at the end of the yellow sand road. Then they were in it, driving down a wide boulevard lined with tall palm trees. There were beautifully maintained flower beds along the dividing strip. Behind pillowy verges stood neat suburban villas, each with its own strip of emerald lawn constantly being strewn with watery diamonds.

They came to a checkpoint manned by Anglo cops – the first time Tom had seen any so employed. They barely glanced at his and Prentice's laissez-passers, being more concerned with establishing that the latter had a prescription for his nicotine gum. Then one of the cops asked them all very politely to get out, and he searched the car thoroughly. In the ashtray he discovered a desiccated butt that must have been there when Tom rented the car, because Prentice always flipped his out the window.

'Ordinarily,' the sergeant said, holding up the evidence bag that contained the butt, 'this would be a misdemeanour, right. But as you folks are new in town I'm gonna let you go with a caution.'

Prentice was fawningly grateful – Tom knew why. Presumably, with Prentice's charges even a misdemeanour could get his bail revoked. Prentice, in the slammer with Anglo truckers coming down off crystal meth' and ravenous for ass. Prentice, stuck in a cell with a haunted Entreati tribesman, too weak to stop it, and forced to watch as the man, crazed by his confinement, cracked open a disposable razor, then drew the thin blade across his throat.

The familiar black tower of a Marriott hauled itself up above the suburban oasis. Gloria said: 'They've gotta excellent mid-week deal, yeah? Room *and* Continental breakfast for thirty-nine bucks.'

Tom smirked, and pulled the SUV into the hotel parking lot.

At reception they checked in, and Tom handed over the two Galil rifles for the hotel armoury. Prentice came struggling through the doors, his shoulder holster slung round his thin neck, a single box of ribaviarin in his scrawny arms. His psoriasis was definitely back; the receptionist noticed it and a wrinkle of disgust bent her lipstick bow.

'I – I say, Tom – Brodzinski, I'm awfully fagged out.' Prentice slumped, wheezing, against the desk. 'You couldn't help me out with the rest of my clobber, could you?'

For hundreds of kilometres Tom had been longing for this: a cool, private space with no flies in it, and a bathroom that didn't stink of shit. But there was no repose to be found in Room 1617. It was a repeat of his experience at the Hilton in the Tontines: the silent valet crushed Tom, the blinds sliced him, the ventilation grilles diced him. He ranged the $39 cage appalled by these things – what were they *for*?

He got his cellphone out and switched it on. There were voice messages; the first was from Adams. 'Ah . . . Brodzinski,' he began hesitantly, and, for the second time, Tom had the impression that he was listening to someone else even as he spoke. 'I think I ought to – not exactly *warn* – but certainly inform you, that your, ah . . . companion may – and I stress *may*, I don't know for certain – have become, ah . . . aware of Mr Lincoln's deteriorating condition. I have no idea if he is in contact with the defen – with . . . well, suffice to say: watch out, Tom. Mind your, ah . . . back.'

The second message was from Martha and the kids, who had put the home phone on conference. Tom could picture them, standing in the living room. The kids were apple-cheeked, snow was falling outside, a too-tall Christmas tree bowed over the mantelpiece and logs crackled in the grate below.

'Hi, Dad!' the kids chorused, while Martha's voice simply stated: 'Tom.' The kids all cried, 'Merry Christmas!' Then Dixie added, 'We're gonna sing you a carol.' They launched into 'Rudolph the Red-nosed Reindeer'. The twins' voices were reedy and off-key, Tommy Junior grunted the words, and Dixie led them by example on to the next line. Martha wasn't singing at all.

Tom unstuck the cellphone from his ear and deleted the message. It would be time to wrap himself in the cosy swag of familial love later on, when the job was done. He picked up his digital camera, then set it down again. The images were consorting in their aluminium cell. Clad in a glittery mail of pixels, Prentice was sidling up on Tom's twins, wheedling them for their little company. While Tommy Junior – who ought to protect them – remained idiotically oblivious: a bulgy teddy bear, the size of a full-grown – yet sexless – man.

Tom could scarcely believe that once upon a time he had cuddled that body; held that hydrocephalic head to his chest and breathed in the warm hay of boy hair, while tenderly exploring the raised scar and wondering what misery had inflicted it. To cuddle Tommy Junior now – what would that be like? He would feel as alien as . . . a Tugganarong cop . . . Football head . . . Flat face . . . Bronze skin . . . Gollyfollyfolly . . .

Tom cupped his genitals through the denim. He thought of masturbating – he hadn't done so in weeks. He thought of Atalaya's breasts pressed against Lincoln's comatose face. He wondered what Gloria was doing in the adjoining room. Could she be toying with herself? Gloria's strange fingers pinching Martha's familiar nipples – pulling the reddening teats up from the pale aureoles. Gloria's unfamiliar hands caressing the curves of the belly he knew so well – travelling down over wrinkles and creases he had watched being scored and stretched by the years. Gloria's interloping thumbs hooking into Martha's panties as the doppelgänger's hips rose . . .

This was as it should be: the two of them separated by concrete, plaster and wallpaper. Exactly the same as any other married couple, unconsciously seeking estrangement to enhance their waning interest.

Suddenly, Tom was no longer interested at all. He got up, picked up his sweat-stained shorts and went into the bathroom. Here he washed them in the avocado-shaped, avocado-coloured sink. Squeezing the froth through the damp cloth, he reached conclusions. Obviously Adams was referring to Prentice, and, just as obviously, he wasn't so much warning Tom as telling him to get on with it.

The idea that Prentice would make a pact with the hated bing-bongs to kill Tom was unthinkable. The Righter of Wrongs, the Swift One – no, that wasn't Prentice at all.

Tom unbuttoned his shirt pocket; the converted tontine was still there. He began to rinse out the shorts, twisting and coiling them into a garrotte. If Prentice were to die, he'd be able to pay off the Intwennyfortee mob, sort out Swai-Phillips's bill and even have some cash left over to give to Gloria's charity. It all made perfectly murderous sense; all he needed now was the opportunity. Tom smiled wryly at the wryly smiling man in the mirror: an average-looking man, an ordinary sort. He'd got into this mess because of an accident that everyone viewed as an intentional act; now he was deliberately intending to do something far worse, then try to make it look like an accident.

There were miniatures of Seagram's and little cans of 7 Up in the minibar. Tom fixed himself a drink – and then a second. He called room service and ordered a club sandwich. He ate this while scanning the contents page of *Songs of the Tayswengo*. He assumed the section on 'Recent Cultural and Social Developments' would cover the charismatic Intwennyfortee leader whom Gloria had spoken of, but this was part of the chunk of pages Tom had cut out in order to hide the $10,000.

Never the less, he continued reading the book, spread out on the bed cover, naked, and investigating his teeth with the toothpick that had pinioned his sandwich. It was dark outside, and Tom had turned the aircon' up to max. So he floated in a lightbox of no-place, while outside the oasis city dissolved into the mirage of night.

'The Tayswengo', Von Sassers were impressing upon Tom, with their usual stolid prose, 'are intensely fearful of public opinion, even deep in the arid wastes of their desert fastness. As we have seen in earlier chapters, this anxiety enforces certain rigid conventions. Lying behind all of them is the Tayswengo fear of *getankka*, or ritual humiliation. To be humiliated – even in ways that might seem trivial to an Anglo – can be a mortal blow to a Tayswengo's fierce sense of dignity.

'Understanding this, even in respect of his own foes, a Tayswengo cannot leave another whom he has so used, and will prefer to watch him die rather than suffer the so-called "shame of the earth" . . .'

It was always the same when he read the Von Sassers: Tom heard the harsh tones of the younger anthropologist's brother – the Chief Prosecutor back in Vance. Each new fact was an accusation, each insight was put forward by the authors purely to show up their readers' ignorance.

Yet it lulled Tom. The heavy tome teetered, then tipped forward on to his bare chest. He slept, then dreamed.

Milford, long since. The streetcar tracks still ran along Main Street, and steam clouds billowed from the foundry at Mason's Avenue and Third Street. This was his sugary childhood: popping Bazooka Joe, slurping Dr Pepper – yet also the early days of his young marriage: keg beer, slap-and-tickle, bashing the books by night for his certification.

'I'm spotting, Tom, I'm spotting . . .' She was sitting on a wicker chair by the open window, a towel rammed between her bare legs, a malevolent Gloria mask clamped on her face. Then she was gone. Gone for weeks. A European tour. He couldn't begrudge her – it was a dreadful experience. He went on studying for his exams and working the day job. Where *had* she gone?

In the dream, Tom was forcibly struck by his own lucidity: a heightened, pinpoint awareness, such as is stimulated by the first heady on-rush of nicotine through the blood. Where had she gone? France, certainly; he remembered a postcard from Arles. And Italy. Then there'd been a few weeks some-where else, staying with family . . . in Belgium? Could it have been? It was such an improbable destination – Tom hadn't paid enough attention . . .

Next, he was lying down on the bedroom floor of the first house they had bought, the frame house in the new Scottsdale development, out towards the reservoir . . . And spring was gusting through the open window, but it remained impossible to pay attention, because Tommy Junior, his adoptive son, was sitting on Tom's chest and punching him in the face with his chubby fists. Pummelling him with a deliberateness that was horribly inappropriate for a one-year-old.

Tom woke up with the fat book crushing him and the sweat chilled on his goose-pimpled skin. He limped to the bathroom and siphoned off the tank full of urine, near-fainting as it hissed into the avocado commode. Then he tottered back into the bedroom, inserted himself between the profane hotel sheets and joined the battle for true oblivion.

14

The fly rubbed its two front legs together: hispid and viscid. Tom couldn't take his eyes off them: back and forth they went, kinking slightly, the motion creating wrists and hands. It wasn't cleaning itself; it was instinctively making a gesture of false humility. 'I'm only a humble fly,' the fly was saying. 'You needn't pay any attention to *me*.'

Yet Tom's attention was unwavering. The fly's six bristled sticky feet were planted on the dash, which, with its terrain of vinyl, mirrored the desert outside the car. The fly's compound eyes – black and shiny – wrapped around its triangular head. Was it Tom's increasingly unbridled imagination, or was there a warty eruption on the insect's mandibles? Mandibles that opened to utter: 'Whoa! Old chap, watch out for that–'

Prentice was cut off as they all rose up to kiss the sky.

At first Tom couldn't figure out what had happened. Then the whine of the whizzing front tyres, and the fact that he was lying on his back, brought home how utter was their reversal. The dumb little SUV – the off-road capabilities of which Tom had always had severe doubts – had tipped backwards and was resting on its tailgate in the sand, while its snub-nosed hood trumpeted engine noises.

In the rear-view Tom saw Prentice supine in a jumble

of cigarette cartons, drug ampoules and baby-bottle nipples. Tom's bad companion peered up at him with an expression of parental dismay.

Gloria broke the spell. 'The water!' she cried. 'And the bloody, fucking fuel!'

She unclipped her seatbelt and struggled out of her seat. Tom did the same, dropping down awkwardly on to the sand, into which a damp patch was spreading from the dented flanks of the incontinent vehicle.

'Squashed,' Tom muttered. 'Squashed like a fly.'

'Move it, you fool!' Gloria screeched, flapping her black robes. 'We gotta get this thing upright!'

They all hung from the auraca bars, and the SUV tipped forward so readily that they only narrowly escaped as all four wheels were reunited with the ground. The water bag was exposed – a popped blister on the silica skin.

Gloria went to the back of the car. 'We're not totally bloody dead, yeah? Amazingly, the gas can is intact.'

'That's a deuced relief,' said Prentice, joining her. He called across to Tom, 'Look here, y'know what's happening, don't you? It was the same on Route 1 before we got to Trangaden. I'd better take over the driving.'

Tom started to argue that it wasn't his fault: after all, they had never driven the SUV off-road before. Then he faltered – an enormous weariness had slumped on top of him. The gelatinous shreds of the previous night's dream still clung to his psyche, making any further protest impossible.

Meekly, he helped Prentice sort out the mess in the trunk. He checked the rifles, but the gas can had protected them. Feeling the fake-wood grain of one of the stocks sent a charge through Tom's hands – this, at least, could vivify him. Silently, Tom climbed into the back seat of the car and took Gloria's egg-shaped parcel in his flaccid arms. Prentice – who, when he was driving, delighted in flouting Gloria's edicts – lit a cigarette and put the car in gear. They drove on.

There were flies in this region of the desert. Flies but no cattle or auraca – and they hadn't seen any moai since before they reached Lake Mulgrene. There were plentiful flies, but nothing that Tom could see for them to feed on. There wasn't even any spiniflex or thorn scrub; only the oceanic swell of the sands, which, as the car strained towards the crest of another dune, were revealed rippling hazily away towards the horizon. Somewhere over there Beelzebub was shooting flies with a needle gun, then feeding their furry bodies to the mutant maggots he hand-reared in underground caverns.

Penetrating his droning reverie, Tom dimly heard a practical back-and-forth between Prentice and Gloria: talk of the route, the diversion they would have to take to Eyre's Pit in order to make good their water deficiency. Gloria studied the map; Prentice changed gear with studious zeal.

Tom interrogated the parcel. What are you and where are you going? What are your intentions, please?

A corner of one of the newspaper sheets had come away from the bundle, and he idly flicked it with a fingernail.

Do I really *want* to do that? Tom considered of each millesimal movement. Is this my sole motivation, to watch the frayed fibres vibrate? If so, can I analyse every link of the chain between my brain and my finger? Can I see the very point where my thought becomes an action? Just suppose that, when the little bit of paper moves, it moves the air, and the air becomes a breeze, and the breeze blows on the sand, and the sand starts to cascade, becoming a landslide that ends up burying somebody. Then what? Is it all down to me? Because maybe I kinda lost sight of that thought as it went along the chain. Maybe I stopped wanting to flick a bit of paper . . . and started wanting to pull . . . a trigger.

The car had stopped in the cleavage between two steeply sloping dunes. The flies were shocked out of their humility for a second, then resumed their supplication on Tom's face.

'Effel,' Gloria said, pointing at the dune.

'What?' Prentice's voice seemed to have dropped half an octave.

'It's a succulent, grows on the back of dunes. The plants are bloody vast – they can put tap roots down hundreds of metres, yeah, and spread for thousands of square clicks.' She got out of the car. 'You could do worse than pull some up, yeah? The bulbs are like little sponges, fulla fluids, yeah? I'm gonna take a piss.'

She strode away over the spur of a dune, wading in its shifting solidity, her black robes riffled by the wind.

Prentice canted round and looked steadily at Tom. 'Honestly, old chap, I wouldn't do it to them if they didn't want me to.'

'You what?'

'I admit, quite freely' – Prentice stroked his smooth, strong jaw – 'that some of them are on the . . . well, let's say, *inexperienced* end of things. Still, you've got to understand how things are for them.'

'Understand what?'

'Come puberty – thirteen, fourteen maybe – they have to go off, leave their mob, lads and lasses both. They stay out in a camp, in the bush. Then, after a month or so, they come back for circumcision–'

'I know all that,' Tom snapped. 'I've read the Von Sassers.'

'Oh, yes, jolly good.' Prentice fluttered a hand, clearly disdaining such book-learning in the light of his own very practical experience. 'Well, then, you'll know what comes next. Bleeding, injured, in dreadful pain, um, *down there*, these poor young things are passed around. First between the makkatas, then all the men in the mob. They're, um, *used* grievously – it's a dreadful shame. Better they be introduced to hunt-the-sausage by someone a little gentler, a chap willing to help them out with a little cash. No one *minds*, Tom – not even their own people.'

'You fucking slime . . .' Tom began, then stopped. There had been a fracture in space and time, or else this confession was only a product of his own fevered imagination. Prentice was at least a hundred yards off, pulling up long tendrils of vegetation from the face of a dune, then squeezing their scrotal bulbs into his parched gash of a mouth. A fly squatted on the headrest of his vacated seat. It was rubbing its front legs together, hispid and viscid, ever so 'umble.

Tom got out of the car. He felt as weak as a half-drowned kitten. His legs, in the thick denim pants, were running with sweat. He tottered to the back of the SUV, unclipped one of the Galils and removed it from its sleeve. He had to rummage in the trunk for the shells, then inserted them into the magazine. Yet with each action his movements became more decisive. This was, he concluded as he rammed the box into the breech, why all along the rifle had felt so instinctively right.

When Tom lifted it to his shoulder and put his eye to the sights, Prentice was in his face. I can touch him, Tom grimaced. Touch him with my metal finger, spreading death ointment. A stray shot – could've been anyone, Gloria . . .

Violent place, the desert – you know that . . . Escaped inmates from Eyre's Pit – crazed smokers . . . Held us up . . .

Tom propped the Galil against the SUV. He began shovelling from the trunk the fresh cartons of cigarettes that Prentice had bought at the last road stop outside Trangaden. He tore a carton open and scattered the fat packs on the sand. Then he stopped and, picking it up, levelled the rifle at Prentice once more.

Get. It. Done. Now. This time Tom Brodzinski could feel the precise weight of every synaptic link in the chain of causality – from intention to action – as it passed between his fingers. His finger tightened on the rifle's trigger. Both cross hairs precisely bisected Prentice's face, slicing it into four equally loathsome sections. Tom felt the first stage of the trigger mechanism fall into place with a click as loud as an explosion. At this range it would be impossible to miss. Death was a twitch away, a butt-flip. Death profoundly and devoutly willed.

Tom froze. He was locked up in his stance – his finger cramped in the trigger guard, the stock grinding against his cheekbone. He could hear his tendons whining with the tension. He was fervently thrusting, with every iota of his will, towards the future – yet unable to breathe, swallow, blink.

It took a long while for Prentice to wade back down the dune. Tom watched, transfixed, as first one of his boots, then the next, lifted from the silvery sand. Prentice's movements were so leisurely that his would-be executioner could hear the individual grains as they trickled over the leather. He was dragging a long net of effel tendrils behind him, trawling the dry sea.

Suddenly, Prentice's face was gone from the sights and

he was standing right beside Tom, his ashtray breath in Tom's nostrils. He carefully – almost tenderly – took the Galil from the spasmed hands and said in a voice that was more parental than any Tom had ever heard before: 'Come on, old chap, we best put this away now. We wouldn't want anything silly to happen, now would we?'

Prentice said nothing of all this to Gloria when she returned; he only drove with the skill and concentration that the desert track demanded of him. Tom hunched in the back seat, quietly whimpering, mourning his potency. The newspaper head stared contemptuously at him, while the flies, forgetting their humility, took disgusting liberties with his eyes and mouth. Little company, indeed.

That night the trio slept out in the desert, cocooned in their swags, their breath condensing in the frozen air. A small white-gold moon sailed along the horizon, leaving a gleaming wake on the dune crests. Tom was a ghost exhaling steam. The lush fruit of other stars was heaped in the bowl of the heavens. In the distance a wild dog yapped.

At dawn, Prentice helped Tom to put on his boots, then served him a breakfast of hot tea and moist porridge. He wielded the little gas stove with diligent economy and, as he passed the vessels, remarked: 'Lucky I had a bottle of mineral water stashed – effel alone wouldn't've got us to Eyre's Pit.'

By mid morning the crescent-shaped dunes were subsiding; then the sands retreated, exposing the desert floor. Ahead, the earth's crust had been playing with itself: fashioning barley sugar twists of basalt and dolloping down lumps of molten rock. In places it had cracked itself open, revealing the mighty vermiculation of subterranean lava tubes.

At noon, when the heat and the flies in the car started to bother even the stoical man of action who was driving, they gained the top of a narrow defile through a range of bulbous, stony hills. Gloria was yakking on about how Eyre, the first Anglo explorer to cross this desert, was deceived by his own 'patriarchal mindset' into believing the Tayswengo to be like himself. Whereas the reality was that the native women had their own powerful traditions, which were taboo to all men.

Martha, Tom reflected, never talked so much. She kept her clapboard mouth – thin, white-lipped – nailed shut. Tom cradled the head for comfort. He stroked the sweat-damp newsprint, and little balls of it came away on his fingers.

'What're you doing?' Gloria rounded on him. 'That contains vital equipment for Erich, yeah? If it's the slightest bit contaminated it'll be bloody useless.'

'Erich? Who's Erich? And whaddya mean, contaminated?' Tom shouted back. He was on the verge of throwing her parcel back in her bossy face, when there was a roaring noise so loud that it undercut the SUV's clanking engine.

'I say, is that the roar of the sands?' Prentice asked. 'It's a sound I've always wanted to hear.'

Now it was his turn. Gloria spat at him: 'No, you bloody drongo, in case you hadn't noticed we left the sands hours ago. That's the roar of the bloody bauxite refinery, the roar of the road-trains carrying the bloody stuff off to the coast, and the roar of all the bloody machinery down the bloody pit!'

A few minutes later they came to a checkpoint. A couple of private security men were manning it. They were Tugga-narong – so bored their faces had gone grey. Like a child who has fallen asleep during a long car journey, Tom woke to find a strange new world stocked with the same old things. He marvelled at the heavily armed guards. How could I have confused these guys with the real natives? They're as out of their element as me.

The guards rousted Prentice out of the car, then Tom and Gloria. Their papers were scrutinized, and Prentice asked if there was any water available. One of the guards told him: 'You'll be able to pick up a water bag at the company store, yeah, no worries.'

Prentice plodded away towards an ersatz massif of slag heaps.

It was too hot to wait in the car, so Tom and Gloria hid from the sun in the shadow of a smoking shelter, where ectoplasm was sucked from dirty-faced miners by powerful ducts. Sitting on the rubble, Tom asked again: 'Who's Erich, and what's that freakin' parcel got to do with him?'

Gloria arranged herself beside him and coyly covered her ankles with the hem of her robe. 'You've known him almost as long as you've known me, yeah?' she said. 'He's one of the authors of that magnificent book you've been struggling with for weeks now.'

'You mean Erich von Sasser, the anthropologist?' Tom pictured the hawkish Chief Prosecutor, pecking at him back in Vance: *If you chance to encounter my brother, Erich* . . . 'Is this some kinduv a set-up?' He struggled to restrain his anger.

'Don't be ridiculous, Tom,' she replied. 'It's common knowledge that the Von Sassers – first father, then son – have been living with the Tayswengo for many, many years now. If you'd made the effort to get through their book, then you'd know how closely involved Erich is with the Intwennyfortee mob.

'Jesus, Tom, I've kids in my bloody orphanages who've seen their parents shot dead over tontines right in front of their eyes. They weren't too traumatized to ask the right questions, but you, you carry on sitting there, yeah? Day after day, letting yourself be dragged along by other people, not even bothering to find out where the hell they're taking you, yeah?'

Another bloody Martha on my back, thought Tom. At least the flies are being kept off by the miners' smoke. He was thirsty; although less, he thought, than he should be, given that he was sweating heavily. Moreover, Tom felt a surge of energy between his shoulders, electrifying his spine. He stretched expansively.

'Did you even hear what I said?' Tom's substitute wife nagged him.

The phone rang in the guards' booth. One of them answered it, spoke for a while, then came over to the shelter.

He addressed Tom: 'It's your man, yeah. Says he's crook, wants you to go down there and give 'im a hand, right.' He went away again.

Tom stood. 'Dragged along by other people, am I?' he said to Gloria. 'We'll see about that.'

He strode off along the road leading to the mine, past DANGER and NO SMOKING signs, then under a banner that advertised: EYRE'S PIT EXTRACTION FACILITY, A DIVISION OF MAES-PEETERS INDUSTRIES. OPERATIONAL DAYS THIS YEAR: 360. ORE EXTRACTED: 75,655 TONNES. INJURIES: 1,309. FATALITIES: 274. The figures, Tom thought, were nothing to brag about.

The background roar gained definition: there was the massed clanking of heavy machinery and the hammering of the engines that powered them, while soaring above it was the bellowing of thousands of voices. Skirting the slag heaps, he made decisively for a stack of Portakabins that he assumed were the mine's offices and stores.

Eyre's Pit yawned open beside him – a massive chomp out of the world, with nibbled edges defended only by a single strand of barbed wire. Tom reeled back and sat down abruptly on the pebbly ground. Then, summoning himself, he crawled forward on hands and knees until he could gaze down into it.

The pit was at least 6,000 feet deep and a mile across: so immense an absence where there ought to be presence that it created its own distortions in natural law. Tom felt as if he were staring into an earthy empyrean – while also experiencing nauseating vertigo. He grabbed handfuls of the ground, lest he be torn down into the subterranean sky.

There were entire weather systems inside the pit: steamy wraiths wrestled with the black clouds spewed by burn-off pipes; turbo-charged thermals carried flocks of grey and black ash high over Tom's head, ashes that seconds before had been floating far below him.

At the very bottom, mechanical diggers tore at the sides of the pit, scouring out ochreous grooves. There were hundreds of these galleries, and thousands of miners stood in them. Some hacked away with pickaxes, while others formed chains to deposit bucket after bucket of ore on to the ever-clanking conveyor belts. Tom was reminded of the leaf-cutter ants on the shrubbery at the Mimosa.

The chthonic pit also created its own warped acoustics, so that while the machinery was muted, the groans of the tormented souls carried up to Tom's ears: the 'hhns' and 'gaars' of the ants hammering at the rock; the 'oofs' and 'aarghs' of their comrades hefting the buckets. Then, very distinctly, a small voice wheedled, 'Gissa ciggie, mate, I'm on smoke-o in ten.'

This wasn't an industrial enterprise at all – it was man-made hell.

Tom found Prentice slumped by the Portakabins, partly resting on the sloppy gonad of a hessian water bag. Tom picked this up by its handle, then helped Prentice to his feet. Together, they limped back to the checkpoint, Prentice leaning heavily on Tom's shoulder.

'Did you see . . .' Prentice croaked, the psoriasis splitting the inflamed skin along his jaw. 'Did you see inside that bally pit, it's . . . it – it shouldn't be permitted.'

'C'mon, Brian,' Tom teased him. 'Get a hold of yourself, man. You wouldn't want a world without aluminium, now would you? There'd be no forks, no planes, no tinfoil to wrap your fags – somebody has to make the sacrifice.'

Tom was still pumped up when he attached the water bag to the back of the SUV. He got in and drove them all away with manly dispatch. But his rejuvenation didn't last for long; by the time they were ten klicks away from the mine, Tom was finding it difficult to keep the car on the track. When they had travelled twenty, he had to pull over and let Prentice take the wheel.

Tom had blundered into a psychic quagmire, and for the next day and a half he floundered there. He was incapable of unzipping his pants without the assistance of his good buddy Brian Prentice. Between feeding sessions – when Prentice coaxed Tom to swallow gritty mouthfuls of oatmeal – and criticism ones – when Gloria hectored him with his ignorance – Tom lay awkwardly along the back seat. The boxes of ribavirin and cartons of cigarettes jabbed his neck, while the desert mutated beyond the filmy windows of the car.

Once they were away from the bled surrounding Eyre's Pit, the track to Ralladayo coiled back into the volcanic badlands. They drove over escarpments of crumbling breccia, then through canyons the cliffs of which were threaded with mineral seams. Rocky outcrops, sand-blasted by the wind, had assumed the most phantasamagoric shapes: cellphones of scoria and obsidian digital cameras rushed towards the car. A Tommy Junior-shaped spire of tufa loomed overhead that had geological indifference etched into its stony features. Tom shuddered and, cleaving to Gloria's parcel, pressed its tattered wrapping to his bristly face. It cooed to him: *soon over . . . soon over . . .*

Towards sunset on the second day the track descended, and the badlands vomited them out. A flock of moai, startled by their approach, rose up from the shade of some gum trees and goosestepped away, their useless pigeon wings flapping. Hypersensitized, all three of them smelled water. Gloria said, 'Nearly there, yeah?'

Then, without warning, they were, jolting between wonky fence posts, past the welcoming sign: YOU ARE ENTERING TAYSWENGO TRIBAL LAND. SMOKING PERMITTED. RESPECT THE ANCESTORS; then a second: RALLADAYO, TWINNED WITH DIMBELENGE, DEMOCRATIC REPUBLIC OF THE CONGO.

Gloria felt moved to hector Tom some more: 'Erich von Sasser has given everything to these people, yeah? They revere him as a – well, perhaps they revere him – and we all do – a little more than we should. But that's no reason for you not to be respectful: he's brought all sorts of benefits to the Intwennyfortee mob, yeah? Fresh water, education, healthcare. Jobs too – and that's had a knock-on effect for the rest of the tribe, who range from here to the Great Dividing Range.

'Most of all, Erich's provided them with a real belief system and a workable social structure, yeah?'

'Given them a real belief system,' Tom rasped, 'what the hell d'you mean?'

But before Gloria could reply, the SUV thrummed over the ties of a wooden bridge and humped into a turning circuit. Prentice hit the brakes – and the flies were upon them, streaming in through the open windows.

In a plantation of widely spaced gum trees stood a long, low building that reminded Tom of the twins' elementary school in Milford. It had the same steel-framed windows and modular construction: one classroom bolted on to the next. A short way off there was a structure in complete contrast, a Tyrolean chalet with elaborately fret-worked doors and shutters, and a wide shallow-pitched roof. The incongruity of this dinky wooden confection was completed by the trio of mismatched men who stood upon its raised veranda, a veranda that was sprinkled with snow-white dust.

Tom shaded his aching eyes. The skeletal figure of Hippolyte von Sasser's brother was unmistakable – they might have been twins. If anything, Erich was even more predatory-looking than the Chief Prosecutor. His skinny legs were emphasized by tight lederhosen; the bib of these and a voluminous cotton shirt provided him with an avian breast. An alpine hat balancing on the sharp summit of his bald head completed the costume. This Von Sasser was a pipe-smoker as well, yet the tiny cumuli that rose from its tall porcelain bowl did little to discourage the flies that preyed on his raptor features.

Standing beside Von Sasser, his naked chest decorated with the medallions of several cameras, camcorders and voice recorders, was Jethro Swai-Phillips; while on the other side of the imposing anthropologist, his bleached teeth showing in a diplomatic rictus, stood the Honorary Consul.

For a long time the two groups stared at one another. Gloria sighed deeply. Prentice detached his hands from the steering wheel with an audible 'tchupp'. Tom hugged Gloria's ovoid parcel. If the three men on the veranda shifted at all, it only confirmed them in their stasis.

Then Swai-Phillips broke the spell. He lunged down the wooden stairs and came towards the SUV. From the way he moved, alone – his head tucked well forward, his arms pumping, his sandalled feet dancing in the dust – Tom saw a complete personality change in the once imposing lawyer. Swai-Phillips was doggy – there was no other word for it. He doggily opened the car door and snuffled Prentice out, then he bounded round and did the same to Gloria. He thrust his moustachioed muzzle into the car, while yapping: 'He's the man, see, Doc von S, yeah, he's the man – c'mon Tommy, man. C'mon and meet him – he's been waiting for you . . . He wants to meet with you . . . tell you stuff, right.'

Swai-Phillips was without his wrap-around shades. His bad eye was gooey, his good one roved crazily. Flies grazed on his furry top lip. 'C'mon, Tommy, yeah. C'mon . . .' He grabbed Tom's hand and bodily hauled him from the back seat. The parcel came too, in the crook of Tom's arm. 'It's here – it's now, it's all times, man,' he blethered, ' 'cause he's the man, the big bloke . . .' His Afro agitated like a wind-blown bush.

Von Sasser stirred. Puffing his pipe, he squeaked down

on high leather boots and came over to where Tom stood, his head reeling. The flies moiled in the deep sockets of Von Sasser's eyes.

'I believe you have something for me, yeah.' Raucous vowels misbehaved on Teutonic bedrock. 'Is that it' – the anthropologist pointed with his pipe stem – 'under your arm?'

Mute, Tom passed him the parcel, and as soon as Von Sasser took it he experienced a fresh surge of vigour; his vision pinged into acuity. Then, over Von Sasser's high shoulder, Tom saw the corrugated-iron humpies of the Intwennyfortee mob. There were at least forty of them, each with its own fenced yard and aircon' unit. They were strung out along an airstrip, at one end of which stood a light aircraft. A wind sock kicked at the sky. A diesel generator hammered in the near-distance. Of the natives themselves there was no sign. Tom stared into the ice-blue eyes. He felt no fear, for once again he was Astande, the Swift One, the Righter of Wrongs.

'Why', Tom demanded, 'was it so important for me to bring this to you? Swai-Phillips or Adams could've, after all; they fucking *flew* here.'

Von Sasser threw back his head and laughed – 'Aha-ha-ha' – then stopped abruptly. He tore away the remaining shreds of newspaper to reveal a translucent pod fastened with two clips. Inside this hermetic egg were five wicked-looking scalpels, formed like embryonic harpoons. 'It's difficult to get hold of such beauties,' he ruminated. 'These are made by Furtwangler Gesellschaft of Leipzig, right. In answer to your very reasonable question, Mr Brodzinski, because of ritual considerations, they had to be brought here together with the individual they're going to be used to operate on.'

Von Sasser darted Prentice a meaningful look. Then, with a 'Hup!', he passed the instrument case sideways to Swai-Phillips, who caught it on the fly and sprinted away towards the school building, still yapping: 'The man, hoo-ee, yeah! He's the man!'

It was an unsettling sight, but Tom focused on what the anthropologist had said. 'Whose ritual considerations?' he queried.

'Why' – Von Sasser smiled – a worrying expression – 'mine, of course.'

Adams had hung back during this exchange. Now he approached them, saying, 'I think all necessary, ah . . . explanations will be forthcoming in good time, Tom. You must be tired after your long journey. I believe you are to be accommodated in the Technical College. Allow me to escort you there. Herr Doktor has invited you – me' – he made an inclusive gesture – 'all of us, to dinner at his house in an hour. I'm sure then he will do us the honour of expounding further.'

But the skeletal anthropologist made no response to this démarche. He swivelled on his heel, squeaked back up the stairs and disappeared into the gingerbread chalet.

The College was derelict but in an anomalous way. Bull dust lay inches deep in the wide corridors, and every classroom had had a rock chucked through its window. There was an air of chronic desuetude – the air musty, drifts of dead flies on all the surfaces. Yet wanton destruction was confined to isolated acts of vandalism: a photocopier broken down into its smallest component parts, steel lockers that had been opened like tin cans, a laptop computer that had been snapped into four equal portions, then neatly stacked on a desk.

Adams allocated one classroom to Tom, the next to Prentice and the one beyond that to Gloria, who hung back, flattening her robe against empty bulletin boards, as the two men ranged along the corridors. Prentice waited outside, smoking against a wall.

Tom pushed four desks together, then unrolled his swag on the capacious platform. He retrieved his shortie suit from the bottom of his battered flight bag. In the boys' washroom he shaved himself as best he could. He had to bend down low to capture sections of his sunburned face in the single remaining shard of mirror.

Back in the classroom he dressed, then got his pocket knife and excised the bundle of currency from its hiding place in *Songs of the Tayswengo*. He had just put it in his jacket pocket when the clanging of an iron bar began reverberating against the sole intact windowpane.

The bar was still being struck when Tom stepped out from the main doors. He had one of the Galil rifles slung over each shoulder; he held the handle of the set of cooking pots in his hand, and as he marched towards Von Sasser's chalet they rattled against his leg. As Tom mounted the stairs to the veranda, Swai-Phillips left off banging and recommenced babbling. 'Yee-ha!' he cried in cowpoke style. 'Howdy, pardner, I see you with my lil' ol' eye.' Seamlessly, he morphed into holy roller. 'You've come to bow down before the *man*, come to reverence the *man*! For he speaks of many things! He has a mul-ti-tude of revelations! And yea! Verily! He speaks the *truth*!'

Tom placed his hand on Swai-Phillips's bare shoulder and, concerned, said, 'What's wrong with you, Jethro?'

Instantly, the lawyer transformed: his clownish moustache and goatee froze on his strong features. From the bunch of accessories dangling from his neck, he hoisted up his wrap-around shades. From behind this reassumed mask he fired at Tom: 'Nothing wrong, Brodzinski. I've gotta job t'do and I'll do it, yeah. I'm the chronicler of this community. I haven't been favoured with the kindest cut, but-that-needn't-concern-you . . .' In his haste to appear sane Swai-Phillips's words leapfrogged crazily: '. . . allnecessarytellyouthat'syoumeimpressionsyourfirst.'

He thrust a voice camera in Tom's face: 'Campthisman-thenjourneyinsurgencykinduvthing,yeah?' Tom pushed it aside, and it was replaced with a camera. Swai-Phillips pumped the shutter, while ranting, 'Importantofpicture AnglojoinsVonSasser'sgreatprojectonthemanspot, right.' Tom placed a hand over the zoom lens and gently pushed it down. Then he sidestepped the lawyer and entered the house.

A long Formica-topped table was set for dinner with Tupper-ware plates, brightly coloured plastic beakers, and plastic knives and forks. The room was far larger than Tom was expecting, and there was enough space for three distinct groups of people to have formed. Standing along the walls were Tayswengo women dressed in black togas and sporting discoid hairstyles. Immediately behind each of the place settings were more Tayswengo women, only these were costumed as Bavarian waitresses in dirndls and aprons embroi-dered with flowers. Their hair had been oiled and twisted into braids. Beyond the table, grouped by a fireplace with pine logs crackling in its grate, were five Anglos: Brian Pren-tice, Gloria Swai-Phillips, Winthrop Adams and Erich von Sasser. Together with them was Vishtar Loman, the doctor from Vance Hospital.

Tom tried to catch Dr Loman's eye, but he was deep in

conversation with the anthropologist. Atalaya Intwennyfortee was among the Tayswengo women, her lissom figure hidden in the heavy black cloth. She too avoided Tom's gaze, instead fidgeting with the hem of her robe.

Seeing that Tom had arrived, Von Sasser broke off and addressed the company: 'Gentlemen, Ms Swai-Phillips, dinner is served.'

Von Sasser took the head of the table, the other Anglos whichever was the nearest seat. The natives hunkered down where they had been standing. The waitresses tripped in and out of the kitchen, depositing dish after dish on the table: sauerkraut, Wiener schnitzel, sausages, boiled potatoes, some sort of broth with dumplings floating in it. The light from the setting sun streamed through the fret-worked shutters, scattering shining heart shapes among the fat-filled platters.

Von Sasser raised his face from his bowl of broth and saw the Galils that Tom had stood by the door. 'Weapons, Mr Brodzinski? We'll have none of those in here. This is a peaceful house.'

'I'm sorry,' Tom said. 'My restitutional payment for Atalaya – for the Intwennyfortee.'

He got up to remove the rifles but was beaten to it by Swai-Phillips, who scampered in the door and snatched them.

'I have the ten thousand here as well.' Tom pulled out the wad of currency from his pocket.

'Really?' Von Sasser sounded underwhelmed. 'Well, Atalaya, no doubt our wayward friends in the north can use the firearms; the cash will go to the common fund. *You* can have the cooking pots.'

She darted forward, took the rifles from Swai-Phillips and slung them expertly on her shoulders. Then she picked up the pots and departed. In the still evening she could be heard rattling off towards the native camp. Swai-Phillips took the cash out of Tom's hands and disappeared into a back room.

Deflated, Tom sat down. This wasn't how it was meant to be. He had anticipated an elaborate ceremony, graceful female dancers, preferably naked, shimmying towards him in a line. Then a tremendous ululation as he was shriven by a prancing makkata. Instead, there was only this odd scene: the Anglos, waited on by fräulein impersonators, stolidly working their way through plate after plate of heavy food, and washing it down with beakers full of dry, light, white wine.

At one point Prentice looked up from his schnitzel and said: 'I've brought the riba—'

Von Sasser cut him off with a wave of his knife. 'No need to speak of that either,' he said. 'Dr Loman will deal with it at the dispensary tomorrow, right.' The anthropologist picked up a chunk of rye bread and tossed it to the Tayswengo women sitting on the floor. One of them deftly caught this and subdivided it among her companions.

Von Sasser acted, Tom thought, more like a monarch than a social scientist. There was ruthless superiority in his every word and gesture to the Tayswengo, while the Anglos were his courtiers: treated with civility, sometimes, yet no more powerful than those who served them.

As night fell, the waitresses brought in old-fashioned brass oil lamps with elegant glass shades. Their soft yellow light welled up, filling the chalet with the distillation of other, more elegant eras. Conversation at the table was general: talk of hunting, rainfall, supply difficulties because of reported bandits along the thousand klicks of track to Trangaden – all matters of predictable importance to an isolated desert community.

Adams, who was seated on Tom's right, was talkative, unbuttoned even. He was also – Tom was amazed to see – smoking. But then all the Anglos were smoking. Smoking before the food was served, smoking between courses and – in the case of Prentice and Von Sasser – even smoking within them, inhaling food and smoke simultaneously. Meanwhile, from the Tayswengo women squatting along the wall, there arose the squelching noise of engwegge mastication.

When the last helping of Apfelstrudel had been served, the cream pot had done its final round, and each of the diners had ladled out a generous dollop, Von Sasser pushed back his chair, relit his pipe and called for 'Schnapps! Coffee! Double-quick time!' The waitresses hurried to do his bidding, their dirndls rusting against the chair backs, their aprons suggestive white patches in the lamplight.

Tom tossed back the first shot of oily schnapps and his glass was immediately refilled. A warm muzziness was creeping over him: there was something almost sexual about this gemütlich scene. Gloria had exchanged her black toga for a high-collared white dress with full skirts, and Tom imagined himself throwing these up and exploring her own suggestive patches.

He – she – *they* had survived, mastered the insurgents, got through the Tontines and traversed the desert. The first reparation payment had been made – so what if there had to be others? Nothing was more terrifying than the unknown. Besides, Tom was properly astande now: he had righted his most egregious wrong. Moreover, even though the tobacco smoke lay as heavily over the table as mustard gas in a trench system, he was also – he exulted – utterly free of smoking, no longer a smoker at all.

He was free to lose himself in the wisps and curls of blue

and grey, to aesthetically appreciate these subtle brush strokes on the glowing canvas of the chalet's interior – a painterly rendition of the very timeless present itself, which, from one second to the next, altered irrevocably. Even Von Sasser had acquired an air of benignity. He was no hawk – but an elegant Audobon heron, his streamlined form garbed in silky, smoky plumage.

Even so, when the anthropologist tapped his pipe stem against his coffee cup, Tom understood that this wasn't only the command for silence; it was also the toastmaster's gavel, signalling the beginning of a long speech – an oration, perhaps – and that the orator himself would tolerate no interruptions.

15

'I am an anthropologist – not an apologist, right.' Amusement sparked around the table, but Von Sasser extinguished it with a foaming hiss of pipe smoke. 'And I view human morality, in the final analysis, yeah, to be a purely instrumental attribute of social systems.'

To illustrate this contention, Von Sasser snapped open the scalpel case that sat beside his place, withdrew one and used it to sever a wispy tumour from the tobacco fug. 'A man's or a woman's very best intentions count for nothing, yeah, when the result of his actions is harm inflicted on another, weaker person.' He levelled the scalpel's tang at Prentice, who quailed, then put it back down.

' "Goodwill",' Von Sasser spat, 'there's a bloody oxymoron for you!' He laughed sardonically, and Prentice, misreading his tone, giggled sycophantically. 'Mind you' – the anthropologist looked in turn at the diplomat, the doctor and the charity worker – 'bad will is equally nonsensical.

'The pols down south, running scared, bleat about winning hearts and minds – and they call this goodwill. Now, setting aside the truth – which is that they'd like to cut out black hearts and wash out black minds – let's tell it like it is: their goodwill is really' – he paused for a beat – 'God will, because all ideas of human free will amount to the same bloody old bullshit. We know, deep in our animal hearts, every last bloody ape of us, that everything we do, we do instinctively. From painting the Sistine-bloody-Chapel to taking a piss, right.

'If you ask me who God is,' Von Sasser declaimed, 'then this is my answer: you see this moth?' All eyes fixed on the moth that fluttered by the lamp. 'Then see its shadow.' The eyes slid to the wall, where the shadow agitated for a moment, then was engulfed by a larger darkness.

'God is dead.' The anthropologist rubbed moth dust on to the tabletop. 'And all ideas of human free will die with him – or her, or it. I put it to you: cannot a man or woman be programmed to perform, like a robot, any action, no matter how contrary to their intentions? You know they can. We're lab' rats, without any Jehova, or Allah, or Yah-bloody-weh sporting the white coat. Only one thing is for deffo: if any given action doesn't contribute to the good, then it is, by definition, a bad action; and that individual – whatever *he* believes' – the anthropologist's hollow eyes bored into Prentice – 'is a bad person.'

A curious thing was happening: as Von Sasser's statements grew more and more adamant, so his tone softened. The raucous vowels were quelled, the harsh consonants churned to Mittel-European slush, the rights and yeahs died a death as the meaningless interrogative swoop flatlined.

'So,' Von Sasser soothed, 'you ask me the next logical question: what is this "good" of which I speak? I'll tell you. The individual, the family, the group, the tribe, the national power bloc – each seeks its own benefit in the exploitation of another individual, family, etcetera, etcetera . . . Who is to be the arbiter, now that the moth's so dusty? A fascist dictator? Or, as in the white parts of this country and the homelands of our visitors, an elective dictatorship – albeit, one voted in by apathy?'

He relit his pipe and had a glass of schnapps. Peering into his own glass, Tom saw a rainbow whorl supported on the clear fluid. He tossed it back, and his eyes swirled with the spectrum. The buttery flames of the oil lamps smeared, then righted. Tom felt keenly the massive void of the desert surrounding them, a cloud chamber, thousands miles wide, across which trailed Von Sasser's vaporous fancies.

'Well, we – *the people*, that is' – he smiled sharkishly – 'have always desired a more perfect union, justice for ourselves, if not our blacker conspecifics. Domestic harmony, mutual defence, common welfare – the blessing of liberty – for now, and for posterity! These are ringing phrases, deffo, but smokescreens all the same.' The scalpel came out again, and he operated on the smoky carcinoma that metastasized from moment to moment.

All but one of the waitresses had joined the women slumped against the wall. Apart from Tom and Prentice, the Anglos were drowsing. During the meal Tom had heard his lawyer's deranged chattering orbiting the room. Swai-Phillips's voice fell from the rafters, flew in through the windows, was even thrown up from beneath the floor: 'He tells it like it is, yeah. He says what he knows, right. Time to lissen up, you bloody buggeraters! Time to foooo–cuss!' But at last he had crept in and huddled together with the tribeswomen.

Von Sasser resumed. 'The more tenderly ambitious the commonwealth in the domestic sphere, the more rapacious its foreign adventuring: the standard of Rome speared in the barbarian heart, Cromwell's mailed fist punched through the Irish kidney, the Belgian neutralists who still run amok here.

Who decides what shall be ordained "the good"? Why, those who have the power – we've always known that.

' "For unto everyone that hath shall be given, and he shall have abundance; but from him that hath not shall be taken away, even that which he hath." The colonized have been taught to turn cheek after cheek, while receiving slap after slap.'

Von Sasser stopped, and Tom wondered where all this was going. Could it be aimed at Prentice, who sat across the table, his face, even in the lamplight, as pale and flat as paper? If so, was it the preamble to even rougher justice than Tom himself had contemplated? The waitress poured him yet another shot, and he injected it into the carburettor of his mouth, where it exploded. Tom gagged, spluttered, headlights bore down on him – from inside his eyes.

Ignoring this, Von Sasser continued: 'Of course, times change, and, rather than admit that he wants to rip off your bauxite, the white man's burden has become the Coke can he made from it, which you're too inconsiderately bloody poor to buy off him. And in their own despotisms of dull, the Anglos abuse their wrinklies, their sickies, their dole bludgers, with a conception of "the good" that reeks of formaldehyde and the morgue. Their utilitarianism – how I bloody despise it! The noble Athenian polis rebuilt – on the never-never – in a general medical ward. Socrates is denied his hemlock and put on a morphine pump – as if that were any kind of death!'

The dirndl rustled by Tom's ear; the shot was poured. Before drinking it Tom had the temerity to interrupt the anthropologist: 'Excuse me, uh, Herr Doktor, but what exactly is in this stuff? It tastes kinda funny.'

'A drop of petrol,' Von Sasser told him. 'Only a drop,

mind. The desert tribes sniff it, and drink it – it's a bloody scourge. I insist on all my guests having a little themselves. As a medical man I can assure you that it'll do you no harm.'

A medical man? Tom was preparing to probe Von Sasser on this, when the anthropologist changed tack: 'When my father arrived here fifty years ago, he found these people' – he gestured towards the bundled-up tribeswomen – 'on the brink of extinction. Winthrop . . . Gloria, Vishtar – they've heard this tale many times before . . .' And besides, Tom thought, they're beyond hearing.

They were: the fastidious Consul had slumped forward on to the table, while both Gloria and Loman were tipped back in their chairs. Gloria's didgeridoo snores were a droning accompaniment to her cousin's continuing jibber: 'He's the man, yeah, the number-one big bloke. Hear him!'

'. . . but I think it's important for newcomers to know the background to what we do here.

'As I say, my father came here as a young anthropologist. He had studied with Mauss, with Lévi-Strauss – he was eager to get into the field and make a name for himself. In those days, well' – Von Sasser dismissed a genie of smoke with a wave – 'the authorities in Capital City had no more shame than they do now. He easily obtained a permit to work among the desert people. Then, when he arrived – in a convoy of bloody Land Rovers! All heavily laden with canvas tents, picks, shovels, all the gear and supplies he needed for six months in the wilderness! Y'know' – he leaned forward, digging at Tom with his pipe stem – 'anthropology itself has always been a kind of imperialism: the noble conquest of authenticity . . . Yes, when he arrived, instead of a state-of-bloody-nature, he discovered that the Belgians had long since rounded up all the able-bodied men, women and even children they could find and put 'em to work in Eyre's Pit. You've seen the pit, yeah?'

'We, uh, swung by on our way here,' Tom said. 'It's . . . I dunno . . . terrifying–'

'Terrifying, exactly! And that's now, when there's mechanization, and Anglo miners are also down there. Then, well, hundreds – thousands – were dying every bloody month. They were being forced, at gunpoint, to dig out the ore with their bare-bloody-hands.

'The mining company had shot all the game – there was nothing for the people to eat. An entire generation – maybe two – had already been decimated. The guvvie encouraged this genocide, cynically offering so-called "development grants" for every native inducted into the certain death of the mine. There were no human-rights monitors in those days, Mr Brodzinski. None of the voyeuristic gear of an international community, which in our own era sees fit to come and see such atrocity exhibitions.

'No, this was the heart of darkness, all right. And my father found out that the indigenous people, most of all, had forgotten its anatomy. The tribal groups – if they'd ever existed to begin with – had been broken up. Isolated mobs of old men and women, and young children, roamed the bled searching for water, feeding on each other's corpses when they fell.

'These people had bugger-all. Nothing. No language but a debased Anglo pidgin, no identity except as concentration camp inmates or escapees. They had no songs, no dances, no myths, no cosmology – not even the most rudimentary creation myths, such as are found among remote islanders. There were no rituals or holy men and women, no leaders – or taboos. These benighted people had only engwegge – and death.'

Von Sasser lapsed into silence and relit his pipe. The drawing of the match flame into the high ceramic bowl cast crazy highlights on Prentice's black button eyes – for he sat in a trance. The other Anglos snored, Swai-Phillips muttered, the Tayswengo squelched their nicotine cuds.

At length, Tom ventured: 'So, uh, if you don't mind my asking, what did your father do?'

'A good question, Mr Brodzinski. I'll tell you what my papa did.' The anthropologist's tone softened still more, to a didactic caress: 'He taught them, that's what he did. He distilled all of his study of other traditional peoples, all of their myths and songs and dances, into a new and viable belief system for these terminally deracinated souls. He devised an entire new vocabulary for them, then grafted this on to the stump that remained where their own language had been amputated. Then he taught this to them as well. Of course, such instruction would've been impossible for a mere rabble, so Papa gave birth to new kinship systems, while inculcating them with the beginnings of a hierarchy.

'This was true bloody fieldwork: meticulous, slow, painstaking – every step of the way profoundly *engaged*. My papa was something that was rare enough in the world in those days, and has now totally disappeared: a heroic man – maybe a superman. He had all the skills he needed. He could hunt, he was a crack shot, he could doctor, speak fluent Homeric Greek, and his embroidery was indistinguishable – to an expert – from that of the most refined Viennese seamstresses. He did the dirndls. Even so, this undertaking tested him to his limits – yet he persisted, for year after year.

'It took him twenty to educate a core group of the natives – the mob that still live here, with me. He called them the

Intwennyfortee mob, for he planned ahead, Papa, way ahead. By 2040 he hoped – *believed* – that this entire land would be under the sway of these new–old traditions. If I'm able to continue the noble work he started for that long, well,' the anthropologist sighed, 'perhaps it will.

'By the time I was finishing school in Bavaria, the process of wider dissemination was under way. From here, emissaries went out to the north and the west. Attracted by these proud pioneers, the tribes now known as the Inssessitti, the Aval and the Entreati coalesced.

'My mother . . .' Von Sasser's voice stretched, then twanged with emotion. 'Fair Elise.' His fingers played a few notes on smoky keys. 'She was a woman of uncommon intelligence – the most refined sensibilities. She supported Papa to the hilt. Not for her the bloody whingeing that women indulge in today, with their drivel about "sexual fulfilment" and "my career", making of their menfolk handmaidens with penises!

'I don't think my parents spent more than three months together in their entire marriage – which lasted over forty years. She understood the enormous significance of her work, she knew her feelings were of no consequence at all, while the knowledge that somewhere, over here, out in the desert, a young girl – or boy – was being infibulated, was fulfilment enough. When Papa sent her instructions, my mother followed them to the letter.

'He decided that I should go to uni, first to read anthropology, while my brother, Hippolyte, came straight out here to law school in Capital City. If either of us had nurtured any other ambitions – to play at poetry or rebellion, travel the world, perhaps – then we made of them mere arrière-pensées. By our late teens *we* already knew our destinies: Hippolyte was to become my father's secret agent, working within the very law itself to undermine the Anglos' hegemony; while I was to join Papa here, once I'd completed my medical training, then qualified as a surgeon.'

'A surgeon?' Tom seized on this inconsistency. 'I thought you said you'd studied anthropology.'

'First with the anthropology!' Von Sasser snapped. 'Then, next, the medicine. Papa had two vital tasks for me – I was, you no doubt realise, the favoured son. First, I was to infiltrate his bold creative synthesis into the relevant academic journals. Those impoverished dullards!' he laughed. 'With their mania for systemization, the ceaseless recycling of mental trash they call knowledge!

'I agitated these people on my father's behalf to obtain the necessary peer evaluations. In due course the academic papers appeared that eventually were assembled and published as *Songs of the Tayswengo*.'

'But . . . you . . .' Tom ventured timorously, 'you, like, made it up?'

'Mr Brodzinski – Tom – there was no *likeness* whatsoever. But then, haven't the sages of the West also, like, made it up? With their World Spirits, their noble savages, their categorical-bloody-imperatives? Isn't what passes for the epitome of Western knowledge no less creative – and, if I may be forgiven a little pride – far less well written than the tales Papa and I spun?

'Ours, Tom, was an *instrumental* morality, not the "will" of a delusory sky god. Papa – he took the long view. In the subsequent years our literary endeavours enabled Hippolyte to campaign for native customary law to be incorporated into the Anglos' civil and penal codes, thus ensuring us – the desert tribes – with a steady stream of income.'

'You mean – my $10,000?'

'Precisely, Tom. It's an elegant form of justice, you might say. Certainly more elegant than theirs, which is what? The crudest calculus of human existence – an abacus of beady little lives slid hither and thither by spiritual accountants.

'What do they want, Tom? Why, you of all people should understand by now. Six billion? Nine? A hundred billion human apes soiling this already fouled little ball of a world – that's their conception of the good. Is that what they – what you – want?'

This was not, Tom thought, a question that demanded an answer – least of all from him. His eyes smarted, and he could feel the oily residue of the last shot of schnapps slick in his gullet.

Now Von Sasser tilted his beak towards Prentice and hawked: 'Then there's the kiddies, eh, Prentice? We mustn't forget them, must we?'

Prentice roused himself. The cigarette between his fingers had burned down. His waxy features had melted in the night-time heat. He was transfixed by Von Sasser, a feeble rodent pinioned by relentless talons. 'Euch, no,' he coughed, 'we mustn't forget them.' Then he jerked upright and pushed his cigarette butt into the crowded ashtray.

A wild dog howled out in the desert, a cry that was taken up by others on all sides of the Tyrolean chalet. Tom thought: perhaps if I open the shutters there will be icing-sugar snow sparkling in the moon-light, a huddle of happy carollers under a cheery lantern. I fucked up in the dunes – but maybe he's gonna give me a second chance?

'The kiddies, yes . . .' the anthropologist mused enigmatically, and set his long pipe down at last. 'They bring us back to where we started.' The hollow eyes sucked in Tom and Prentice's tacit assent. 'We are in complete agreement, then: morality is *always* an instrumental affair. For the Anglo governments those instruments are the survey, the bell curve, and the statistician with no more imagination than this plastic fork.' He held it up and deftly snapped off a single tine. This then became a diminutive baton, with which he conducted his own final remarks.

'I spent a further decade acquiring the necessary skills needed to facilitate Papa's conception of the good.' The little baton swung in the direction of the scalpel case. 'He had reached an impasse. He had cultivated these people, right enough – yet he had failed to harvest them. They still remained passively in the path of the Anglo combines. What was needed were mystics, firebrands and charismatics who would galvanize the embryonic body politic! Papa – who had no formal medical, let alone surgical, training himself – was relying on me to provide them.'

Von Sasser flexed the spillikin between his slim surgeon's fingers; with a scarcely audible 'ping', a bit snapped off and hit the Consul's forehead, then dropped to the tabletop. Adams stirred, groaned, drool looping from his slack mouth.

'And that, gentlemen, is enough for one night.' Von Sasser scraped back his chair and rose. 'We will resume our discussions tomorrow. Very good!'

Discussions, Tom thought, was hardly the right word.

The anthropologist strafed the natives slumped against the wall with the tracer phonemes of his father's made-up language. They got up – penitent, monkish in their black togas – and filed out. Swai-Phillips brought up the rear with his jazzy plainsong – 'Oh, yes! The man, OK, the man – he's said it all, he's done it all. He's the big sharp 'un . . .' which faded into the silvered negative of the starlit desert.

The Anglos' exodus was a more awkward affair. Perversely, Adams, Loman and Gloria all chose to behave as if they had been lapping up their host's every word. They took their time to say their grateful goodbyes, praising Von Sasser's food, his drink, his conversation. But when they stumped across the veranda and stumbled down the steps, their sleep-cramped legs betrayed them.

Tom and Prentice followed on behind.

'Until the morning, then.' Von Sasser bade them goodnight from the top of the stairs. 'There are some things I'd like the two of you, in particular, to see, yeah.'

Tom went to his swag in the classroom of the abandoned school, musing on how it was that, for so long as he was lecturing, Von Sasser's accent was located in the Northern Hemisphere; yet as soon as he ceased, the squawking indigenous vowels came home to roost.

As he undressed, Tom admired the scissoring of his lean heat-tempered limbs. He slid into the canvas pouch and was soon asleep.

In the night, first one of his twins and then the second crawled in with him. Tom buried his face in their downy little backs. Later on, more disturbingly, Dixie joined them. Tom had to manouevre a twin in between them, lest he inadvertently press his groin against her thigh. Finally, shortly before dawn, Tommy Junior came into the classroom. 'Where are you, Dad?' he called out in the anaemic light. 'Where are you?'

Tom wanted to respond to his adoptive son, but he was encumbered by the fleshy straitjacket of his own flesh. He could see Tommy Junior plainly enough, but the boy wasn't helping himself. He refused – or was unable – to remove the hand-held games console from right in front of his eyes, so he bumped into the desks and collided with the walls.

He persisted, though: 'Where are you, Dad? Where are you?' His own wanderings in the maze of furniture replicated those of the tiny avatars on the screen he was fixated by.

Dixie, the succubus, rolled over and grasped Tom's thigh between her own legs. It was she who had the impressive morning erection: a pestle that she ground into him. He screamed, but there was a rock rolled across his mouth, and the cry echoed only in the cave of his skull.

Between sleep and waking, paralysis and flight, myth and the prosaic, the existential and the universal, Tom watched, horrified, as Tommy Junior at last found a way through. He flopped forward on to the swag, and his adoptive siblings splattered into nothing. Now, there was only the overgrown cuckoo child bearing down on Tom, crushing the life out of him.

Tom ungummed his swollen lids. Gloria Swai-Phillips was sitting in a chair by the window. She wore a cotton dressing gown patterned with parrots, and her hair was wet from the shower. The sunlight flared on its damp sheen, but her face was deep in shadow.

'You're gonna haveta get your shit together today, yeah?'

Why, thought Tom, did no one in this country ever prefix their remarks with the verbal foreplay that made it possible for humans to rub along with each other? Every conversation was as brusque as a military briefing. He slid upright in the sweat-lubricated sheath of the swag.

'I know that,' he replied, groping underneath the mattress for the reassurance of the envelope with his tontine in it.

'So long as you know, right?'

She stood and her gown fell open. Her pubis was bare but for a pubescent tuft. The mousetail of a tampon dangled from her cleft. She moved to the door in wifely déshabillé. *I'm spotting, Tom . . . and it's your fault . . .*

As he dressed, Tom reflected on the previous evening. They were all – Adams, Gloria, Loman, the mentally ill Swai-Phillips – in thrall to Von Sasser. It was equally plain that the anthropologist thought little – if anything – of them. However, with Tom himself there was surely a shared bond: the matter of Prentice. Tom may have had a failure of nerve back in the dunes, but Von Sasser's manner towards him suggested that this need not affect the current situation. The important thing was to act. 'I am the Swift One,' Tom said aloud as he splashed brownish water on to his tanned face. 'I am the Righter of Wrongs.'

Breakfast was already under way. Last night's company were seated at a long trestle table that had been set up on the veranda of Von Sasser's chalet. An awning protected them from the fierce sun. There were thermos jugs of milk and coffee, cartons of juice and cereal boxes dotting the tabletop; among these were salvers heaped with the scary fruit that Tom remembered from the Mimosa.

'See, Brian,' he said bumptiously to Prentice, who was nursing his hangover with a can of Coke. 'Aluminium bowls and aluminium cans – even the Intwennyfortee mob can't do without Eyre's Pit, so no need for you to become a bleeding heart after all.'

The long night of serious schnapps-drinking had paradoxically agreed with Tom. It occurred to him, as he munched his Rice Krispies, that this might have been because of the small quantity of gasoline Von Sasser put in the spirit: maybe

I was running on empty after all that damn driving and just needed to refuel.

Ralladayo was less intimidating in full daylight. Tom could recognize that, despite the neglected school building, and the anomaly of Von Sasser's dwelling, it was a proper settlement – in marked contrast to the hell-hole of the Entreati on the shores of Lake Mulgrene. The Tayswengo's humpies were roomy tubular shacks of galvanized iron. There was a shower block, and a number of cinder-block buildings were scattered on the bare ground beneath the overarching eucalyptus, one of which had a red cross painted on its tin roof. Most reassuring – with its air of being a steelily efficient conduit to the outside world – was the hundred-metre-high radio mast planted beside the airstrip.

Tom sprinkled more sugar on his cereal and, as he did so, added generous pinches of salt to the eccentric diatribe that his host had delivered the night before. The kids who were playing in the shade with a tame auraca foal were well fed and dressed in clean clothes. The women doing their laundry in a long trough next to the shower block were chatting merrily. It struck Tom that Von Sasser was probably no different to the other people he had met who dedicated themselves to such development projects: cranky, perhaps, and inclined to take the high moral ground – but this was all understandable, forgivable too, for they had a right to be proud.

If Tom was feeling refreshed, the same could not be said for the other Anglos. Gloria, Adams, Loman – all were subdued. They spoke little, concentrating on rehydrating themselves with reconstituted orange juice. Gloria had a painful-looking pimple in the dimple of her chin. Vishtar Loman's hands shook.

There was no sign of Von Sasser, but Swai-Phillips – who Tom now thought of as the witchy anthropologist's familiar – emerged haltingly from the chalet and joined the party. There was no 'He's the man!' gibbering this morning. The lawyer stumped up to the table dragging his right leg behind him. His right arm hung uselessly by his side, and the right side of his face was palsied: a sluggish lip trailed down from his moustache.

The others ignored Swai-Phillips, while his wrap-around shades pre-emptively deflected Tom's half-formulated remarks. But, watching him struggling with some muesli, Tom realized that yesterday's highly unlawyerly behaviour had – quite as much as today's debility – been the function of an all too common pathology: he must've had a stroke. *He's come out here to stay with his pal while he recovers. I guess he must be under Loman's care . . .*

Dr Loman's presence in Ralladayo did nag at Tom. Was he on a vacation of some kind or doing Peace Corps-type work? More worrying still, did his being here mean that back in Vance Reginald Lincoln the Third was . . . gone altogether?

Pouring himself another cup of coffee from the thermos jug, Tom decided that Gloria had been right back at Eyre's Pit when she hectored him over his passivity; it was high time he got some answers to all these questions. He took an oblique line, by gaining Adams's attention: 'What brings you all the way, er, over here to Ralladayo? Consular business?'

Adams's manner was more diffident than ever, his pauses seemingly taken up by the conduct of a diplomacy he alone could hear. He slowly inclined his Polaroids to Tom: 'Ah . . . not exactly. It's true that Erich's, ah . . . community has the same semi-autonomous status as the other tribal home-lands, and on that basis a consular official might be called on to assist any of our nationals who were, ah . . . over here. But in this case, Tom, it isn't *all* about you.'

Tom bridled. 'I hadn't imagined that for a second.'

'No.' Adams gave a fastidious shudder. 'I've a long-established involvement with the work that Erich does here. I first visited Ralladayo on my drive north after my retirement. His ideas, his, ah . . . vision, his personality too – they all had a profound, ah . . . effect on me.'

Adams was looking old this morning; he was even unshaven: a silvery blaze on his horsy cheeks. Tom speculated on the hiatuses: was Adams rummaging in the lumber room of his own consciousness, trying to find a useful phrase? Or might there be an Entreati sorceress in there with him, composing these near-instant communiqués? If it was the latter, then the Honorary Consul had received all the instruc-tion he currently needed, because he snapped back to his usual full attention: 'Erich is unavoidably detained with important work in the dispensary until lunchtime. However, he asked me if I'd be prepared to show you and Mr Prentice over the place – if you'd like me to, that is?'

'Sure,' Tom said.

Adams seemed relieved. 'That's good. I've been coming back here every year since that first visit. Dry season vacations I spend with my, ah, friends in the hill country – but Christ-mases are always devoted to Ralladayo. It may be something of an exaggeration, but Erich – and the Intwennyfortee mob, of course – have given me a little, ah, job – communications, PR, that kind of thing. It's undemanding work, but my diplomatic experience can be put to, ah, use.'

Tom was going to point out that it had been highly unprofessional of the Consul to withold this information from him when they were back in Vance, but Adams was already on his feet, slurping down the last of his own unsweetened, undiluted coffee.

Prentice had also got up. He stood, looking nauseous and rubbing the raw patch of red skin on his neck. Adams leaned over and whispered something into the wiry cloud surrounding Jethro Swai-Phillips's left ear. Gloria and Vishtar barely glanced up, only muttering 'Bye' as the three men quit the veranda. When Tom looked back, he saw that the lawyer had risen, and was awkwardly dragging his stricken leg back inside.

There were noisy galah birds mucking about in the eucalyptus trees. Their pink plumage and grating cries were faintly uncanny: were they tiny airborne Anglos or had the white interlopers on this island-continent mutated to resemble these plumed natives, whose every song burst ended with a query: 'Kraa-kra-kraa?'

First, Adams took them to see the domestic interior of a Tayswengo humpy. Obediently, Tom chatted to its proud inhabitant, a grave matron in a black toga, whose cheek bulged with engwegge. She pointed out cooking pots similar to the ones Tom had bought in Vance, and mimed the preparation of auraca meat.

Next, they walked to the far end of the airstrip. Hidden behind a low hill was a galvanized-iron barn two storeys high. The noise of machinery — incongruous in this desert fastness — echoed beneath its roof. When they stepped inside, Tom was surprised to find the menfolk who were so conspicuously absent from the rest of Ralladayo. He had assumed they were away hunting; instead, they were hunched over industrial sewing machines and automated cutting equipment.

It was a sweat shop – and the garments the Tayswengo were piecing together were the black togas.

'Initially, they were a bit of a novelty,' Adams explained as they strolled from stage to stage of the manufacturing process. 'Certain, ah, bohemian types down south adopted the togas as, ah, fashion statements. But increasingly the Anglo market is coming to appreciate that these are beautifully designed for outdoor pursuits.'

Tom almost laughed at Adams's attempts to play the marketeer – they were so at odds with his studied circumspection. But then, as they left the baking-hot barn, the Consul threw back at his charges: 'Erich's idea, naturally.'

They doubled back to the airstrip. Here, in a small shack, was the grandly titled 'Communications Center'. Adams pointed out every part of his little fiefdom – the PC, the photocopier machine, even the water cooler – with unaffected enthusiasm. Tom was reminded of a kid with its playhouse. In a small inner room, Adams introduced the men to a new-looking two-way radio. 'Feel free', he said to Tom, 'to call home. We can patch in to the phone network via a, ah, sympathetic operator in Trangaden.'

After that, they proceeded in the direction of a double-sized humpy that stood near by, at the end of the main drag. 'This', Adams said, 'is the orphanage I mentioned to you. It's really only a, ah, marginal undertaking for the community, but Erich is particularly devoted to it . . .' He broke off and eyed his tour party sceptically.

Tom had subsided into tedium as the tour progressed: Amish village, historic town centre, Ralladayo – where was the difference? As for Prentice, he had lagged behind the whole way, fiddling with his cigarettes, and now he was baulking at the orphanage.

'I say, Mr Adams,' he wheedled, 'I expect you'll be heading over to the dispensary after this, yes? If it's no bother, I'll pop back to the College and pick up the ribavirin, then I'll meet you there.'

If Prentice had been requesting permission, he didn't wait to have it granted. He walked away as fast as he could, with his stiff-legged silent-movie gait. Tom waited until he was a way off, then said snidely: 'Surely the ribavirin is needed here, at the orphanage?'

'Don't be, ah, silly,' said the Consul dismissively. 'You can't have barely trained care assistants administering powerful medication like that, can you?'

'Look.' Involuntarily Tom felt the blistered nap of Adam's seersucker sleeve. 'I – I tried my darndest back there, before Eyre's Pit–'

Adams shrugged him off. 'I don't want to hear about it, Tom, it's not relevant any more. Besides, you're forgetting who I am.'

The Consul put an end to the exchange by opening the gate in the wire fence. Tom sighed, then followed Adams's long back into the big humpy.

Inside, there were utilitarian steel cots clustered under the whale-belly curve of the corrugated iron. A few lurid plastic toys were piled on the old piece of carpet that had been laid directly on the earthen floor. Three toddlers were sitting in silence by these injection-moulded bubble cars and sectional toadstools. In the dim light their pupils were dilated, and they emanated bemusement. A young Tayswengo woman sat watching them on a stool; at least, so Tom assumed, for it was completely hidden by the skirts of her toga. She curled forward from this invisible plinth to wave the flies off the little kids with a switch of leaves.

'Is Miss Swai-Phillips here, Olympia?' Adams asked her.

'No.' The girl was as listless as her charges. 'She stopped by, yeah, now she's . . . Oh . . . I dunno.'

A rustling noise coming from one of the cots at the back of the humpy attracted Tom's attention. Not wanting to – although the resistance also seemed to be in the treacly air – he strolled over to it. A baby lay awkwardly curled in a damp skein of sheet. Distractedly – for the mite was a pitiful sight – Tom fixated on the mattress, which had the same covering of frangipani blossoms as the ones at the Mimosa. The child was the size of a one-year-old, but, on examining it more closely, Tom realized it was much older: maybe two or even three – not a baby at all. Its face was wizened, its skin lumpy and scaly – in places, cracked and weeping. The child was of mixed race.

Adams joined Tom.

'Is it . . . AIDS?' Tom asked.

'No' – the Consul was blithe – 'although we do see cases here. The young women go off to the road stops. They get themselves into, ah, difficulties. No, this little guy has psoriasis – Vishtar tells me it's, ah, hereditary.'

As the Polaroids revealed the Consul's eyes, so Tom sought them. 'Is this,' he asked, 'what you wanted me to see?'

Adams wouldn't look at him. 'I never wanted you to *see* anything, Tom,' he snarled sorrowfully. 'I wanted you to *do* something.'

Prentice was sitting waiting for them outside the dispensary. He eyed Tom through the smoky veil he always wore, presumably trying to gauge Tom's reaction to the orphanage visit. Rather than respond to this, Tom extended his hand and helped the pathetic fellow up.

'The dispensary' was a misnomer for this cinder-block building, which was nearly as big as the derelict school. It had an extensive waiting area that was thronged with Tayswengo women holding babies who were sick enough to be there, yet strong enough to bawl about it. There were also a few native men in evidence – and they too exhibited a reassuring lack of stoicism. They had sustained a variety of cuts, bruises and, in one particularly vocal case, a minor gunshot wound. Whenever one of the harassed nurses appeared, the Tayswengo all pounced on him or her, proffering the afflicted portion – or baby – while pleading to be seen by the doctor.

They all got the same answer: 'Dr Loman is busy assisting the surgeon today – you all know that, yeah.'

Prentice handed over his boxes of ribavirin to one of these nurses, who whisked them off without comment. The making of his reparations had been as anticlimactic as Tom's. 'Wampum,' Adams muttered, then he led them down the corridor that ran the length of the building, pointing out the treatment rooms to one side and the wards to the other.

The dispensary, Tom thought, had been built and equipped perhaps two decades before as a small state-of-the-art hospital. Some time during the intervening years, it had begun to be severely neglected. Now the floors were unwashed – stained with blood, and worse. Perished rubber hoses dangled from oxygen cylinders, while used hypodermic syringes lay in the drifts of dead leaves that had blown in through the warped un-shuttable windows. In one ward there was a waist-high heap of soiled gauze pads; in a second, a broken pipe leaked bilious water on to the cracked tiles. The aircon' wasn't working, and the flies – unlike the medical staff – were in constant attendance.

They reached the end of the corridor and stood there,

looking through the dirty window which faced the airstrip. On the far side of this some young Tayswengo men were breaking in an auraca bull. They circled the enraged animal, chucking dust and pebbles in its supercilious face. When, inevitably, it lunged at one them with its tiny head, the youth leaped up and neatly pincered its long neck with his legs. They both crashed to the ground and writhed there, their spasmodic movements compellingly pornographic. Tom looked away.

'The scalpels I brought,' he said to Adams. 'They were for these operations, then?'

'That's right.'

'And the surgeon is—'.

'Erich – Herr Doktor von Sasser, you must've guessed that. I address him as "Herr Doktor" because he holds a medical degree. His father, Otto, had a Ph.D. in anthropology, but Erich's own contribution to *Songs*, well, academics can be incredibly, ah, narrow-minded.'

'He has to do lots of these operations?' Tom persisted, while out of the corner of his eye he noticed Prentice, up against the wall, arms and legs crossed defensively.

'As many as he possibly can,' Adams answered. 'These are relatively straightforward procedures, Tom, not too invasive. The patients can, in most cases, leave the dispensary the same day. At a modern hospital – say in Trangaden – they would be entirely routine; the costs are, ah, minimal. Out here, with the particular problems a community like this faces, they're absolutely essential. That's why Erich has devoted himself to them so, ah, single-mindedly.'

Lunch was on the veranda. Tom was hungry. He was finally getting accustomed to the local Anglos' proclivity for stuffing themselves with wads of hot food in the very baking oven of midday. At Von Sasser's the culinary accent remained resolutely Germanic: ham hocks stood in the top of a double-boiler, paddling in apple sauce. A fresh hayrick of sauerkraut had been pitch-forked, steaming, on to an aluminium platter. The potato was mashed today – and piping hot.

Gloria joined the three men at the table and poured herself a beaker of lemonade. At breakfast she had been in her black toga; now she was wearing the same cotton dress she'd had on when Tom first encountered her at the Swai-Phillips compound. It did flattering things to her bust – which Tom admired while eating. There was no sign of her crazy cousin.

Loman and Von Sasser came ambling through the eucalyptus grove from the direction of the dispensary. They climbed on to the veranda and helped themselves to large plates of pig, cabbage and carb'. Neither man had troubled to take off his scrubs, but only undone the tapes at the back, so that the green garments gaped open. Both were wearing short pants, and when they came to the table, the blotches of blood on their chests gave them the creepy – yet comic – appearance of patients who had escaped the knife in order to enjoy a hearty meal.

16

The others had finished their own food, yet no one made to leave the table; they stayed to watch a bravura performance by the men in theatre costumes. Von Sasser and Loman steadily tunnelled their way through their food mountains, pausing only to call for salt, water or beer. The anthropologist, predictably, drank his beer from a stein half a yard high. Overhead, the awning rat-a-tat-tatted in the rising sirocco. In his blood-stained scrubs, the skeletal Von Sasser was a giant praying mantis devouring its mate.

Tearing his eyes from the grisly spectacle, Tom saw the little SUV standing where Prentice had parked it the evening before. Some Tayswengo kids were sitting inside. The one in the driver's seat was wrestling the wheel; the others were aiming pretend cameras, miming Anglos on vacation. They captured the occupants of the veranda in their invisible boxes, then turned them on the tame auraca grazing the sparse grass in the paddock.

With the air of men who had for a long time been working as a team, Von Sasser and Loman finished their plates at the same time, then pushed them aside. Von Sasser called for coffee, and the Tayswengo waitress swished away in her humiliating dirndl. Von Sasser produced his long-stemmed pipe. He filled it with tobacco from a leather pouch, then lit it. The assembled company were all riveted by this matinée, but Tom was now convinced that Von Sasser's spoken lines were intended for him – and Prentice – alone.

'How does it all end?' was how the anthropologist began today's homily. 'Isn't that the question that torments the Anglo – bothers him like a fly in his eye? The Third Act problem, the thrilling climax . . . then the drowsy resolution. Yes, yes, the Anglos' lust for this is blatantly bloody sexual – they're not like the true natives of this great land. Those poor bastards have had it hammered into them for so long that they're shit, that they just sit on their arses while the flies eat them! Especially the children – the poor bloody kids. It's almost as if,' – he shifted to confront Prentice – 'they're born with this fatalism.'

Von Sasser stopped. Prentice no longer had the energy to even quail beneath his raptor's stare: his psoriasis was back with a vengeance; the badlands of cracked and humped skin had spread right up on to his face. 'You!' Von Sasser spat. 'You can do whatever you like to the poor bloody kids . . . except' – the shotgun eyes came back to Tom – 'tell them stories with clap-happy bloody endings!'

He took a long draw on his pipe, then resumed more evenly: 'You're probably wondering why the Technical College is such a dump, when the rest of Ralladayo – thanks, in no small part, to those present' – he nodded to Adams, Loman and Gloria in turn – 'who have given *their* hearts and bloody minds to the community – is ticking over pretty damn efficiently.'

'Uh, yeah, I guess I was kinda intrigued,' Tom said lamely.

'My father, Otto, is buried at Gethsemane Springs, forty clicks east of here, yeah, on the track to the coast. The Technical College was his own brainchild, right. He laboured for it – strived to make it a reality. He even went south, put on dress kit and gave after-dinner bloody speeches to raise money for it from Anglo fat cats, who – once his back was turned – went back to cursing the bloody bing-bongs.'

With forensic fingers, Von Sasser picked up his tiny espresso cup and took a sip. He smacked his lips with an 'ah', then went on. 'Be that as it bloody may, when my dad was dying he made me promise that I'd sack the Anglo teachers and let the College decay back into the bloody dust.

' "Erich," he said. "It doesn't matter whether our people study the sciences, the arts, maths or languages – the result is the same: it makes them lust for an end; that, Erich, is the true leitmotif of Western civilization, and it's the very one we've come here to rid them of. Don't let our people fall victim to the narrative fallacy of the Anglos!"

' 'Course, I'm not claiming that those were his actual last words – that'd be a bit bloody rich! But he was dead in days, and I respected his final wish – why wouldn't I? By then I'd already begun the work he'd had me trained for; it's true, the first results were not exactly, er . . . conclusive' – Tom noted the hesitation – 'but in spite of that we were both confident we'd found a way forward, so that these people' – he threw an arm wide to encompass all of Ralladayo – 'would never, ever waste their lives waiting for the bloody end. Sitting in the dark and smelly multiplex of their minds, gagging to know how their lives would turn out, while completely neglecting to bloody live them!'

There was silence for a few seconds, then Tom heard an electronic whirr. Its source was Swai-Phillips: the lawyer was hovering at the corner of the chalet, a camcorder held to his good eye. He switched it off and let it fall by its lanyard on to his bare chest. He approached the table, walking normally and banging his big, square hands together with slow, resounding claps. He stopped, bowed low, then gravely intoned: 'Here endeth the second lesson.'

Von Sasser ignored him, instead rattling off a series of commands: 'Winnie, take Brodzinski here over to the comms shack; he'll be needing to call his people. Brodzinski, you take your man Prentice along with – you wanna keep a close eye on that one. Vishtar and I've got more bloody carving to get on with s'arvo.' He rose. 'Till sundown, then!' And, with Dr Loman in his train, swept off the veranda and back through the gum trees towards the dispensary.

Adams came to life. ' 'C'mon,' he said to Tom. 'Erich's right; the early afternoon's the best time to patch across.'

Tom was about to protest at this assumption that he even *wanted* to call Milford, but something in Adams's tone prevented him. This wasn't to do with his calling home; it was about Prentice not being allowed to. Prentice, who was now a pitiful sight: a pile of dirty dude's clothes slung over a seat back. Not one for his good lady's album.

Tom, with an access of hypocritical pity, helped him to his feet and said, 'D'you want me to get some ointment for you? I don't mind putting it on . . .'

'Don't bother, old chap,' Prentice muttered. 'Let's go make your call.' Then he gave the lopsided smile of a beaten cur, and added: 'Not long now.'

In the comms shack Adams adopted the persona of a radio ham. He put on headphones – or 'cans', as he pretentiously referred to them – and played with the switches and dials on the transmitter. Prentice dumped his bundle of a body form down on an upturned crate, while Tom took a swivel chair beside Adam's. The ether whistled and warbled, then, once the appliance was humming nicely to itself, Adams took his headphones off.

'There's some news you, ah . . . might like to tell the folks back home,' he said. 'It's, ah . . . concerning Mr Lincoln.'

Tom marvelled at how such a heavy lunch could rise up his gorge so easily: here it came, another hateful display of amateur dramatics by the Queen Ham. 'What?' Tom yelped. 'Has the old man died?'

'On the contrary.' Adams chose his words as fastidiously as a spinster selecting Scrabble tiles. 'Dr Loman spoke with one of his colleagues in Vance this morning. It would appear that Mr Lincoln has, regained, ah . . . consciousness. It's an astonishing case – the infection is, ah . . . subsiding. It's early days, but the feeling is that he may well make a full, ah . . . recovery. Of course, the consequences for your own, ah . . . situation – especially now an initial reparation payment has been made – can be nothing but, ah . . .' – the longest pause, dry-stick fingers fondling the slack vocab' bag – '. . . good.'

And with that Adams resumed his other communication duties, rapping out a call sign into the mic' once, twice, a third time. Between each announcement his equine face quivered with the strain of listening. He pointed to some other headphones, and Tom put them on. He was in time to hear the radio operator in Trangaden say: '. . . receiving you RAL20–40. You're faint – but you're there, yeah. How can I help ya today, Winnie? Over.'

Adams read out the Brodzinskis' home phone number and asked to be patched through. The sounds of the Trangaden man dialling were suddenly very loud: each digit a klaxon beep, then there came the leonine purring of the ringing phone. 'WE'LL LEAVE YOU TO IT,' Adams mouthed exaggeratedly, and Tom revolved to see him hoik Prentice unceremoniously to his feet and lead him out the door.

Tom pressed the headphones firmly against his ears, and the purring lion padded into his head: 'pprrrupp-prrrup; pprrrupp-prrrup; pprr–' Then stopped. 'Martha Lambert speaking,' said Martha's voice. Hearing it, Tom allowed himself to fully accept what Prentice had said: it wasn't long, now. Long before he would be back in Milford; long before he would be able to mend this crazy breach between them; long before he would be at home with her – and the kids.

He pushed his mouth into the mic's steel mesh: 'Martha, it's me, Tom, can you hear me, honey?' The etheric birds had been netted; every one of his words sounded as clear as a bell that resonated with cravenly hopeful expectation.

'Tom, is that you?'

'Yes, yes, I'm in Ralladayo, where Atalaya's – Mrs Lincoln's – people live. Lissen.' He couldn't stop himself gabbling. 'There's fantastic news – it's incredible. The old man – Mr Lincoln – he's, he's making a recovery, and I've, I've made the, like, restitution I hadta, so, it looks as if – I mean, I can't be certain – but it looks like I might be home soon.' He stopped. There was no sense of the half-world that separated them, only a voracious nullity, sucking on his ears with foam-padded lips.

'That's . . . excellent news, Tom . . .' Had her voice ever sounded more like *her*? More completely *Martha*: each snicked syllable and sharply enunciated consonant a tight brush stroke, vividly describing her slim body – so very dear, so very familiar, so utterly strange. 'I'm so happy for you . . .' There was a small yellow-tinted perspex window in front of the table the transmitter sat on. As he listened to his wife, Tom Brodzinski stared at this acrylic of an alien land: the streaks

330

of the gum trees' trunks, the pointillism of their foliage, the brown splodge of a humpy in the mid-distance, the painterly distortions of the sun's own strokes. 'It'll be good to have you back home, sometimes I think you don't realize . . .' Looking like Death, a figure in a black native toga walked into the picture from the left. '. . . how much the kids've . . .' It turned towards the comms shack, and in the shadow of the hood bloomed a pale face. It was Gloria Swai-Phillips, talking on a cellphone. '. . . missed you . . .' Martha's words, which had pulsed along wires, been thrown into space, bounced off a satellite, then cast back down to earth, were now dubbed precisely on to Gloria's lips. Tom registered this, because Gloria completed Martha's sentence: '. . . especially Tommy Junior.' Then she looked through the window straight at him and gave him a playful little wave.

Hispid and viscid: the sweat-damp hairs on Tom's nape lifted and stretched themselves, each chafing against its neighbour. Hispid and viscid: Beelzebub's proboscis was nuzzling at the sweet nooks and crannies of Tom's cerebrum. It tickled.

Tom found himself outside without any awareness of having torn off headphones or slammed through doors. He was temporarily blinded – than he groped his way, hands on sunbeams, to where Gloria stood in her sack. The race was over; she snapped the cellphone shut and disappeared it in the folds of her robe.

'You – she . . . W–What? W–What have you done? Are you – have you been fuckin' copying my wife?' He spluttered his childish accusation.

Gloria looked him up and down matter-of-factly. 'If you want me to be your wife, Tom, then that's fine, yeah?'

'I – I dunno . . . Have you been talking – on the phone, to me?' He ranged back in time to the night before the prelim' hearing in Vance, and the rhythmic jingling trudge he had heard when he held his own cellphone to his ear. The Martha voice impersonating Gloria. What was it she – they – had said: *you've gotta say these things to keep 'em happy, yeah? I mean, their pathetic little egos require it, yeah?*

But that was then.

Gloria Swai-Phillips led Tom back towards the Technical College by the arm. She guided him between the gum trees, holding him firmly in case he should trip on their roots. As they walked, she gave him an explanation – at least, that's how she saw it.

'Squolly – Commander Squoddoloppolollou – he read your rights to you when you were arrested, right?'

'Rights?' Tom murmured. All he remembered was Swai-Phillips ridiculing him for even raising the matter.

'What I mean is, Squolly would've told you how the police were gonna investigate you, yeah? How they were gonna tail you, check out what your intentions were, yeah? Figure out what kinduv a guy you are.'

'And those were my *rights*?'

'So far as the Tugganarong and Anglo communities here are concerned, yeah, those are your rights. The thing is, Tom' – still holding his arm, Gloria drew Tom round so that he was facing her – 'Squolly's men've been tailing you for a long time now – years in fact, yeah? Y'see, when you were a young bloke, Tom, you kinduv took your eye off the ball.'

'Eye off the ball?'

They had reached the low wall that bounded the Technical College. Tom's eye – still off the ball – rolled over crab grass, cracked earth, the sawn-off stumps of a mulga thicket. The thrift-shop donation that was Prentice was piled on top of the wall, smoking. There was something different about this small prospect – a change that bothered Tom. He fixated on this, instead of listening to the harpy.

'Not acting – y'know, that can reveal a lot concerning a bloke's intentions. After her miscarriage, when Martha came to visit us in Liège, then, when she came back, and a few months later you guys adopted Tommy Junior, well, you didn't act: you never asked the questions a conscientious man – a man with good intentions – would've asked, yeah?'

It was the SUV – that was the difference. It was gone. Tom scrutinized the patch of dirt where the little vehicle had been standing only half an hour before. Why were there no tyre tracks to show that it had been driven away?

'But you're not a conscientious man, are you Tom? You're the kinduv man who feasts his eyes on a young black girl's tits, then wants to screw his wife with the hard-on, aren't cha?'

There was *something* where the SUV had been, and bizarrely it was car shaped. Ignoring Gloria, Tom moved towards it. He felt a perverse affection for the SUV, whatever its design weaknesses; it had managed to carry him all this way.

'You're the kinduv man who pays no attention to a woman at all unless she's a sexual-bloody-prospect.' The ghastly crow came pecking after him. 'Winthrop's Handrey women friends? They're only fuck-buddies, fat gals beneath your contempt – same goes for my cousin Betsy, who you never so much as said "hi" to. Daphne Hufferman saves your life, but she has to ride in the bloody back like a kid.'

The object that had replaced the SUV *was* a car; or, rather, it was a 1:10 scale model of one. Tom squatted down and picked up the Gandaro spirit wagon. He ran his hand over the artfully bent and hammered sides of the tiny MPV, marvelling again at the skill with which it had been soldered together out of tin cans.

Glancing up, Tom saw that Prentice was as intrigued by the spirit wagon as he was; although, of course, Prentice could have no idea what an astonishing coincidence it was to find it here, thousands of miles from where Tom had first seen the cult object.

'I wonder what you think Atalaya Intwennyfortee *feels* about her husband – a respected elder of this community – being so viciously bloody assaulted, yeah? Then lying for all these weeks on the brink of bloody death? You sure as hell don't *know*, Tom, 'cause you've never once taken the time to talk to her, despite having big mobs of bloody chances, right?' *I'm spotting, Tom . . . I'm spotting . . .*

Tom set the spirit wagon down on the wall next to Prentice, who, somehow managing to summon his famed national reserve, gave him a look that implied – at one and the same time – that he too was withering under Gloria's onslaught, while never the less being too polite to have heard a single word of it. He touched his waxy finger to the flying vee of the spirit wagon's spoiler.

'It's bloody incredible how you've behaved since you flew in, Tom, when all Martha was ever trying to do was show the kid his roots, and get you to face up to your bloody responsibilities as his father!'

This penetrated – and Prentice flinched as if it had been aimed at him. Tom thought: bloody this, bloody that, bloody every-bloody-thing. *I'm spotting, Tom . . . I'm spotting . . . and it's your fault.*

He rounded on his Jesuitical tormentor. 'Are you telling me' – Tom was amazed by the control he was exhibiting; he must still be astande – 'that I, we – the whole damn family – weren't here for a vacation?'

Squolly was sitting in the deliciously air-conditioned interview room. Tom was opposite him, sipping a soda, the bubbles fizzing on his culpable tongue. Attached to the shiny peak of the squat Tugganarong's complicated cap was a Tommy Junior mask. It fitted perfectly.

But Gloria refused to be interviewed. 'What did Erich say to you at lunch, Tom? You Anglos are always the bloody same; you're as happy as a pig in shit – and this is shit, Tom, believe it – so long as there's an ending to the sorry bloody tale. Well, I'm happy to provide you with one, Tom, and like I said, I'm happy to be your wife too. You wanna know why? Aw, I'll save you the bloody bother of asking, yeah? It's 'cause, exactly like Martha, I'm gonna leave you.'

Tom was still righteously empowered, yet finding it hard work to maintain what he knew to be the correct perspective. Instead of looking out through his own eyes, he kept seeing the three of them from off to one side and slightly above.

It was a stagy scene: the two men, identically costumed in jeans, bush shirts and elastic-sided boots, being berated by the one-woman Greek chorus. What was needed, Tom thought, was an entrance by another character, otherwise this could go on for ever, strophe and antistrophe, until the audience got bored and went home.

Providentially, Von Sasser materialized. The anthropologist stepped out from behind the derelict Technical College. He had his bunched-up scrubs stuffed under one of his arms, while in his free hand he held Tom's roach motel. Coming up to them he said: 'Some of the kids have taken that SUV of yours off to be cleaned. They found this wedged under one of the seats – yours, is it?' He held the roach motel out to Tom, who took it, stuttering, 'Y – yes, it is.'

'Walk with me, Tom,' Von Sasser said, draping his bony arm over Tom's shoulder. 'There's some stuff we need to talk about, yeah.'

Apart from the 'yeah', it was exactly the same phrase that Tom's own father had used when he wanted to have a man-to-man chat with his son. Momentarily gulled into thinking himself back with Mitch Brodzinski, swishing through the fall leaves that lay deep on the farm track out to Hermansburg, Tom went respectfully along.

Von Sasser unhitched the gate to the auraca paddock and guided him through. They were halfway across before the older man began to speak. 'I've been hacking away since 8 a.m., and I can tellya, I'm tuckered out. Still, at the end of a stressful day in the oppo theatre, a stroll out here never fails to relax me. 'Course, it's too bloody far to go the whole way, but from the top of this rise we'll be able to see Gethsemane Springs in the distance.'

The familiar, leaden inanition was creeping up Tom's legs: his arteries were sucking up sand, his veins were choking with dust. So he said nothing, concentrating only on forcing one clod of a foot in front of the other.

'The mobs way out in the desert – the Aval, the Inssessitti, the Entreati – even some of the hill mobs and the feral Tuggies squatting on the north-west coast – they all send their cases down to me, here in Ralladayo.' Von Sasser talked as he walked, with an easy, loping rhythm.

'We-ell, some of 'em are A-1 bad fellers – murderers, kiddie-fiddlers, rapists – you name it. Others, we-ell.' He laughed shortly. 'I s'pose in your part of the world people'd say they were minor offenders – but that's not how we see things here. You've gotta remember, right, for the Tayswengo – for me too – nothing happens by accident.'

On they went up the hill. They reached the next fence, and Von Sasser pulled the top wire up so that Tom could drag himself beneath it. The roach motel was a deadweight, its sharp corners cutting into his hand. The grass had straggled away, and, as they went on, Tom's footfalls scraped the bare earth. The sun slammed into his head – he regretted having left his hat behind.

'Ho-hum,' Von Sasser sighed. 'I've gotta say, Tom, the primary purpose of this procedure was never intended to be behaviour modification, right. It was more or less by chance that we found out how well it worked.'

'So . . . you – you, like, castrate them?' Tom managed to ask. And once the words were out, they became incontrovertible: this was where the makkata's blade had been tending, this was why Prentice's white thigh had remained unmarked.

But Von Sasser was consumed by merriment. He swept off his odd little Tyrolean hat and beat it against his leather-clad thigh.

'Ha, ha, ha! Oh, no. No – no. What the hell would we want to cut their balls off for? We're not bloody *vets*, right. Papa didn't want big mobs of bloody eunuchs roaming the desert.'

'But I thought . . . Prentice – the kids–?'

'Didn't you listen to what I said last night?' Von Sasser admonished. 'Papa invented these people's culture himself, ex nihilo – from bloody nothing. He knew what they needed: mystics, firebrands, charismatic makkatas who'd take the Anglos by the bloody neck and shake 'em till their brains rattled!'

They reached the top of the rise, and Von Sasser urged Tom down on to a flat rock. He didn't take much persuasion. The sun was plunging, and Tom's remaining energy reserves were falling with it. Straight ahead there was a vertical escarpment parted by a wide gorge; through this could be seen the drained sea bed of the desert floor, a tired expanse of tide-ground hills and wave-scoured depressions.

The anthropologist got out his pipe and began to fill it. ' 'Course,' he meditated, 'I don't mean that literally, but the trouble with Anglo civilization is that it's a left-brain business, all to do with order, systematization, push-button-bloody-A. Papa understood this, as well as knowing enough anatomy – and anthropology – to see the solution. He became the first neuro-anthropologist the world has ever seen, and I' – he inflated with pride – 'am the bloody second.' He paused to light his pipe, his limbs twisting into a protective cage for the wavering flame.

'The corpus callosum – that's the bloody enemy, Tom, it's a tough little bugger.' He swished his pipe stem in the gloom, slicing grey matter. 'Information-bloody-super-highway of the human brain, that's what it is, yeah. Same as the internet, the corpus callosum fuses together two hemispheres, the right and the left. Movement, speech, sensation, visual recognition – they dominate, yeah, they're the *Anglos* of the brain. But over on the right, well, that's where dreams are, that's where the spirits find their voice, and that's where humans have the imagination to actually hear what they're bloody saying!

'Look.' The neuro-anthropologist put an avuncular hand on Tom's leg. 'I'll grant you, we may've got our act together now, but quite a few of the early oppos . . .' *The boy's hair with its scent of warm hay. The dreadful scar seaming the back of his sweet, small head.* 'But even these, er, failures, have turned out to be pretty useful. Obviously, with better equipment – scanners, lasers, that kinda thing – it'd be a whole heap easier, yeah.' *It wasn't as if he was stupid – he was in the same grade as other kids his age, he was just a bit . . . cut off.* 'We either go straight down through the longitudinal fissure . . .' *The white trough of a scar that bisected the old wino's grizzled head from nape to crown.* '. . . or angle our way in between the parietal lobe and the parieto-occipital salens. 'Course, wherever we make the incision, we stretch and suture the scalp so the scar won't be below the hairline.' *Adams, was bent over the three-panelled mirror on the vanity table, examining the back of his head.* 'The important thing to hold on to, Tom' – for once Von Sasser had a kindly twinkle in his deep-set eyes – 'is this: it isn't painful; it doesn't hurt.'

The foody perfume of pipe smoke braided with the clean-smelling desert breeze; the sunset, as ever, was spectacular: a ruddy blush rushing up the face of the sky. Tom found his external voice. 'B – but a little kid, a baby?'

'Like I say, mate, there were some balls–ups, but b'lieve me, by far the majority of those early oppos were done on patients that already had some, y'know, neuroses – or even actual brain damage. It wasn't like we were messing with something in working order, right.'

Tom, dodging dream fists, levering the weight off his chest, searched for the sympathy he knew he didn't have. Yet if only he could find it, he was sure the appropriate outrage would be there too.

'He – Tommy, my, uh, son. Y'know he isn't . . .' He dredged up one of Martha's weary pronouncements: 'Adequately socialized.'

Von Sasser snorted. 'Tell me about it, Tom. Those boys

up in the north aren't adequately-bloody-socialized either! Some of 'em can be pretty vicious – we aren't talking clean-kills here, yeah. There's rape – torture even. Lissen, I'm not saying I condone such behaviour, but you've gotta offset it against the positive impact the insurgency has on the left-brain hegemony: their infrastructure, mines, their financial-bloody-services, their drinks industry, and especially the Tuggy foot soldiers who do the Anglos' dirty work for 'em.

'Thing is' – the neuro-anthropologist brought his sharp knees up under his sharper chin, a surprisingly adolescent posture for a middle-aged man – 'say they don't, I dunno, *function* that well, at the very least they can advance the desertification programme. I mean, y'don't haveta be a makkata to string a length of chain between a couple of utes, now do you?'

Despite the impression that he and Von Sasser were speaking wildly at cross purposes, Tom persisted: 'If – if you can't be, uh, can't know, definitely, what the results are gonna be, then how does this, like, operation, work to, y'know, modify behaviour? I mean, it seems to me that in this case, uh, castration might be, I dunno, more effective.'

Von Sasser sighed, a long exhalation of waste-compassion: 'Ye-es, it's true, the human brain is – viewed with the Western medicalized paradigm – a complex system; it seems always to be striving to reach homeostasis. Even with all connection between them severed, left-brain functions can be re-established on the right, and vice versa. Still, these are only minor drawbacks, while the benefits can be astonishing, and anyway, when it comes to a case such as this, I don't think castration is a good comparison at all, yeah. I mean, that's a punishment, isn't it? Whereas you can try thinking of the oppo – and I suggest you do – as a reward.'

'A reward?'

'You've got it: a reward, a reparation payment that I can help you to give, if you help me.'

'Me? In the, uh, oppo?' A cut – a nick even – the very image of scarlet pulsing from capillaries made Tom gag. 'H – how? How the hell can I help?'

'Lissen.' Von Sasser smiled at him again. 'What's your idiom . . .' He thought for a second. 'That's it: "sucks". Coercion, Tom, *sucks* in my view, right. I mean, I could *make* you, but I'm certain once you get to considering all the possible benefits – the goodwill of my brother, Hippolyte, Atalaya and the Intwennyfortee mob's as well – you'll come round to the idea of volunteering, yeah.'

And Tom, who no longer had any power to resist this outrageous proposition, understood that, by default, he had already come round and round again, and round once more, until he was all dried out, the last desiccated guest in the roach motel.

'Schweinsaxe?' Von Sasser asked Adams, holding up a pair of serving tongs with a whole pig's trotter wedged in them.

'Thanks, Erich,' the Consul replied. 'Don't mind if I do.'

Von Sasser deposited the truncated foot on a plastic bowl, then ladled thick brown gravy on top. The Tayswengo waitresses in their starch-stiff dirndls were still loitering by the kitchen door, but this evening the neuro-anthropologist had elected to serve the food himself.

Tom supposed this was partly to promote an atmosphere of cosy domesticity, but also because – with some sensitivity – Von Sasser didn't want to draw attention to Prentice. After all, if the Tayswengo had refused to serve him, he might have made a scene. At the very least, it would've looked as if a 'Nil by mouth' sign had been hung from his scrawny neck. In the event, when it was his turn, Von Sasser simply passed over Prentice in silence, and dished up for the next person at the table.

When Tom's turn came, Von Sasser neglected him as well. For a moment, Tom thought to protest, but then his volunteer status came back to him, and he appreciated that a full stomach wasn't something he wanted to have on his first outing to an operating room.

Prentice wasn't remotely discomfited by his fast. He helped himself to the bottle of Hock, and sat smoking and chatting, more animated than he had been at any time since his arrival at Ralladayo. He discussed, quite openly, the two mixed-race children he had 'fathered': one in the Tontines, and one who had recently been transferred here, to the orphanage.

Was it only Tom who could see the parentheses around 'fathered'? It can't be, he thought, because without them Prentice's remarks were psychopathically unabashed. 'I've made a decision,' he was now telling Gloria. 'No matter what the consequences are for my marriage, I'm going to tell my lady wife the entire truth.'

Gloria nodded sympathetically, then said, 'That's good, Brian.'

'I've made the first reparations to two of the ladies involved, so I've got to jolly well do right by the third as well.'

'That's excellent, Brian.'

'Yes, honesty is the best policy and all that sort of thing. I – I'm not terribly articulate, you know, but it did something to me – seeing the kiddies. I've never thought of myself as a fatherly sort of chap, but it stirred me up, and I want to – if I'm allowed, that is – try and, sort of, look after them.'

It stretched the bounds of Tom's credulity that Gloria Swai-Phillips – who had cared for the results of Prentice's paedophilia – could sit there encouraging this grotesque fantasizing. Yet he found himself sitting and listening to it, and, perhaps by his very passivity alone, encouraging him as well.

Walking back to the settlement, Tom had been so unsteady on his feet that Von Sasser had to hold him up. Never the less, with his head already swimming, Tom still couldn't prevent himself from taking shots of schnapps from the bottle that had thoughtfully been left beside his empty plate. The oily aftertaste of the spirit was curiously moreish.

With no food of his own to eat, Tom was at leisure to examine each of his dining companions in turn, and analyse what they were saying with the benefit of his new background knowledge. With his, ah . . . harkening to his master's inner voice, and his slavish espousal of Von Sasser's made-up folkways, there was no doubt that Adams had had the 'oppo'. Tom deduced that Vishtar Loman must have had it too. Gloria? No – she didn't need it, she was one of life's self-appointed Head Girl scouts, ever ready to boss a troop, whether of baboons or bankers. If her corpus callosum had been cut, Tom thought ruefully, the only spirit voices Gloria would hear would be those of sullen inner-children refusing to respond to her remorseless questioning.

As for her cousin, who had joined them at table, he was definitely one of the neuro-anthropologist's less successful outcomes. This evening, Jethro Swai-Phillips was part-way between his two impairments: he could move his crabbed right hand – although he accidentally dabbed it in the gravy – but couldn't prevent himself from intermittently slurring: 'Heesh the ma-an!'

Tom speculated: had Jethro had his oppo recently? Or

was his violated brain mysteriously reacting to the enviroment itself? Back in Vance, Jethro had been such a vivid character – decisive, self-possessed, the courtroom colossus of the Tropics. Yet, Tom now understood, the lawyer had always been serving this other, far more heavyweight client.

Was this why Martha had reacted so vehmently to him? Tom shook his muzzy head, desperate to gain purchase. But it was no good; he'd never be able to get a grip on the conundrum of his wife's intentions; the well-oiled links of the chains that dragged effects behind her causes simply slid through his hands.

What was it Jethro had said, sitting under his hunting prints in his office at the top of the Metro-Center? That it didn't matter a damn if Tom began smoking again – that the entire apparatus of prohibition was solely a product of race politics?

Tonight, the dense tobacco smoke alone identified the chalet as the command centre of the insurgency. Long pennants of it furled and unfurled in the warm draughts. A particularly thick standard of pipe smoke was draped behind Von Sasser's chair, and now, rallying to it, the neuro-anthropologist addressed his staff, who, with the exception of Tom and Prentice, were working their way through big wedges of Black Forest Gateau, slathered with cream.

'You cannot conceive', the rhetorician of Ralladayo began, 'of a cannibal sending back his enemy pie simply to avoid a statutory fine or a short term of imprisonment, any more than a Parsee would forgo the excarnation of his mum, or an Inuit his hunt for the narwhal's tusk – but this, yeah, is precisely what the Anglos have done.

'I'm not saying that this is all t'do with smoking, right, but you've gotta admit it's pretty bloody key. Y'see,' he said, shaking his hatchet head incredulously, 'that's the way an Anglo thinks – that's the way he conceives of himself. He thinks: I'm giving up smoking and that's a *good thing*; it's such a bloody *good thing* that I better go looking for some other poor bastard I can impose it on. No, it's this – this imposition, this sixteen-metre line we all haveta stand beyond, because we're bad little boys and girls, that my father – and now me – have dedicated our entire lives to getting rid of, yeah.

'I'm not saying, yeah . . .' But he was saying, and saying, and bloody saying some more, his sharp words cutting into Tom's very flesh, his bloody convictions splattering the lapels of Tom's crumpled, sky-blue suit. '. . . I'm not saying that what we do here isn't similar – that's bloody obvious! We come from the same bloody tradition. But see, when me and Vishtar do an oppo, yeah, we're not simply imposing our idea of the good, we're turning people into living, breathing, walking-bloody-instruments – instruments that can hear a voice right inside their heads telling them, loud and clear, what they should actually bloody do!

'Y'see' – relighting his hideous pipe, Von Sasser dribbled smoke – 'you've gotta fight fire with bloody fire.'

But Tom Brodzinski didn't see this at all. What he did see – and what he cleaved to, even now – was that the best thing he had done in years – perhaps in his entire life – had been to give up smoking. He felt much better, despite his current weakened state; indeed, if he hadn't quit, Tom felt sure he would now be seriously ill – what with the stress and the fatigue, and the sheer monotony of listening, for hour after hour, to this insane man lecture his lobotomized confrères.

Tom thrashed in smoky whirlpools, struggling to stay

afloat on the wreckage of his reasoning, but it was no use – he shouldn't have had that last schnapps, and so he submerged into unconsciousness . . .

. . . And popped back up to be dashed with song spray:

> This golden realm of unutterable promise . . .
> We give it to you, O Lord, our country,
> We give . . . it . . . to . . . you–ooo . . . !

The lamps had long since been lit and now burned down low. The paraffin fumes were choking, the tobacco smoke was stale, and the meat was already putrefying between the gaping teeth from which these words spewed. They were all standing to attention behind their chairs. Prentice even had his hand on his heart. His angular Adam's apple bobbed as he sang, stretching the smooth healthy skin of his neck.

They finished the anthem. There were tears in Gloria's eyes, and Von Sasser's, the latter said: 'There she blows! Poor bugger's had a skinful of grog, you better get him to his swag, Brian, yeah.'

Tom had no real awareness of the walk back to the derelict College; nor of Prentice, once again, readying him for bed. He switched off the lights and shut the door, but, as soon as Tom shut his eyes, he found himself back out in the dusty corridor, together with Tommy Junior, who mooched up and down puffing a cigarette. What was the slob of a teenager *doing*? Cutting class was one thing – but smoking in the *school*; that wasn't merely delinquent, it was *insane*. Tom would've berated his adoptive son – as he had so many times before – with his lack of concern for anyone's feelings other than his own, were it not for the uncomfortable fact that what the boy was smoking was Tom himself.

Tommy Junior stuck Tom's feet in his mouth and slobbered on them: a suck of incestuous satisfaction. His father's head burned with shame. Then the boy pinched Tom's legs, hard, and flipped him. Tom flew, end over end over end, yet never reached the end of the dusty corridor; while up ahead the woman that was Martha, that was Atalaya, that was Gloria – that was all of them – turned and turned and turned the corner, avoiding him for an eternity, her words floating back, over and over, to her rejected spouse: 'I'm scared, honey. I'm scared . . .'

It was still early when Prentice came to wake him. When they got outside the Technical College, the first dull light of the pre-dawn showed up the sloppy grin on Prentice's face. He had changed his clothes as well as his complexion; the slogan on his too-tight, white T-shirt read NEXT PUB 859 KMS. *He must've scored last night and the T-shirt is his sick trophy* . . . Prentice took Tom's hand and led him into the eucalyptus grove.

As they walked towards the dispensary, he prattled away: 'Have you ever noticed, old chap, how the water here goes down the plughole the other way? Y'know, anti-clockwise. I'm not good at expressing myself at all, but it did occur to me that this was a sort of meta-thingy.'

'Metaphor.'

'That's it, metaphor – for what's happened to me. I mean, a good deal of pressure was applied, don't get me wrong. Jethro told me I'd be seeing the inside of the old prison walls. Then there's the racialism thing. Well, I'd be the first to admit that my, um, standpoint – rumpy-pumpy aside –

was pretty old-fashioned, but, well . . .' He laughed. 'Seeing your behaviour – how *crass* you were – and then meeting my own children for the first time . . . Well, it turned me completely round, twisted me anti-clockwise. Now I believe in what I've done, Tom. It's like Erich says: it doesn't matter what my intentions were, I was a good tool.'

There was barely enough current in Tom's brain for the connections to be made – but then they were. At high speed the entire narrative spooled through the viewfinder of his awareness, and the depth and complexity of the set-up, and the shallowness and simplicity of his own responses, stunned him with blow after blow.

Adams – who'd known so very much about Tom without even having to ask, right down to the fact that he drank Seven and Sevens – had been omniscient in the breakfast room at the Mimosa – and then there was Swai-Phillips, who had already known that Tom had met with the Consul. The indifference and then hostility of the junior embassy attaché – who had been got to long before Tom called.

Then, once things were up and running, they had a legman keeping an eye on Tom's every move. First there were tails from behind – Squolly's men – and then they were replaced by a better tail, one who worked from the front and was able to anticipate which way he'd go before Tom knew himself.

The man who knew what the inside of the courtroom was like – even knew that it had good airconditioning; the man the car-rental clerk knew the name of without having to be told; the man who'd slipped it to the clerk in the Goods Shed Store that the rifles weren't for Tom; the man who was never marked by the makkata in Vance to begin with, and whose thigh was checked by other makkatas along the way, purely to confirm that he was the plant. Yes, the man whose case was being handled on a no-win-no-fee basis, and who performed brilliantly as an instrument to be played upon by the wills of others.

Lincoln, Tom kicked himself. The old man was the only damn one of them who had told the truth. He tried to warn me – the rest of them were all in on it. And to Prentice, he croaked: 'That makkata.'

'What's that, old chap? Speak up.'

'That makkata, back in Vance, he was a fucking fraud, wasn't he?'

'Oh, absolutely,' Prentice laughed. 'Pissed out of his brains, the ceremony was a total cock-up. You must've realized, Tom, you were inquivoo all along.'

They had reached the dispensary, and Prentice let go of Tom's hand to withdraw an envelope from the back pocket of his jeans. It was identical to the one that Tom had left under his swag – the one that contained Tom's copy of the tontine.

'All tontines are, of course, fully reciprocal, Tom,' Prentice said, waggling the envelope. 'You may have thought you could convert it unilaterally, but I'm afraid you couldn't. I'm surprised the man at Endeavour didn't spell it out for you, but then insurance salesmen aren't the most honest of chaps. The natives are easy to rook; however, it's different with an Anglo – they couriered a copy round to me at the Hilton within an hour.'

Prentice smiled complicitly. 'Our tontine covers – you'll've noticed, if you've read the small print – severe mental impairment, as well as injury and death. In the absence of your having appointed someone to hold your power of attorney

. . . Well, let's just put it this way, since I can see you're still a little groggy: it seems I'm on the verge of coming into a considerable sum of money.

'But don't think I'm going to be selfish,' he continued, holding the dispensary door open for Tom. 'By far the bulk of it will go to support my kids – and to help Erich's work, naturally. So, best not to look on this, um, procedure as a punishment at all; rather it's your way of giving a lot of people a much deserved reward.'

Erich von Sasser was waiting for them in the anteroom to the operating room, together with Vishtar Loman. The doctors were already in their gowns and masks, but a third shrouded figure – smaller, slimmer – was scrubbing up at a sink in the corner.

Prentice helped Tom on to the gurney, then went to take his turn at the sink. The other operating assistant was Atalaya Intwennyfortee, and it seemed she was playing the part of of anaesthetist, because she came over to where Tom lay bearing a kidney dish, and looked down at him. Her beautiful dark eyes were joined by Von Sasser's hollow sockets.

'I'm afraid, Tom,' the neuro-anthropologist said breezily, 'that a lack of funds means we aren't able to give you a pre-med', but Ms Intwennyfortee here has something that should help you relax.'

Atalaya took a quid of engwegge from the kidney dish and pushed it into Tom's defenceless mouth. Biting down on it, feeling the nicotine immediately perfuse through his gums and into his bloodstream, Tom ruminated on what a pity it was that his last smells were so bitterly antiseptic.

In gown and mask, Prentice joined the other two standing over Tom, and Von Sasser put one rubber-gloved hand on his shoulder and the other on Atalaya's. 'Well, Tom,' he said, 'if you're puzzled as to why Brian is helping out with your oppo, cast your mind back to Papa's *Songs*. You'll recall that there's nothing a Tayswengo fears more than *gettanka*, or ritualized humiliation, and that he – or she – would rather see a man die – or at any rate, experience an ego-death – than suffer such a fate.'

However, Tom wasn't casting his mind back anywhere; he was adrift in his engwegge trance, and faintly amused by the way things had turned out. After all, he was only doing what he had always done: passively conforming to an invented belief system.

The Butt End

Some years later . . .

The Honorary Consul, Winthrop Adams, stood on the casino steps together with his two friends, Jethro Swai-Phillips and Brian Prentice.

Prentice, who had a good deal of ready cash, was known around Vance as something of a high-roller, and, although he only blew into town from time to time, he liked to cut loose and enjoy himself. Treating his mates to a few hundred bucks' worth of chips, so they could fritter them away on blackjack or craps, gave him immense – and not altogether discreditable – pleasure.

The three men lingered, chatting on the white marble steps, under the white marble pyramid of the vulgarly grandiose building; then Prentice waved his arm, hoping to gain the attention of one of the cab drivers waiting in the shade of the ornamental palms on the far side of Dundas Boulevard.

'Can't I give you a ride, Brian?' Swai-Phillips asked.

'No, that's all right, old chap,' Prentice said. 'I've got my Hummer to pick up from the garage, and I need to do a few errands in town before I head over–' He stopped abruptly. Something – or, rather, someone – had caught his eye.

An old wino was shuffling along the arc of the sixteen-metre line, bending down to pick up cigarette butt after butt, then lifting each in turn up to the sky and scrutinizing it, before letting it fall. Every time he bent down he displayed the back of his cropped head to the three spectators, and the white trough of a scar that bisected it from nape to crown.

'I say,' Prentice exclaimed. 'Isn't that Tom Brodzinski?'

'Yes,' Adams said. 'I believe it is.'

'What's he still doing here?' Prentice demanded.

'Well, Brian.' The Consul couldn't avoid sounding official, if not officious. 'There have been numerous, ah, complications with his, ah, status. Seems his passport was, ah, mislaid and, given his record, it's proving tricky to get him another one. He's stuck in limbo, poor fellow.'

'He looks like he's getting a bellyful of grog in limbo,' Swai-Phillips caustically observed.

'Well,' Adams said pedantically, 'I shouldn't imagine there's a lot else he can do, given his, ah, mental-health problems.'

'At least he's doing now what he should've bloody done in the first place, yeah,' the lawyer persisted.

'Oh, and what's that, old chap?' Prentice was genuinely curious.

'Picking up the bloody butts, of course!'

And, although this wasn't a particularly adroit witticism – even by Swai-Phillips's unexacting standards – his two friends still rewarded it with laughter: Prentice giving voice to manly guffaws, while the Consul emitted a dry 'heh-heh-heh'.

Tom heard everything the three men were saying with perfect clarity, and he entirely understood its relevance to him. If he made no response, it was because Prentice and the others were so ridiculously tiny and insignificant: buzzing flies, settled for a split-second on the side of a termite heap, before some still smaller perturbation triggered them into flight.

Astande, who stood beside Tom, enormous and black and beautiful and proud, now pointed out another cigarette butt and said: 'Pick it up, Tom, yeah.' Tom did as he was told. 'Now hold it up, mate.' Tom held it up, turning the butt this way and that. 'Yup,' Astande boomed, 'I reckon that's the one, d'you see?'

Tom did see. The crumpled paper tube, with frayed tobacco at one end and its bung of synthetic cellulose acetate at the other, had been accidentally moulded by the sole that had ground it out. The butt was a mashed vee that, from the right angle, was exactly the same shape as the great island-continent itself.

Tom asked his spirit guide: 'Can I smoke it?' And Astande said, 'Sure, why not?' So Tom scurried into the thin passage-way that had been left behind in the scar tissue lining his longitudinal fissure. He burrowed deep inside his own brain, to where Von Sasser's scalpel had negligently created a small cavity while in the process of clumsily cutting through the tough cells of Tom's corpus callosum.

Over the intervening years since this slight, Tom had worked away at the cavity with his bare hands and whatever tools he could find lying around, until he had managed to excavate a sizeable den.

The pulsing, pinky-grey walls of the brain-cave sparked with neurones – an unearthly display; but the furniture that Tom had dragged in from his memory was rather prosaic: a couple of plastic-backed chairs taken from Squolly's inter-view room, Tom's crap bed from the Entreati Experience and a gateleg table that he had carried away from Adams's bedroom. There were plenty of ashtrays.

Tom straightened out the butt and lit it with a match from a book advertising SWAI-PHILLIPS ATTORNEYS, NO WIN-NO FEE. CALL: 1–800-LAW. He took a deep drag and handed it to Astande, who sat opposite him on the other plastic chair. The Swift One took a companionable pull, then passed the butt back.

A NOTE ON THE AUTHOR

Will Self is the author of four collections of short
stories (the first of which, *The Quantity Theory of Insanity*,
won the 1992 Geoffrey Faber Memorial Award), six
novels (of which *How the Dead Live* was shortlisted
for the Whitbread Novel of the Year in 2002),
three novellas and five non-fiction works. He is a
regular broadcaster on television and radio and, as a
journalist, a contributor to a plethora of publications.
He lives in London with his wife and four children.

A NOTE ON THE TYPE

The text of this book is set in Bembo. This type was first used in 1495 by the Venetian printer Aldus Manutius for Cardinal Bembo's *De Aetna*, and was cut for Manutius by Francesco Griffo. It was one of the types used by Claude Garamond (1480–1561) as a model for his Romain de L'Universitë, and so it was the forerunner of what became standard European type for the following two centuries. Its modern form follows the original types and was designed for Monotype in 1929.